Women and the Media

Diverse Perspectives

Edited by
Theresa Carilli
Jane Campbell

UNIVERSITY PRESS OF AMERICA,® INC.
Lanham • Boulder • New York • Toronto • Oxford

Contents

List of Illustrations

List of Figures

Acknowledgements

We assembled this collection of articles in response to the notion that we live in a post-feminist era where women have achieved equality. These articles point to the reality that all over the globe, women must strive to overcome their marginalized status. We hope this book will further contribute to the dialogue about how the media affects and interprets women's lives.

We are grateful to a number of individuals for their support on this project. We would like to thank all the contributors for their patience and belief in this book. We also wish to thank Purdue University Calumet, especially Dr. Dan Dunn, Dean of Liberal Arts and Social Sciences, Dr. Dennis Barbour, Department Head, English and Philosophy, and Dr. Yahya Kamalipour, Department Head, Communication and Creative Arts, for providing us with research release time to complete this manuscript. We offer a special thanks to Dr. Colette Morrow, Director, Women's Studies Program at Purdue University Calumet, for building a curriculum which recognizes the importance and value of women's issues and experiences.

We would like to thank Anastasia Trekles for her technical support, patience, and attention to the manuscript. Without her help, this project would not have come to fruition. Finally, we thank Christina Camedeca for assisting us.

We dedicate this book to all the women who have influenced us and shaped our way of thinking. Thank you for feeding our renegade spirits!

Introduction

Combining the words "women" and "media" is a challenging task because the words are so at odds with one another. According to one of the earliest mass communication theories, "agenda setting," the media shapes public opinion by telling people what to watch and how to experience what they witness. For women around the world, agenda setting has meant exclusion and marginalization. While women have been active participants as journalists, filmmakers, and broadcasters throughout the media's history, they have been relegated to the sidelines, where they have attempted to change the agenda while watching themselves being subjugated by the agenda. In her 1992 book *Girls in the Balcony: Women, Men, and The New York Times,* Nan Robertson addresses how female journalists during the 1950s and 1960s were quarantined off on the National Press Club balcony:

> No woman who was a reporter in Washington during the 1950s and 1960s would forget the balcony at the National Press Club . . . After World War II, every man of consequence on the globe who wanted to deliver an important speech in the capital preferred to do so at the club. . . . Women reporters never covered such speeches. They were not allowed even to set foot inside the press club doors for any reporting events. . . . And then in 1955, after years of pressure from the Women's National Press Club, the men thought of a solution. They would put women reporters in the balcony of the ballroom. Of course, they would get nothing to eat during the speeches, which were usually delivered at lunch. And there would be no place to sit up there—if there was any kind of crowd. But by God, no woman would be able to say that the club didn't let her in to cover the assignment. (pp. 99–100)

The balcony becomes a metaphor not only for the way women are treated as media personnel but also for the treatment of women in the media. Women appear as saviors and sex objects, villains, vixens, and forces to be squelched. Rarely do they have an opportunity to express their unique experiences and strengths. But when they do, they are changing the status of life for women around the globe.

We come to this anthology as feminists who have been involved in women's studies and in media. Having worked in radio and television, we acknowledge the bind facing women. Women who work in the media can make delicate contributions by challenging some of the implicit patriarchal values. In America, these challenges have been made through individuals like Lesley Stahl, Helen Thomas, Barbara Walters, Diane Sawyer, Oprah Winfrey, and Ellen DeGeneres. Such women serve as role models of strength and intelligence, inviting younger women to work in positions of power outside the domestic arena. Yet, the statistics tell us that these women are still anomalies, constituting approximately 30% of newspaper and broadcast journalists (Media Report to Women), 38% of actors (Screen Actors' Guild), and 10% of all international film directors (Redding and Brownworth, 1997). In spite of statistics that show that women are severely underrepresented in the media, these women and others are re-configuring the agenda and allowing women to question how the media represents them. The book has been divided into four sections, *Commodifying and Exoticizing the Female Body, Stereotypical Depictions, Portrayals of Political Activism,* and *Media Pioneers.*

In *Commodifying and Exoticizing the Female Body*, authors point to the relegation of women into the traditional categories of mother and tramp, mammy and Jezebel, and to the prevalence of the male gaze. Despite protestations to the contrary, women are expected to adhere to the age-old, patriarchal values of self-sacrifice and nurturing, once they have passed the age of being nubile sex objects. Abhik Roy examines women's highly sexualized representations in Indian television commercials. Orly Shachar argues that Israeli women's reproductive capabilities have been seen as synonymous with their national loyalty. Catherine Gilotti analyzes voyeuristic portrayals of lesbians' romantic overtures in mainstream films, contrasting them with the more realistic images offered by lesbian directors. Kimiko Akita explores the ways Japanese media encourage women to subscribe to culturally-derived manners that ultimately demean and disempower them. Giovanna Del Negro explores the Argentinian *telenovela's* commodification of chastity, suffering, and self-sacrifice, reifying values spanning continents.

In *Stereotypical Depictions*, writers deplore the limited portrayals women face in advertising, print media, and film. Women and women's issues suffer from invisibility and marginalization in all media. When women do appear, they are predominantly represented as white, young, glamorous, heterosexual, and less influential than men. Women of color continue to be underrepresented. Portrayals of African American women are limited, even in films and print media that target Black audiences. Through content analysis, Barbara King and Tom Reichert show the multiple ways advertisements reinforce gender roles, rendering women invisible, powerless, decorative, or traditional. Theresa Carilli explores film representations of Italian American women as oversexed, uneducated, and unambitious. Michelle Tracy Berger analyzes the one-dimensional, often degrading depictions of African American female drug users in films. Gloria Gadsden demonstrates how *Essence Magazine* reinforces the mammy/Jezebel dichotomy and marginalizes lesbian sexuality. Reiko Ishiyama and Shinichi Saito argue that Japanese print media rarely cover gender equity issues, leading to a lack of knowledge and reinscribing stereotypical gender roles.

The essays in *Portrayals of Political Activism* celebrate female participation in the public sphere at the same time as they interrogate the restrictions women still face. Xin-An Lu and Linda Y. Devenish expose the "insidious oppression" that post-liberation Chinese propaganda posters telegraph, despite their aura of gender-equity. Tina Richardson and Audrey Vanderford critique popular culture's repackaging of ecofeminism through patriarchal depictions of Julia "Butterfly" Hill and Erin Brockovich. Lori Montalbano-Phelps looks at how gender roles influence the performance aesthetics women have needed to adopt for high profile political campaigns. Angela High-Pippert examines the framing of women's political participation, arguing that "mom discourse" is a double-edged sword.

The essays in *Media Pioneers* offer hope and inspiration to women of all ages. These four pioneers remind us that regardless of obstacles, discouragement, and setbacks, women will survive, prevail, and transcend. Linda Brigance excavates the life of Maria Kowalska, a second-generation Polish American who navigated the rocky waters of gender and ethnicity to publish a Polish American newspaper in the early part of the twentieth century. Margaret Finucane celebrates the vision of Joan Ganz Cooney, whose idealism and talent enabled her to found the Children's Television Workshop and Sesame Street. Cynthia Lont investigates the life and work, the determination and spirit, of Frances Benjamin Johnston, whom Lont calls the mother of photojournalism. Finally, Dacia Charlesworth showcases two groundbreaking episodes of *Cybill*, the feminist sit-com developed and produced by the remarkable Cybill Shepherd.

We offer this anthology as an exploration of the status of women in the media. Despite the constraints women have faced in achieving equality, they continue to forge ahead undaunted. With this book, we hope to initiate a global dialogue about this subject and build partnerships with women around the world.

REFERENCES

Diversity Update from the Screen Actor's Guild. (2001). Retrieved April 21, 2002 from http://www.sag.org.

Industry Statistics from Media Report to Women. (2001). Retrieved March 25, 2002 from http://www.mediareporttowomen.com/statistics.com.html

Redding, J. M. and Brownworth, V.A. (1997). *Film Fatales.* Seattle, WA: Seal Press.

Robertson, N. (1992). *Girls in the Balcony: Women, Men, and the New York Times.* New York: Random House.

Part One

COMMODIFYING AND EXOTICIZING THE FEMALE BODY

Chapter One

The 'Male Gaze' in Indian Television Commercials: A Rhetorical Analysis

Abhik Roy

Advertising is a major cultural institution that reflects and molds our lives. The constant bombardment of advertising images of gender, types of persons, social classes, and other groups influences our social learning process (Roy, 1998). According to Ewen and Ewen (1992), advertising not only sells us products and services, but it also indirectly tells us ways to understand the world. Similarly, Goldman (1992) points out that advertising is a major social and economic institution that seeks to maintain cultural hegemony by providing us socially constructed ways of seeing and making sense of our world.

Like any other industry in a capitalist system, advertising is subject to the same principles of competition, accumulation, and profits. In order to survive and grow, the advertising industry has to generate sufficient profits for manufacturers by maintaining current markets and creating new ones (Roy, 1998). In this marketing process, women play a crucial role. By carefully studying women's habits, lifestyles, and psychological makeup, advertisers woo them to buy products for the home and family. Galbraith (1974) observes that women make a significant contribution to society by facilitating a continuing and unlimited increase in consumption. While advertising encourages women to consume, it also induces women to perceive themselves as commodities. Winship (1980) argues:

> Femininity is recuperated by the capitalist form: the exchange between the commodity and 'woman' in the ad establishes her as a commodity too . . . it is the modes of femininity themselves which are achieved through commodities and are replaced by commodities. (p. 218)

The sexual objectification of women in advertising is frequently achieved by exploiting their sexuality, or by fragmenting the female body into eroticized

3

zones such as hair, face, legs, breasts, etc. Mills (1995) reminds us that the fragmentation of women's bodies has two main effects: (a) the body becomes "depersonalized, objectified, and reduced to its parts" and (b) since the female model in the commercial is not represented as a "unified conscious living being, the scene cannot be focalized from her perspective" (p. 172). Thus, fragmented bodies are associated with male focalization—the female is objectified for the male gaze.

Traditionally, in any patriarchal culture, it is always the female body that has served as the object of the male gaze in advertising as well as other forms of mass media. Kuhn (1985) argues that this cultural way of seeing a female body as a sex object has deep material and historical roots. She argues that "whenever we look at painted, drawn, sculpted or photographed images of women, it is important for us to remind ourselves that images of women have traditionally been the province and property of men" (pp. 10–11). According to Coward (1985), the male gaze shown in photographic images is an extension of how men view women in the streets. She points out that it is perfectly natural for men to stare at women, and they "assess, judge and make advances on the basis of these visual impressions" (p. 75). In a patriarchal culture, in his hunter's role, the male can and will feast his eyes on any female object that catches his fancy. Women, on the other hand, have to beautify themselves, make themselves all the more desirable and "siren-like" to catch the men's attention (Coward, 1985).

While there are several feminist works that have looked at female spectatorship and the male gaze in Western film and mass media, there is still no work that has examined how women in developing countries, such as India, are visually sexualized to become the object of the male gaze. By deconstructing ways of representing women in Indian television commercials as a spectacle for male voyeuristic pleasure, my essay aims to fill the existing lacuna. While my study does not attempt at making any generalizable claims, it uses selected commercials to serve as what Kenneth Burke (1969) calls "representative anecdotes" to help demonstrate how women are constructed as objects of desire and fantasy for men in Indian television advertisements.

In this study, a rhetorical analysis was done to get behind the 'broad distribution of manifest content' to the 'latent, implicit patterns and emphasis' (Hall 1975, p. 16). In such a rhetorical analysis, a text acts as a means to the study, not an end. The aim of the critic is to deconstruct the text: " 'The text' is no longer studied for its own sake, nor even for the social effects it may be thought to produce, but rather for the subjective or cultural forms which it realises and makes available" (Johnson, 1987, p. 62). Thus, in order to determine the underlying meanings, a critic takes into account the verbal, rhetorical, and presentational codes that advertisers employ to create advertising commercials. For analyzing the text, I paid careful attention to appearance, manner, and activity of the female models in the commercials. Additionally, I looked at the technical events such as framing, camera shots and angle, lighting and color, music, sound effects, and voice-over. Semiotic studies can inform us about how femininity and womanhood are constructed on television by examining the varied cinematic techniques such as camera distance/angles, shot composition, lighting, music, and voice-over, among others. These devices are connotative because they are subjective decisions on the part of directors to create an impression of unmediated reality to the viewers.

Television advertising is a complex rhetorical form, involving an amalgam of strategic choices in order to persuade the audiences, including the rhetoric of the camera and text, with its figures and tropes in the patterns of lighting, editing, voice-over, and sound effects. A critic's job is to discover and deconstruct the symbols that inhere in the text of the commercial. One must, however, bear in mind that any critical piece lends itself to divergent views and interpretations, and it is practically impossible for anyone to say everything about a critical piece, nor should one endeavor to do so. This is why a reader may find that I have chosen to focus on some particular symbolic aspects in commercials while de-emphasizing others.

GENDERED WAYS OF SEEING

Many feminist media critics argue that women's self-consciousness is created through the complex interaction between women and the media. According to Keohane and Gelpi (1982), the feminine self-consciousness regards the female body as the object of another person's attention. In mass media, a woman, in Simone de Beauvoir's (1974) terms, is often defined by the male gaze, construct, and desire. She becomes the sex object in a patriarchal society. This gaze becomes a site for power when the viewer is male and the one gazed at is female. The male gaze, however, is not exercised exclusively by men. Patriarchal systems ensure that the male gaze is internalized by women, as explained by art critic, John Berger (1972):

> Men act and women appear. Men look at women. Women watch themselves being looked at. This determines not only most relations between men and women but also the relation of women to themselves. The surveyor of women in herself is male: the surveyed female. Thus she turns herself into an object—and most particularly, an object of vision: a sight. (p. 47)

Berger argues that women are rarely in a private space. They are constantly under this male gaze, which provides voyeuristic pleasure to men. Berger's concept of the male gaze is founded on Marxist criticism of the economic and social structures that perpetuate a patriarchal power base.

Unlike Berger, Laura Mulvey (1975), in her seminal essay, "Visual Pleasure and Narrative Cinema," writes about the power of the male gaze from the Lacanian psychoanalytical perspective. She argues:

> In a world ordered by sexual imbalance, pleasure in looking has been split between active/male and passive/female. The determining male gaze projects its phantasy on to the female figure which is styled accordingly. In their traditional exhibitionist role, women are simultaneously looked at and displayed, with their appearance coded for strong visual and erotic impact so that they can be said to connote *to-be-looked-at-ness*. (p. 11)

Mulvey offers scopophilia, where pleasure comes from "using another person as an object of sexual stimulation through sight" as a primary driving force behind the male gaze (p. 10). Mulvey's concept of the male gaze can be found in three distinct points: first, the look of the camera when the situation is being shot. This is often voyeuristic and presents a patriarchal perspective to the viewer. The second point involves the gaze or look of the male characters in the screen that makes the women an object. The third point involves the look or gaze of the spectator that imitates the first two looks. These three factors combine to replicate the structure of uneven power relations between men and women. Although Mulvey's work in 1975 is still hailed as a pioneering work in feminist film criticism, she was criticized for failing to explain adequately how her theory affected women as spectators. In her original work in 1975, Mulvey consistently used the male pronoun while referring to the spectator. Later, Mulvey (1989) defended herself by arguing that the spectator was not necessarily male but "masculine," who adopts a masculine subjectivity or subject position while viewing the film.

Both Berger (1972) and Mulvey (1975) argue that women are the object of the gaze as opposed to the subject of the gaze. Mulvey contends that the pleasure of looking is always split between "active/male and passive/female" (p. 11). Similarly, Berger has outlined a pattern of looking for voyeuristic pleasure that is very similar to Mulvey's: "Men act and women appear. Men look at women. Women watch themselves being looked at" (p. 47). Berger and Mulvey's concept of the male "gaze" can be found in both print and television advertising, where a woman's body is represented as an object of the masculine gaze and a producer of voyeuristic pleasure. The gaze in advertisements provides codes to the viewer to make sense of the social behavior. According to Fiske (1987), the mass media construction of a masculine reading position for a woman from which she can make sense of her own body through masculine eyes is a deliberate economic strategy of the media industry. Macdonald (1995) also points out that advertising messages consistently present women in "narcissistic poses, enthralled by their own mystery. Self-contemplation and self-absorption envelop the woman in a shrine of her own making, and poise the spectator uneasily between the contradictions of identification and voyeurism that Mulvey sees as the characteristic of the 'male gaze'" (p. 107).

WOMAN AS AN OBJECT TO BE VIEWED

A close reading of the text of the commercials revealed that men were shown in the voyeuristic role of a "surveyor." The commercials treated Indian women as objects of the male "gaze" to gratify a man's ego and sexual desire. The woman was either surveyed by males featured in the commercial, or the camera focused on the woman's body, imitating the way men survey women. In all these commercials, the dominant use of the male voice, juxtaposed with what Mulvey (1989) describes as the masculine "look" of the camera, transformed the woman into a sex object.

The following two commercials show how the female body was constructed as a sex object for men's voyeuristic pleasures. In the advertisement for Sir mouth freshener, a young woman walked into a college cafeteria where a group of men were milling around. The camera slowly panned the legs and hips of the woman, who wore a mini-dress. The music kicked in on a dramatic note while the camera focused on her face and red lips as the men ogled her figure with gaping mouths. As she walked toward the men, they were busy primping in order to impress her, and the least attractive man opened up a packet of Sir mouth freshener to prepare himself, should she happen to "choose" him. She walked through the group straight to this same man and took a pinch of the freshener from him. The camera angles focusing on the contours of her body and her mini-dress, while juxtaposing these shots with the leering glances and slack-jawed expressions of the men, suggested that it was all right to be gawked at by men; after all, that was what she expected and wanted. Also, her half-smiling face implied that she did not mind the ogling and was probably used to such leering; she had successfully packaged and "sold" herself. By the woman approaching the most unattractive man in the group for his Sir mouth freshener, it was suggested that the product was so desirable she was available for anybody who carried it. The image conveyed was that someone who wears western dress and appears progressive was "loose" and thus deserved what she got from the males: a hungry, lustful look, and perhaps more. The woman was presented as though she were solely there for male enjoyment. She was open for sexual use by the men ogling her, ready to comply with their fantasies.

In the commercial for Fem Fairness Bleach cream, another woman was depicted as a sex object. In this advertisement, a young, attractive woman in her
bathroom applied the cream to her face. After applying the cream, her complexion became light and glowing. She was the epitome of beauty: "lily-
white, rosy-cheeked, soft and dewy and free of blemish . . . a sentimental at-
tribute of virginal innocence . . . evidence of a sheltered life and male sexual
preference for a serene young female in mint condition" (Brownmiller, 1984,
p. 130). By glorifying a fair complexion, this commercial upheld the elitist
aesthetic that a woman's light skin reflects her higher class and aristocratic
fragility. This bias for light skin is incongruous in the Indian context, where
a majority of the population is not fair-complexioned. In the next few shots,
she was shown wearing a sexy, pale pink dress, singing and preparing her dinner table for a mystery man. Her alluring smile and delicate hand gestures,
along with her pale pink dress, suggested a soft, feminine sexuality. In between her actions, several men peered at her through various windows of her
home; her soft, fair skin had lured them there. Infatuated by her looks, the
men sang in praise and approval of her fair complexion. Showing these young
men praising the lightness of her complexion indicated that loveliness equals
fairness. The windows of her home, standing between her and the male
voyeurs, constructed her as an object of the spectator's curiosity, arousing a
desire among the males to unravel her mystery. Since she could not be touched
by the leering males, the knowledge about her had to be secured through
voyeuristic peering, clearly objectifying the woman with the focus of their
gazes.

In both the Sir mouth freshener and the Fem Fairness Bleach commercials,
the male gaze was omnipresent; his look seemed to hover around the woman,
staring at her and undressing her with his eyes. One could feel in his look the
desire to possess the woman, his involvement in what Mulvey (1975) has described as the voyeuristic pleasure of looking at a woman as an erotic object.
The implicit message in both commercials was that leering was a compliment
to her physical appearance. Inevitably, men's attitudes toward women and
women's attitudes toward themselves are influenced by this voyeuristic approach. It is these kinds of sexual portrayals of women in advertisements that
convey the invidious message that they are morally "lax" and therefore de-
serving of this kind of sexual harassment.

While the previous two commercials suggested that the woman was complicit in attracting the male gaze, the following set of five commercials
demonstrated a different dynamic of the male gaze. These advertisements
showed the woman involved in successfully beautifying herself to attract the
gaze of men. She was portrayed as someone whose goal in life was to either
catch a man or obtain her husband's "look" of approval about her appearance.

The following commercials demonstrated how the advertised products performed "black magic" by helping the woman become desirable in the eyes of the male.

Sometimes products transformed a woman's plain appearance to obtain the look of admiration from a male, as in the Velvette Shampoo commercial. As in the story of "Cinderella," the youngest sister in this commercial was the plain Jane in the family. Her two attractive sisters went to a party while the youngest one, looking forlorn, stayed home, asking the mirror on the wall, "Why is my hair so dry and without any life?" Suddenly, to her surprise, a shampoo appeared in a magic bottle. Applying the shampoo to her hair, she was transformed into a beautiful woman. With her new-found, gorgeous-looking hair, she appeared at the same party where her sisters were and became the center of attention. The handsome young man, who was talking to her sisters, was captivated by her beauty and could not stop staring at her. He then took her hand for a waltz and fell in love. Throughout the commercial, a male sang the glory of the shampoo's magical qualities: "Velvette Shampoo is the magic of the hair. It wakes your hair and makes it alive; it makes your hair flowing and radiant, spreading it like a fan, making you irresistible [read: 'to men']."

Like all fairy tale romances, this commercial created what Barthes (1975) calls a sense of *plaisir*, pleasure or satisfaction in happy and orderly outcomes. Thus, we had the predictable, all-too-familiar ending—"And they lived happily ever after." Reality and the magical fairy tale world of romance were deliberately blurred in this commercial. Like the fairy tale heroine, the woman in this commercial was young, innocent, pure and beautiful, and she rose to a higher state of happiness and contentment with her lover, implying inevitable matrimony and consummation. The magical qualities of the shampoo not only transformed her hair but also changed her life: a life of loneliness and despondency became one of joy and happiness. The shampoo made her life complete by helping the woman find her Prince Charming. After all, her efforts to beautify herself did not go to waste; she found her man who gave an approving "look" of her beauty.

However, not all the commercials were so drastic as to invoke the magical powers of the products to transform a woman's appearance and life. Sometimes a woman who was attractive and feminine needed only the right soap to succeed in obtaining a man's "look" of admiration and love.

For example, in the Jai Soap commercial, a young man caught a whiff of a woman's soap as she walked past him. As in any stereotypical romance, the man was bold, the woman, coy. He fell in love with her at first sight and declared his tender feelings toward her. The close-up of her face captured her demure expression, and although she liked him, she could not reciprocate his feelings right away because that would make her appear too accessible, needy, and unappealing. In keeping with the patriarchal tradition, she was never shown actively pursuing the man; if she had she would have lost her innocence and charm. On the other hand, if she remained passive, she could not get her man. Thus, she had to await another opportunity. In the next shot, the woman was shown caressing her body with Jai soap. After her bath, she was walking in a meadow amidst green trees and blossoming flowers, wearing a long, flowing white gown, when the man appeared from behind a tree and gave her a bouquet of flowers as a token of his undying love, which she accepted with delight. In this commercial, the camera took the position of the male observer following her around. One could feel his presence everywhere: walking behind her in the meadow or catching a view of her body in the bath scene. The accompanying song also evoked the romantic mood of the commercial: "My first love brings a springtime feeling in life . . . when the soap touches the skin, it talks to it. The skin smells from moment to moment like first love feels." One could easily substitute the soap in this commercial for the male lover who would be "touching her soft, gentle skin and talking to it."

Like the male in the commercial, the viewers were invited to gaze at the woman in her private moments and feel her smooth skin. The commercial conveyed a virginal and innocent sexuality: the woman waiting for her man, typified by the image of a young woman in a long white dress. The surrounding flowers and greenery also evoked her purity and femininity. Moreover, the correlation of the feelings of "first love" with "spring-time feeling" was important in what these represented: youth, freshness, anticipated romance and excitement about the woman, all thanks to Jai Soap.

In the two previous commercials, Velvette Shampoo and Jai Soap, the products helped a woman to draw the man's attention to her loveliness. However, gaining a man's attention was not enough. The following commercial for Pond's cream exemplified a woman's need to be reassured that she had the right looks that men appreciated. Since her own critical observation of her appearance was not enough, she had to have a man for validation; his approving "look" was important for her to convince herself about her desirability. In the Pond's advertisement, a young woman was visiting her sister-in-law when she ran out of her face cream. She used Pond's cream instead, which made her skin feel "soft;" it "blossomed and started to look young," making her beautiful. She could not decide for herself if her new beauty resulted from her imagination or the magic of the product working on her face. Her lover's look of approval assured her that she was not dreaming.

The woman's need for an approving look from a man continues throughout her married life. To keep the romance going and hold the man's interest, a woman has to continue performing her beauty rituals as a wife, as was observed in the following two commercials for Charmis cream and Breeze soap.

The spell-bound husband was also present in the Breeze Soap commercial, where he was "intoxicated by the rose-like fragrance" emanating from his wife's body. The commercial featured a song in a male voice [ostensibly the husband's], capturing his romantic mood: "Your rose-like New Breeze soap intoxicates me . . . its heady fragrance intoxicates me." The accompanying visuals showed the husband and the wife together in an outdoor scene, in the suggestive situation of lying together on rose petals. In another shot, the woman was shown in a narcissistic pose, caressing her body with the fragrant soap. The male voice-over intoned, "Breeze makes your skin soft, young and beautiful." In the final scene he caressed her face with a rose, and the close-up shot showed the woman canting her head with a dreamy look as she turned her face away from the husband's. For Goffman (1987) both the head cant and the turning away of her face are significant. He describes the lowering of the head as a "ritualization of subordination," suggesting "an expression of ingratiation, submissiveness, and appeasement" (p. 46). Goffman calls the turning away of the head a "licensed withdrawal." When a woman is shown turning her face away from a man and it does not suggest flight, it indicates her submission to and trust in the man. The roses signified the love and passion the couple had for each other, while the soft pink lighting of the commercial captured the romantic mood. The petals strewn all over the woman's body and on the ground symbolized her delicately sensual image. Like the petals, she was soft, fragrant, moist and inviting. The whole show of petals and fragrance could also signify a woman's fertility, as suggested by Bataille (1985). The camera assumed the male point of view once again. His gaze seemed to be omnipresent, and there was no reprieve from it; whether outdoors or in her private bath, his eyes followed and surveyed her "soft, young, beautiful body."

THE WOMAN AS SIGNIFIER FOR THE PRODUCT

The male "look" was not always so obvious as in the previous four commercials for Velvette, Jai, Charmis, Pond's, and Breeze, where women seduced men with their physical appearance and succeeded in attracting their gaze. Although no males appeared in the following commercials, the camera's "male gaze" positioned viewers to adopt the masculine voyeuristic perspective toward the featured celebrity models, based on Mulvey's theory of the gaze (1989). In the following commercials, beauty, glamour, and the sexuality of celebrity models were exploited to symbolize the advertised commodities and to function as an object of voyeuristic pleasure for the viewer. By using the model's body and looks, the commercials implicated her in perpetuating the male-defined ideals of beauty. She was shown interpellating the female viewer/consumer to think of herself in terms of the advertised glamour image and purchase the products with which she would be able to catch her man or keep him enamored. As Stannard (1971) puts it:

> Glittering and smiling in the media, looked at by millions, envied and ogled, these ideal beauties teach women their role in society. They teach them that women are articles of conspicuous consumption in the male market; in other words, that women are made to be looked at, and that females achieve success in the world by being looked at (p. 123).

Like the chic models in the commercials, the female viewer/consumer was expected to have an alluring smile (Colgate toothpaste), luxuriant hair (Brahmi Amla Hair Oil), and a soft, fair complexion (Lux International Soap), among other physical attributes.

In a commercial for Colgate toothpaste, former Miss World winner, Aishwarya Rai, was featured endorsing the product. She lay on her stomach on the sofa while hugging a pillow like a teddy bear. According to Goffman (1987), the recumbent figure of a woman on a sofa is a "conventionalized expression of sexual availability," and it is women and children who are depicted in what Goffman calls a "ritualization of subordination" pose (p. 41). The close-up shot also allowed the viewer to get within an intimate distance of her alluring green eyes and sparkling white teeth. With her head tilted to one side and looking somewhat coy and kittenish, the beauty queen shared with the viewers her story: "Colgate toothpaste is the best protection. My mom trusted it and I do the same. From childhood, Colgate has protected me, and it will continue protecting me all my life. It will always remain with me." Aishwarya's testimony about the toothpaste had rhetorical implications: on a denotative level, the toothpaste was sold for its protective qualities for teeth and gums. However, on a connotative level, Colgate toothpaste, like a male lover, not only protected her but also gave her confidence about her appearance. Most importantly, with Colgate's help, she possessed a radiant smile to catch the man's attention.

An Indian film star was used to endorse Brahmi Amla Hair Oil. The camera captured her beauty and sexuality in different ways: she was portrayed as a sexy nymph, playing in a pool of cascading water, while the camera focused on her low-cut halter top, emphasizing her body. In another setting, she was projected as a demure yet alluring woman, draped in a beautiful saree, hair flowing in the breeze, while she looked at herself in a hand mirror. The significance of the actress' gaze into a hand mirror was to depict her as a narcissistic woman observing herself with a critical eye to make sure that she had what it takes to be glamorous. Barthel (1988) writes that a "mirror is the symbol of femininity. It is not vanity; it is necessity. It reflects the commandment that women see themselves as others see them; it is the means by which they can be at once both (self critic) and other (object)" (p. 60). The medium close-up shot of her in the final scene suggested virginal and innocent sexuality, typified by the young woman's white dress, braided hair, and the canting posture of her body in front of the camera in a childlike, playful manner. As she smiled, while looking straight at the camera, she said, "My beauty is in my hair, and my hair is fed by Brahmi Amla Hair Oil. And what is good for my hair is also good for you." This commercial underscored and reinforced the male-defined ideal of beauty, reinforcing that the only identity for a woman is her visible beauty. The first impression is important when it comes to catching a man's eye; therefore, by using this hair oil, the female viewer/consumer would not only succeed in having luxuriant hair like the film star, but she might also receive appreciative gazes from male admirers. This commercial projects a woman's existence only through her physical appearance. In this case, the beauty of the woman is not attributed to any of her intrinsic qualities but to the physical attributes of her hair, and in the process, she becomes commodified.

The beauty and sexuality of a famous Indian model, Tabu, were used as correlatives in order to signify Lux International soap, as in the previous two commercials. Although there was no male present, the camera captured the male gaze. In the first shot she did yoga, remarking (off-camera), "Beauty begins with feeling beautiful and looking after your skin," while in the background soft, light choral voices were heard. In the next shots, the Indian model enjoyed a private moment, taking a bath in a narcissistic pose. The camera focused on her face that looked away from the direct gaze of the viewers, appearing ecstatic, almost orgasmic. At this point, the music changed from light choral voices to a dramatic crashing sound. Juxtaposed with the music was the visual of a bar of Lux suggestively plunging into the water in slow motion. The choral voices became louder as water sprayed the model's feet and legs. She was in a cascade of water, which soaked her as she playfully splashed in it, looking content. The woman appeared to have been caught by the camera in a moment of autoeroticism. She was enjoying her own body behind the soap suds and mistiness—the soft, silky smoothness of her skin, her own touch; an apparent erotic fancy. She was transported by her own pleasure. This self-absorbed, narcissistic woman was a source of voyeuristic pleasure to the viewer as well, as pointed out by Kuhn (1985):

> an attractive woman takes a solitary bath and is carried away by the sensuousness of it all. The spectator sneaks a look at her enjoyment of an apparently unselfconscious moment of pleasure in herself: the peeping Tom's favorite fantasy.

Since she does not know he is there, he can take a good look at what a woman gets up to when she is on her own (p. 30).

This commercial, which was primarily aimed at women, invited them to adopt the masculine point of view while watching it. While female viewers saw themselves as men perceived them, they were encouraged in this commercial to "enjoy their sexuality through the eyes of men: "It [was] a narcissism which at the moment of self-masturbation and scopophilia (looking in this instance at one's own body) [was] also exhibitionist, inviting voyeurism from men" (Winship, 1980, p. 25).

WOMAN AS A NON-THINKING, DECORATIVE OBJECT

Another frequent portrayal of an Indian woman was purely decorative without any functional relationship with the advertised product. Her sexuality was exploited not only to sell a variety of products but also to provide visual pleasure to male viewers. In these commercials, the woman as a sign/signifier was wrenched from the concrete socio-historical context and attached to these commodities in order to lend meaning to them. Irigaray (1985) points out the commodification of women in another context: "The body of a commodity thus becomes, for another such commodity, a mirror of its value" (p. 179). As a decorative object, a woman was frequently depicted as a brainless body, almost a piece of equipment, singing vacuous jingles, dancing provocatively, or posing as a mannequin for a wide variety of products.

The commercial for Copper men's cologne, for example, showed a young man standing in a rugged-looking landscape under a scorching sun. Nearby was a scantily clad young woman who moved her body like a wild animal, writhing to the pulsating music of the commercial. She was portrayed as a lustful woman ready to be taken by the man. The close-up shots focused on the woman's physical dimension, most notably her legs, midriff, bust, and mouth, while she caressed her own body in an erotic manner. A husky female voice-over said, "Before you get close, get Copper," implying that the woman could be obtained as a prize for any man wearing this cologne.

Similarly, in another commercial for Videocon Bazooka (television), the husband surprised his wife with his newly purchased television. The authoritative male voice described the "pulsating" quality of its sound while the wife's cocktail dress was lifted up by the suggested power of the sound, and the camera helped the viewer catch a glimpse of her legs. The name "Bazooka," juxtaposed with the visual signifier of the woman's dress billowing up, suggesting a sexual act.

The advertisements for Bajaj Almond Drop Hair Oil showed two nubile women in a variety of revealing outfits, playing and dancing on the beach. With the gentle sweeping movements over the women's body, the camera displayed the women as a visual feast for the voyeuristic pleasure of men. Additionally, in the commercial for Nirma Bar (detergent), women's sexuality served to sell the product. In this commercial, two female models in sexy clothes gyrated provocatively to the music while the camera, focusing on their bodies, provided visual pleasure to the viewers.

WOMAN AS A FRAGMENTED OBJECT

A plethora of Indian television commercials encouraged women to perceive their bodies as a kind of *project* that needed constant improvement and embellishment. These advertisements consistently showed parts of the female anatomy. The underlying message of these fragmented women's bodies was that the various parts needed care and attention so that they would become as perfect as the ones shown in the commercials to provide visual pleasure for men. For example, the disembodied images of a caressing hand, the beckoning eye, or the seductive lips, among other body parts, suggested allure and availability. Export (1988) argues that society defines femininity in terms of a woman's body parts—lips, breasts, legs—parts that are so interchangeable and generic that the woman herself becomes interchangeable and, in the process, becomes depersonalized, dehumanized and objectified. By showing the fragmented images of women's bodies "each part becomes eroticised and sexual, to-be-looked-at and marveled in. The whole outer surface of the body is transformed into an exquisite, passive thing" for the visual pleasure of the male (Root, 1984, p. 60).

Since almost all the Indian commercials featured women whose bodies were fragmented, I will only list a few of the advertisements that best illustrate the disembodied images of women. The Krack (foot cream) commercial, for example, emphasized a woman's feet, and the rest of her body was not visible. Also, in the commercial for Center Fresh (chewing gum), the camera focused on the woman's face and her mouth as she was putting the gum into her mouth. In almost all the detergent commercials, a woman's body was fragmented by showing her arms or hands washing the clothes. Many beauty health and beauty products focused on women's body parts to sell their products. For example, the Camay International and Coty Vitacare commercials showed a woman's beautiful face severed from the rest of her body while the advertisement for Sunsilk emphasized the luscious hair on the back of the woman's head. Winship (1980) notes that fragmentation of this nature in advertising traps a woman's sexuality within commodity relations. A part of a woman—lips, hair or face—signify her whole, but these individual parts also function as signifiers for the advertised products and, in the process, she becomes the advertised commodity herself: the shampoo, the hair oil, the face cream, and the soap.

CONCLUSION

The profusion of images of women in Indian commercials as beautiful sexual-ized bodies or parts of bodies celebrated and endorsed the patriarchal ideology that women were not differentiated complex minds but just bodies to be looked at. The underlying message in all these commercials was that an Indian woman's job was to be an attractive sexual object, and all the beauty and personal groom-ing products were her tools of the trade. The constant barrage of messages ex-horted her to transform herself and look better to be desirable to men. In this commodification process, an Indian woman was made a co-conspirator, not only in the exploitation of her own body but also in the occlusion of her intelligence. Frequently, she was portrayed as a decorative sex object with no functional re-lationship with the advertised product and as a woman who was absorbed in beautifying herself in order to get a man's attention and approval. In this beauty ritual, her body was packaged and displayed for the pleasure of the "male" view-ers. These images of women were constructs from a masculine perspective. In keeping with the dominant patriarchal structure, the camera adopted the mascu-line "gaze" to produce masculine reading subjects among the female audiences of these commercials. This masculine gaze need not be a man's, of course; women involved in the construction and reception of advertising can incorporate and replicate the ideology represented in these commercials. As Fiske (1987) ob-serves, "women can be constructed as masculine subjects and can consequently experience masculine pleasures. They, like men, can subject the female body to a masculine gaze" (p. 225). The commodification was accomplished through signifiers created by the visual dissection of the female body into zones of con-sumption. Consequently, a woman's image contained nothing intrinsic to herself as a whole person but was limited to the visual signifiers such as hair, skin, teeth, lips, and eyes. In other words, an Indian woman was frequently depicted as a synecdoche for the commodities she incorporated in her "persona": the sham-poo, the soap, the facial cream, the lipstick, etc. were "woman." Irigaray (1985) argues that this kind of commodification of women is inherent in a patriarchal system:

> In our social order, women are 'products' used and exchanged by men. Their sta-tus is that of merchandise, 'commodities'. . . . So women have to remain an 'in-

frastructure' unrecognized as such by society and our culture. The use, consumption, and circulation of their sexualized bodies underwrite the organization and reproduction of the social order, in which they have never taken part as subjects (p. 84).

Like Irigaray, Doane (1989) indicates that a woman is always the "object of exchange rather than its subject" in relation to the commodity (p. 23). The process of commodification in advertising underlines the tautological nature of the woman's role as a consumer: she is the subject of a transaction in which her own commodification is ultimately the object. Bowlby (1985) explains the reciprocal commodification process between the woman and commodity in terms of an amorous relationship:

> Seducer and the seduced, possessor and possessed of one another, women and commodities flaunt their images at one another in an amorous regard which both extends and reinforces the classical picture of the young girl gazing into the mirror in love with herself (p. 32).

The paradoxical position of women in this commodification process was underscored in Indian commercials. The focus on women's physical parts not only commodified them but also positioned them as consumers of these hybrid product/persona "selves": to buy the same products which objectified them. Thus, these commercials made them complicit in their own exploitation. Sexual objectification of this kind of Indian woman in television advertisements has serious implications in India, where violence and oppression against women are often closely liked to the male perceptions of their bodies and notions of femininity (Thapan, 1995). According to Thapan, such degrading portrayals make the "female body appear no more than as a 'body-for-others,' socially constructed, and therefore under the constant gaze of the [male] other" (p. 72).

REFERENCES

Barthel, D. (1988). *Putting on appearances: Gender and advertising*. Philadelphia: Temple University Press.

Barthes, R. (1975). *The pleasure of the text*. (R. Miller, Trans.). New York: Hill & Wang.

Bataille, G. (1985). *Visions of excess: Selected writings, 1927–1939*. (A. Stoekl, Ed., and A. Stoekl with C.R. Lovitt & D.M. Leslie, Jr., Trans.). Manchester, England: Manchester University Press.

Berger, J. (1972). *Ways of seeing*. London: British Broadcasting Corporation: Penguin Books.

Beauvoir, S. de (1974). *The second sex*. New York: Vintage Press.

Bowlby, R. (1985). *Just looking: Consumer culture in Dreiser, Gissing and Zola*. New York and London: Methuen.

Brownmiller, S. (1984). *Femininity*. New York: Linden Press/Simon & Schuster.

Burke, K. (1969). *A grammar of motives*. Berkeley, CA: University of California Press.

Coward, R. (1985). *Female desires: How they are sought, bought and packaged*. New York: Grove Press.

Doane, M.A. (1989). The economy of desire: The commodity form in/of the cinema. *Quarterly Review of Film and Video*, *11*, 23–33.

Ewen, S. & Ewen, E. (1992). *Channels of desire: Mass images and the shaping of American consciousness*. Minneapolis: University of Minnesota Press.

Export, V. (1988). The real and its double: The body. *Discourse*, *11*, 3–27.

Fiske, J. (1987). *Television culture*. London: Routledge.

Galbraith, J.K. (1974, May). How the economy hangs on her apron strings. *Ms.*, 74–77. Goffman, E. (1987). *Gender advertisements*. New York: Harper & Row.

Goldman, R. (1992). *Reading ads socially*. London: Routledge.

Hall, S. (1975). Introduction. In A. C. H. Smith (Ed.), *Paper voices: The popular press and social change, 1935–1965* (pp. 11–24). London: Chatto & Windus.

Irigaray, L. (1985). *This sex which is not one*. Ithaca: Cornell University Press.

Johnson, R. (1987). What is cultural studies anyway? *Social Text*, *1*, 38–80.

Keohane, N. O. & Gelpi, B.C. (1982). Foreword. In N.O. Keohane, M.Z. Rosaldo, and B.C. Gelpi (Eds.), *Feminist theory: A critique of ideology* (pp. vii–xii). Chicago: The University of Chicago Press.

Kuhn, A. (1985). *The power of the image: Essays on representation and sexuality*. London & Boston: Routledge & Kegan Paul.

Macdonald, M. (1995). *Representing women: Myths of femininity in the popular media*. London: Edward Arnold.

Mills, S. (1995). *Feminist stylistics*. New York: Routledge.

Mulvey, L. (1975). Visual pleasure and narrative cinema. *Screen*, *16*, 8–18.

Mulvey, L. (1989). Afterthoughts on 'Visual pleasure and narrative cinema' inspired by King Vidor's *Duel in the Sun* (1946). In L. Mulvey, *Visual and other pleasures* (pp. 29–38). Bloomington: Indiana University Press.

Root, J. (1984). *Pictures of women: Sexuality*. London: Pandora Press.

Roy, A. (1998). Images of domesticity and motherhood in Indian television commercials: A critical study. *Journal of Popular Culture*, *32*, 117–134.

Stannard, U. (1971). The mask of beauty. In V. Gornick & B.K. Moran (Eds.), *Woman in sexist society: Studies in power and powerlessness* (pp. 118–130). New York: Basic Books, Inc.

Thapan, M. (1995). Images of the body and sexuality in women's narratives on oppression in the home. *Economic and Political Weekly*, *30*, 72–80.

Winship, J. (1980). *Advertising in women's magazines: 1958–1974*. Stencilled Occasional Paper, University of Birmingham, Centre for Contemporary Cultural Studies.

Chapter Two

The Israeli Womb:
Images of Gendered Nationalism
in the Israeli Press

Orly Shachar

"Increasing the Jewish birth rate is a vital need for the existence of Israel. . . .
A Jewish woman who does not bring into this world at least four children . . . is
defrauding the Jewish mission" (Ben Gurion, Ha'aretz, December 8, 1967).

INTRODUCTION

The concern over reproductive issues in many developed countries is reasonably clear: inadequate population growth. Currently, many countries facing
low birthrates are trying to move in a pronatalist direction. As of 1995, about
45 countries had pronatalist policies designed to maintain or raise fertility
levels (United Nations [UN], 1996). For example, in Canada, the Quebec
government created in 1997 the Ministry of Family and Children's Services
with a budget of C$500 million (Krull, 2001). In Europe, the Italian govern-
ment has called for European Community directives to encourage European
women to have more children, in response to what is being coined as a demographic crisis (Johnson, 1990). Currently, French families benefit from extensive allowances: lengthy maternity leaves—sixteen weeks for the first two
children and twenty six weeks for a third child, coverage of maternity and infant health care through the national health care system, government supported nurseries and parenting allowances (King, 1998). Germans are being
encouraged to have more children in spite of the stigma that is still attached
to the concept of population policy dating back to Nazi Germany (Cleaver,
2000). And in Asia, with its birthrate falling below that of Singapore and
Japan, Hong Kong is planning, for the first time, a population policy in support of large families (Manuel, 1999).

Accordingly, public information campaigns concerning reproductive issues in industrial societies differ from country to country. Most lack clarity and appear to lead in various directions, from a printed guide to maternity benefits distributed by request in some countries (*A Guide to Maternity Benefits*, 2000), to a governmental internet site explaining information concerning maternity and parental benefits (*Changes to Maternity and Parental Benefits*, 2000), to public proclamations of liberal abortion policies in others (Yishai, 1993). Further, these strategies have not been solely demographic in character but more broadly social, economic, environmental, political and humanitarian (Francome, 1997; Oppenheim Mason, 1997; Yuval-Davis, 1989).

It thus becomes important to examine social institutions which participate in the public discourse regarding issues of population control. One such social institution is the media. This essay maps media treatment of reproductive issues in a particular setting. The country under study here is Israel, a modern, urban and industrial society. Israel provides a unique opportunity to illuminate the power of the popular press to direct social dynamics and propagate certain gender images at times when a society is forced to deal with issues of survival and continuity. Mostly, this study will focus on the Israeli print media in two periods, the 1967 War and the 1973 War. Images from later time periods also will be presented as Israel continues to be a society at war. Wars oftentimes facilitate a social climate responsive to change. The impact of stress on society tends to affect, in different ways, its social milieu. Some will argue that the Israeli society can be characterized as permanently at conflict with its Arab and Palestinian neighbors, rendering Israelis, among others in the region, with long term distressing effects. The aim here is to shed some light on social self-perceptions of a society under siege.

A major part of this project is the analysis of the themes indicative of the way the popular press handled reproductive issues. In this article, I will examine four illustrations of media imagery that have been used in the Israeli press in wartime. First, I will provide a brief review of the literature on Israeli Jewish women. A discussion will follow, focusing on the idea that the Israeli media produce ideology conducive to the preservation of nationalistic objectives. My primary aim here is to provide a framework for the imagery of wartime presentations of Israeli women. I carry this image in my mind, that of a quilt or a fish-net where all the little squares come together to create a daunting visualization of what women ought to do, be, or feel. It is daunting not only because of what these images encompass, but because it assumes one character with no variation. My intent is to document this discourse, providing illustration of the use of women as national icons—biological reproducers and nurturers of their people.

JEWISH WOMEN IN ISRAEL

Scholars who studied the position and status of Israeli women in the first 30 years of its statehood argue that Israeli women have been perceived as achieving equality greater than that enjoyed by most women in Western nations (Golan, 1997; Izraeli, 1979; Lahav, 1974; Padan Eisenstark, 1973; Van Creveld, 1992; Weiss and Yishai, 1980). In fact, Jewish women in Israel have been firmly anchored to the private sphere, where they are mostly responsible for their families and their households (Izraeli, 1992; Yuval-Davis, 1997). Much scholarly attention was given to the relevancy of the social and psychological effects of the Arab-Israeli conflict on the traditional role-orientation of Israeli women, implying that Israel is a "garrison state" overwhelmed at times with a siege mentality. Constant fear of war and periodic eruptions of fighting with its neighbors propelled Israeli women towards traditionalism and imposed cultural obstacles on their entry into the public sphere (Herzog, 1998). As part of this central theme, Nira Yuval-Davis positions Israeli women within the lines of ideological constructions as "national reproducers" (1997), and Nitza Berkovitch (1997) postulates that the Arab-Israeli conflict serves as a framework for the "womanhood equals motherhood" theme. Concurrently, Hanna Herzog writes, "in a cultural conception of this kind, women's place in the sphere is not only strengthened, it is magnified" (63).

Other scholarly works on Israeli women tend to explore the complex influences of gender roles on social construction within the context of nationalistic ideology. Studies vary in their focus, ranging from gender related personal decision making to microeconomics. Delila Amir writes about the politics of sexual behavior, reproduction, and family planning in Israel. Amir and Orly Benjamin (1992, 1997) demonstrate how contraceptives became a pivotal issue in regulating morality. Amia Lieblich (1994, 1997) narrates various women's experiences as they relate to the role of the "hero's wife" assigned to Israeli women, among them, Israeli wives of prisoners of war. Dafna Izraeli (1992) focuses on equality issues related to Israeli women in the workforce. Tamar Rapoport (1988, 1997) concentrates on socialization agencies and gender issues, and Marilyn Safir and Barbara Swirski (1993, 1994) provide significant insights into the past and current state of feminism in Israel.

Only recently did some scholars begin to delve into the attitudinal differences between secular and orthodox Jewish women towards their traditional collective societal roles (Moore, 1998; Moore, 2000). Interestingly, Moore found that although religious Jewish women seem to accept the patriarchal system and therefore are more obedient than secular Jewish women, they are just as politically active, especially against the peace process, and in support of the reactionary right wing coalition. This same segment in the Israeli population—orthodox Jews and especially ultra-orthodox—produces a high rate of fertility which, combined with below replacement fertility of the non-religious population, still accounted for the high average fertility of the population as a whole (Friedlander & Feldmann, 1993).

Israeli women did not fare well by the country's popular culture. In the literature that spanned the first decade of Israel's statehood (1948–1958), women were frequently portrayed as "deceptive, egotistical, devious, and overly sexed" (Fuchs, 1999, 212). In Hebrew contemporary fictions of the 1960s and 1970s, the Israeli woman was painted as a "vampiric bitch" that was out to destroy the Israeli male (Fuchs, 1989). While analyzing modern Hebrew literature, Esther Fuchs noted the near reversal in female and male characters' roles. She writes, "The cultural acceptance of Thanatos brings about a reversal where woman, the giver of life and the principle of Eros, is depicted as a deathly victimizer, while man, who does the killing, is perceived as a victim" (1989, 276). Ruth Ginsburg (1997) writes about the representation of the Jewish mother in Israeli literature within a span of a century. She concludes that the neglected and even suppressed mother figure in the earlier novels returns in more recent fictions with "excessive vengeance."

In recent years a handful of studies examined the portrayal of women in the Israeli media. Some studied television coverage of political campaigns concluding that women received less visual exposure and were portrayed in their traditional roles as nurturing care-givers (Lemish & Tidhar, 1991; 1999). Others analyzed images of women in Israeli advertisements focusing on subordination of women and their representation as sex objects (First, 1998; Lemish, 1997). And a recent study looked at the absence of Israeli women broadcasters during the Gulf War (Lemish & Tidhar, 1999).

However, lacking from this scholarly investigation is an inventory of images that exist within the Israeli media when women are described and discussed during national security crises. The following is an attempt to catalogue and categorize these images.

THE MYTH OF THE WOMB: A NATIONALISTIC SYMBOL

The primacy of motherhood in Israel is well documented (Katz & Peres, 1986; Izraeli & Tabori, 1988; Matchan, 1983; Safir, 1991). Illustratively, Solomon writes, "certainly women in Israel have little worth if they are not mothers" (1991,106). Likewise, fertility is a primary priority in the Israeli society. Thus, there are more fertility clinics per capita in Israel than in any other country in the world (Kahn, 1998). Israelis do not suffer inexplicably from more fertility problems than people in other parts of the world. In Israel, however, fertility is regarded as a supreme calling for both men and women. Safir quotes a clinical psychologist who reports that infertile "couples experience stress and guilt, and anger towards each other, their fertile friends ('are we inferior?', 'What's wrong with us?'), and towards their own families ('we are depriving them of their grandchildren')" (1991, 58). Remennick's study (2000) of infertile Jewish Israeli women suggests that their experiences include stigma coping strategies such as selective disclosure, avoidance of exposure of their "hidden disability," and passive-conformant versions of living.

Modern Israel lives in the shadow of the past. Biblical stories have a great impact on the image of the Jewish mother within the country and outside. Consider the story of the biblical Rachel. Genesis' well-known story of conceit and enduring love places Rachel as the beloved barren wife of Jacob. After years of frustrating yearning, Rachel bore Joseph, only to die while giving birth to a second son, Benjamin. Genesis tells us about her burial place, "on the way to Ephrat, which is Bethlehem. And Jacob set a pillar upon her grave; that is the pillar of Rachel's grave to this day" (35:20). Unsurprisingly, the Matriarch Rachel is the only biblical woman around whom an Israeli cult has been formed (Sered, 1999). Women suffering from infertility have frequented her tomb for centuries. In 1990, on the week marking the anniversary of Rachel's death, 100,000 women visited that site. A popular custom with these pilgrims has developed, one that links the mythological matriarch and fertility: a red string wound seven times around her tomb is then worn as a charm for fertility by her followers.

Several other Rachels amplify the place of the biblical Rachel in the Israeli mythology. Among them is Rachel Blubstein, perhaps the best-known Israeli female poet who published her poems under only her first name, Rachel. She died at a young age in 1931 in Palestine. One of her most famous poems, "The Barren One," explores her yearning for a child of her own. Later, this poem was heralded as the cry of every infertile woman in Israel. Her gravesite near the Sea of Galilee in northern Israel has been attracting many visitors, who perform rituals including reciting her poems and leaving notes at the grave.

The emphasis on physical continuity is part of the Jewish heritage. Keeping the distinction between past and future to a minimum, an ancient image resurfaces. This primal myth is the metaphor of the womb as the personification of the cycle of life. Wilshire (1989) describes this cycling from birth to death and rebirth: "The Mother's body, the earth, was perceived both as the womb out of which we are born and the tomb into which we are buried—that automatically again is the womb out of which we are reborn in the unending cycle. Both womb and tomb. Not either/or" (100).

In Israel, the womb plays a major role in defining a crucial element of its citizenry. The Knesset, the Israeli Parliament, passed the Embryo Carrying Agreements Law in 1996, publicly legislating surrogacy contracts by a government appointed commission. Israel is the first country in the world to do so. This law stipulates four conditions for surrogacy. Grippingly, the second condition mandates that the surrogate and the contracting couple must come from the same religion. This condition was made part of the law as a concession to the Israeli Orthodox rabbinical authorities. Accordingly, "a child conceived with the genetic material of a Jewish couple and born of a Jewish womb is considered to be Jewish. By contrast, if the embryo of a Jewish couple is gestated to parturition in a non-Jewish womb, the child is not considered to be Jewish" (Kahn, 1998. p. 31). Strikingly, as Kahn explains, not only the surrogate's womb is up for rent, but the Jewishness of her womb can be rented as well.

The following are four illustrations of the womb metaphor used in Israel to describe women.

The Womb as a Political Buffer

In 1966, about 20 years after Israel achieved its statehood and successfully directed a massive Jewish immigration wave into the country, a government-based natality committee charged with examining population, fertility, and reproduction policies concluded that "a reduction in the rate of growth of the population in the future seems undesirable from several viewpoints. The demographics-economic condition is such that an increase in the present size of the population and a substantial rate of population growth might stimulate economic development. . . . By means of an increased birth rate, the Jewish population of Israel would make an important contribution toward the rebuilding of world Jewry, whose general demographic situation is very unfavorable at present. A high rate of population growth seems most desirable from the standpoint of political and national security factors . . ." (Friedlander, 1974, 63). In 2001, 53 years into statehood, Israelis still worry about their demographic composition. Arnon Sofer of Haifa University, one of Israel's leading demographers, predicts that by 2020 the area comprising Israel and the occupied territories will be 58 percent Arab. As reported by *Newsweek*: "For Israel, the Palestinian problem is going to get more difficult with each passing year. Arafat well understands this, which is why he has often said that his strongest weapon is 'the womb of the Arab Woman'" (Israel's Best Plan, 2001, 33).

If there is a symbol or a central message propagandized to the Israelis it is the symbol of the womb. "The womb of the woman belongs to the motherland," wrote an Israeli journalist, Amos Kenan, in the aftermath of the 1973 War during the political campaign to reform the abortion law (10). Kenan referred to the use of the womb symbol for political and national purposes, "As to the holiness of life, many wrong deeds were done in its name. One of them is the suppression of the woman and making her a tool in the hand of the state. The womb of the woman belongs to the motherland, but a man is free to do as he pleases" (10).

Kenan was referring to the politicization of the womb, also known as the demographic threat. It is a double threat, since first, it relates to the security problem of a few million Jews in continuing conflict with 150 million Arabs. Second, it refers to the difference in the birthrate between Arabs and Israelis, and in particular, between Israeli Jews and non-Jews.

Writers and politicians placed woman in the heart of the national security problem. The "Israeli womb" was made the source of the problem. Not enough Jewish children were born in Israel. The suggested solution was to produce more children.

In the aftermath of the 1967 War, an Israeli morning daily published an article written by David Ben Gurion, the former first Prime Minister, attacking the practice of birth control in Israel. He wrote, "A Jewish woman who does not bring into this world at least four children—assuming it is up to her—is defrauding the Jewish mission" (13).

Ben Gurion called upon women's organizations to explain the needs of "our unique nation to women of European origin, to women born here, and to every Jewish woman who is capable of listening and understanding. A family should have four children, preferably in the first 8–10 years after the wedding. This is a woman's first responsibility" (13).

Ben Gurion was aware that the exclusive childbearing role assigned to Israeli women seemed demanding. Yet he proclaimed that this task was a form of service to the country. ". . . Almost every Jewish mother sends her son to the army without hesitation, even though she cannot be sure that he will stay alive or that she will see him again. She must understand, and she does, that she bears a secret . . . to assist as much as she can, in the rapid increase of our people in our land" (13).

Even women called upon other women to have more children. "We women must fight, not to decrease, but to increase the birthrate," wrote a female reporter in 1967 (Tora, 1967, p. 309). She cited national security reasons for her position.

In the 1970's, fear of zero Jewish population growth was a hot issue, not only in Israel, but also among Jews around the world. A conference on Jewish fertility in which scholars presented papers exploring this problem from various historical and sociological perspectives was held in New York in

February 1967. An organization was founded for "population regeneration union," punning the Hebrew commandment "Pr'u ur'vu" (be fruitful and multiply). Rabbi Norman Lamm, then the president of Yeshiva University, advocated that "each Jewish couple should have four or five children [because] Jews are a disappearing species and should be treated no worse than the kangaroo and the bald eagle" (*The Disappearing Jews*, 1975, p. 39).

The Heroic Womb

First and foremost, Israeli women fulfilled their duty to their people as mothers. In an article devoted to a newly published album celebrating the contributions of the Israeli servicewoman, a reference was made to the book's preface, written by Golda Meir, then the Prime Minister of Israel. She wrote, "The servicewoman of today is the daughter of yesterday's servicewoman and the mother of tomorrow's servicewoman and serviceman. Thus, this continuation safeguards the existence of the nation" (Ofer, 1972).

In particular, this one-dimensional presentation was typical of Israeli women in wartime. The press portrayed the Israeli woman as a heroic war mother who taught her son to be brave. "Mother brought us up to be soldiers," said a regiment commander who was quoted in the daily press a few days before the 1967 War (Lev, 1967, p. 5). Also, according to another account in the press, a mother of five soldiers expressed her feelings in the following manner, "When I felt my baby kicking inside me, I used to sing to him,`Kick son, kick, and when you come out you will become an Israeli hero and you will kick out all the enemies of Israel'" (Cohen, 1967, p. 17).

Literally, the wartime mother evoked an image of a symbolic womb in the wartime press. When interviewing a soldier's mother, a reporter noted, "Without raising my eyes to the face of Mother Biton, I thought that instead of her face I was seeing one big womb. Warm, soft, flowing and alive" (Cohen).

The Vulnerable Womb

The heroic womb myth was reinforced by another symbol, the vulnerable womb. Certain activities were believed to dislodge a woman's womb or make her infertile. This myth has even been enshrined in law. The 1959 Employment Services Act states that "the Minister of Labor may regulate, prohibit or limit the employment of a female worker in any specific work, production process or workplace employment in which it is likely, in his opinion, to be especially prejudicial to the health of a female." Hazelton (1977) reports that until the mid sixties, army doctors would not allow servicewomen to parachute because the jumps supposedly damage the womb. She also writes about her conversation with a kibbutz woman who claims that driving a tractor "can upset your menstrual cycle, makes you infertile, [and] can cause stillbirths" (88).

In addition, the Women's Labor Bill, which was introduced by Golda Meir and passed in 1952, granted special protection to female workers. According to this law, women could not work in industries connected with lead. Neither could they work in the proximity of, or operate, dangerous machinery. Also, women were not allowed to work night shifts, except those employed as nurses, waitresses, maids or those who obtained a special permit from the Ministry of Labor (Albeck, 1972).

Since women's reproductive abilities should be guarded in service of the nation, women's military service, especially in combat, is heatedly debated in Israel. The concern is three-fold: women's primary contribution to the society is actualized through their role as mothers; a physically demanding military service may compromise a woman's chance to become a mother; and participating in combat may result in captivity and possible rape of female soldiers, further putting at risk their ability to bear healthy Jewish children. This last reason is rooted in a deep fear among Israelis. The issue at hand is not only the concern for the welfare of the fighting soldiers but also the potential threat regarding the welfare of the (future) nation. In a newspaper profile of a young woman soldier, she provides an interesting twist in her own assessment of the restrictions put on female service in combat. Orit, a trainer in an infantry course, says: "It's nonsense—the whole issue with POW. If they want us in combat, order us to put in an IUD for five years. Then, I'll think about it seriously" (*Women of Valor*, 1994). Orit's comment demonstrates the extent to which Israeli women internalize the dominant discourse concerning women's roles in this militarized society (Ben-Ari, 2000).

The Defense Service Law of 1949, still in effect at present time, exempts married women as well as mothers from service. A woman becoming pregnant during her military service is discharged immediately. In dissenting from the majority opinion in a 1995 Supreme Court decision allowing female soldiers to partake in the pilots' training course, Justice Tal reasoned that a soldier's pregnancy could deny her entry to the course (Green Light, 1995).

With recent advances in research about human reproduction, a great deal of attention, coupled with generous public funding, has been provided for couples experiencing reproduction problems in Israel. The Public Health Insurance Law of 1995 entitles infertile couples an unlimited number of in vitro fertilization treatment cycles for producing not one but two children. Patients bear only modest co-payment for these costly services. Not surprisingly, Israel has among the highest per capita ratio of assisted reproduction clinics in the world (Romanic, 2000).

The Privileged Womb

Israel sustains a relatively high fertility level among its Jewish population. The Jewish fertility rate is about 3 children per woman compared with 1.4 in Western and Northern Europe and 1.9 in the United States. Fertility levels among religious Jewish women are even higher: 4.5 to 7. 5, depending on their level of orthodoxy (Friedlander & Feldmann, 1993).

Another version of the womb myth focuses on its privileged aspects. It presents femininity as a series of privileges that no woman could dream of forgoing. Few women dare express a desire to remain childless. Israeli women of reasonably high socioeconomic status who see childbearing as an unparalleled privilege tend to share this concept also. As Golda Meir told an Italian journalist, ". . . it is the greatest privilege we women have compared with men" (Fallaci, 1973, p. 100). Even though she abandoned her personal role as a mother, in the eyes of many Israelis, she became the national grand-mother. Often, reports of her habit of making tea and cakes for "the boys" guarding her house were published in the press.

Large families are referred to, in Israel, as "Bruchot Yeladim"—blessed with children. "Zehavi," an organization formed in 1972, works for the rights of large families. Among other suggestions, the organization requested that every mother of many children be recognized as an "approved government enterprise," so that they may receive special tax benefits and grants. The explanation of this suggestion calls for some comparison between men and women's contributions to society. It seems that while men serve the country as soldiers, women serve it as mothers.

THE WOMB AS A FIXATION IN THE
ISRAELI NATIONAL CONSCIOUSNESS

The focus on population planning in Israel has always been political. Prior to the establishment of the state of Israel, the Jewish community in Palestine had aimed at increasing the size of the Jewish population as rapidly as possible since this was considered to be an important issue in determining the country's political future. Following the establishment of the statehood, one of the first laws passed by the Israeli government was the Law of Return, according to which every Jewish person is entitled to immigrate to Israel. During the time between 1948 and 1951, Israel's population more than doubled.

After 1952, immigration to Israel declined, and the pressure to increase the population by natality was felt within the Israeli society. In addition to political objectives, rapid growth of the Jewish population has been viewed as an integral part of the religious values of Judaism.

However, these political and religious considerations have not led to a deliberate governmental policy against the provision of family planning services in Israel. By contrast, there are no such services within otherwise extensive public health services. In addition, until the late 1970's, a British law that was left untouched from the period of Mandatory Palestine prior to 1948 prohibited abortion in Israel. A 1977 law legalized abortions under very restrictive conditions, coupled with a bureaucratic process of petitioning abortion committees that were set up only by public hospitals (Yishai, 1993). Linked to public debate over the issue of legalizing abortions, a governmental committee was formed. Named after its chair, the Efrat Committee for the Encouragement of Higher Birthrates issued a plea to Jewish women to have more children, thus fulfilling their national duty (Sharoni, 1995a).

Because of the lack of family planning services, there is much public ignorance surrounding matters that concern family planning. At the same time, the absence of easily accessible family planning advice makes no positive contribution to the political or other national agenda.

This notion is not only accompanied by the lack of any communication programs or strategies aimed at the Jewish population, but also by popularly held images of women within the Israeli society. These images or metaphors, taken together, constitute a mythology. In her analysis of popular mythology of women in science, Keller (1983) argues that "this is not to imply that they are not true (they may or may not be) but, rather, to remove them from the realm of irreducible fact and to locate them in the realm of social construct . . . culturally shared myths . . . inevitably (at least in part) both reflect and shape the realities we observe" (133).

The two Freudian symbols, Eros and Thanatos, can explain the mystification of the womb as a primary mythology within the Israeli social context. In 1977, Hazleton wrote,

> Israelis . . . live and work out these constructs by assuming that war and the womb are antitheses. The womb is life, personal life, and future life in the bodies and persons of created others. And if life has to be protected by death, as it does in Israel, then as much life as possible must be created before death . . . (68).

These wartime media images are an integral part of national imaginings. Anderson's *Imagined Communities* put forward the idea of a strong sense of connection between the world of journalism, fiction, and national consciousness (1983). Building upon this important insight, David Koester, in his study of gender ideology and nationalism in Iceland, suggests "culturally based orientations toward gender enter into both the imagery of nations and the manner in which they construct themselves" (1995, p. 573). Koester describes the

Icelandic national discourse arguing for the centrality of "mother" and "the feminine" in Iceland's lingacultural, nationalist ideology. Similarly, Simona Sharoni (1995b) plays out the importance of the Hebrew language and some other cultural practices to the centrality of the theme of nation-as-woman of Israeli nationalism. The words used to describe the land of Israel are all feminine in Hebrew, "moledet" for homeland, "adama" for earth, "eretz" for country, and "medina" for state. Closely related is the concept of one's love of the country, since in this context, Parker, Russo, Sommer & Yaeger argue that it can be defined as "eroticized nationalism" (1992).

Sharoni adds that both Israeli and Palestinian women in the aftermath of the 1967 war were encouraged to participate in nationalistic projects assuming primary responsibility for reproduction. In this context, she pronounced that the "women in both the Palestinian and Israeli collectivities were encouraged to be nationalistic but were publicly praised only when they participated as women" (120).

Intriguingly, it was an American President, Bill Clinton, remarking on another American President, at a 1998 state dinner in Jerusalem, who allied a woman's womb with the sanctity of her role in Israeli nation building. He said: "It was in the White House that Harry Truman recognized the State of Israel only 11 minutes after you had declared your independence. And, I might add, he did so over the objection of some of his most senior advisers. It was in the White House a year later that President Truman wept when Israel's Chief Rabbi told him, 'God put you in your mother's womb so you would be the instrument to bring the rebirth of Israel after 2000 years.' Mr. Prime Minister, every President since Harry Truman has been strongly committed to the State of Israel and to Israel's security." (*Remarks at a Dinner,* 1998). Ironically, this time it was an American woman's womb (nevertheless a womb) that acted as a midwife at the birth of modern Israel.

CONCLUSION

When women are defined by their wombs, their entire existence is validated by that one bodily part and its function. A key element in pronatalist thought is the idea that a woman's role must involve maternity and that a woman's destiny and fulfillment are closely related to the birth experience (Peck & Senderowitz, 1974, p. 1–2). This approach has been both studied and challenged by feminists and social scientists for decades, commencing with Firestone's important work (1970).

While much of the research has focused on the coercive aspect of pronatalist policies, its reductionist aspect has been somewhat disregarded. This is not to say that reductionism—treating women not as whole beings, but only as parts—has not gained prominence among feminist scholars in recent years as a research subject but that the role of popular imagery in portraying women as reproducing machines needs further investigation.

REFERENCES

A Guide to Maternity Benefits. (2001, April). Guide NI17A, Leeds, UK: DSS Communication.

Albeck, P. (1972). The Status of Women in Israel. *American Journal of Comparative Law*, 20.

Amir, D. & Benjamin, O. (1992). Abortion Approval as a Ritual of Symbolic Control. In Feinmann, C. (Ed.), *The Criminalization of a Woman's Body.* New York: Haworth Press, 5–26.

Amir, D. & Benjamin, O. (1997). Defining Encounters, Who Are the Women Entitled to Join the Israeli Collective? *Women's Studies International Forum,* 20:5/6, 630–650.

Anderson, B. (1983). *Imagined Communities, Reflections on the Origins and Spread of Nationalism.* London: Verso.

Ben-Ari, A. (2000). Fresh Mattresses: Sexuality, Fertility and Soldiering in Israeli Public Culture. *Race, Gender & Class,* 7:1, 71.

Ben Gurion, D. (1967, Dec. 8). Increasing Birth Rate—How?. *Ha'aretz,* 3, 13. In Hebrew.

Berkovitch, N. (1997). Motherhood as a National Mission, The Construction of Womanhood in the Legal Discourse in Israel. *Women's Studies International Forum,* 20:5/6, 605–619.

Changes to Maternity and Parental Benefits. (2000). Retrieved from: http://www.hrdc-drhc.gc.ca.

Cleaver, H. (2000, August 1). Germans Used to Have More Babies. *The Daily Telegraph* (London), 13.

Cohen, G. (1967, June 2). A Private Conversation With Mother Biton. *Ma'ariv,* 17. In Hebrew.

The Disappearing Jews. (1975, July 14). *Time,* 39.

Enloe, C. (1983). *Does Khaki Become You? The Militarization of Women's Lives.* London: South End Press.

Fallaci, O. (1973, April). Golda Talks to Oriana Fallaci. *Ms.,* 74–76, 100–104.

Firestone, S. (1970). *The dialectic of sex: the case for feminist revolution.* New York: William Morrow.

First, A. (1998). Nothing New Under the Sun? A Comparison of Images of Women in Israel Advertisements in 1979 and 1994. *Sex Roles,* 38:11/12, 1065–1077.

Francome, C. (1997). Attitudes of General Practitioners in Northern Ireland toward Abortion and Family Planning. *Family Planning Perspectives,* 29:5, 234–236.

Friedlander, D. (1974). Israel. In Berelson, B. (Ed.), *Population Policy in Developed Countries.* New York: McGrawHill, 4297.

Friedlander, D. & Feldmann, C. (1993). The Modern Shift to Below-Replacement Fertility, Has Israel's Population Joined The Process? *Population Studies*, 47, 295–306.

Fuchs, E. (1989). Images of Love and War in Contemporary Israeli Fiction, A Feminist Re-vision. In *Arms and the Woman, War, Gender, and Literary Representation*. Chapel Hill: University of North Carolina Press.

Fuchs, E. (1999). The Enemy as Woman: Fictional Women in the Literature of the Palmach. *Israel Studies*, 4:1, 212.

Ginsburg, R. (1997). The Jewish Mother Turned Monster, Representations of Motherhood by Hebrew Women Novelists 1881–1993. *Women's Studies International Forum*, 20:5/6, 631–638.

Golan, G. (1997). Militarization and Gender: The Israeli Experience. *Women's Studies International Forum*, 20: 5/6, 581–586.

The Green Light for Women Pilots. (1995, Nov. 27). *The Jerusalem Post*.

Hazleton, L. (1977). *Israeli Women, The Reality Behind the Myths*. New York: Simon and Schuster.

Herzog, H. (1998, Spring). Homefront and Battlefront, The Stares of Jewish and Palestinian Women in Israel. *Israel Studies*, 3:1, 61.

Israel's Best Plan: Build More Walls. (2001, Aug. 13). *Newsweek*, 33.

Izraeli, D. (1979). Sex Structures of Occupations. *Sociology of Work and Occupation*, 6, 404–29.

Izraeli, D. & Tabori, E. (1988). The Political Context of Feminist Attitudes in Israel. *Gender & Society*, December 2, 4, 463–481.

Izraeli, D. (1992). Culture, Policy, and Women in Dual-Earner Families in Israel. In Lewis, Izraeli, D. & Hootsmans, H. (Eds.), *Dual-Earner Families, International Perspectives*. London: Sage.

Johnson, B. (1990, November 26). Italians Urge 'Have a Baby' EC Directive. *The Daily Telegraph* (London), 9.

Kahn, S. (1998). Putting Jewish Wombs to Work: Israelis Confront New Reproductive Technologies. *Lilith*, 23:2, 30.

Katz, R. & Peres, Y. (1986). The Sociology of the Family in Israel, An Outline of its Development from the 1950s to the 1980s. *European Sociological Review*, 2:2, 148159.

Keller, E. F. (1983). Women, Science and Popular Mythology. In Rothschild, J. (Ed.), *Machina Ex Dea, Feminist Perspectives on Technology*. New York: Pergamon Press, 130–46.

Kenan, A. (1975, Jan. 27). Artificial Abortion. *Yediot Achronot*, 10. In Hebrew.

King, L. (1998, Winter). 'France Needs Children': Pronatalism, Nationalism and Women's Equity. *Sociological Quarterly*, 39:1, 33–53

Koester, D. (1995). Gender Ideology and Nationalism in the Culture and Politics of Iceland. *American Ethnologist*, 22:3, 572–88.

Krull, C. (2001, Nov/Dec). Quebec's Alternative to Pronatalism. *Population Today*, 29:8,3,6.

Lahav, P. (1974). The Status of Women in Israel, Myth and Reality. *American Journal of Comparative Law*, 22:1, 107–29.

Lemish, D. (1997). The Ripple Effect: Pornographic Images of Women in Israeli Advertising. In S. G. French (Ed.), *Interpersonal Violence, Health and Gender Politics*. Toronto: McGraw-Hill, 285–295.

Lemish, D. & Tidhar, C. (1991). The Silenced Majority, Women in Israel's 1988 Television Election Campaign. *Women and Language*, 14:1, 12–21.

Lemish, D. & Tidhar, C. (1999). Still Marginal, Women in Israel's 1996 Television Election Campaign. *Sex Roles*, 41:5/6, 389–412.

Lemish, D. & Tidhar, C. (1999, Fall). Where Did All the Young Girls Go? The Disappearance of Female Broadcasters in War Times. *Women and Language*, 22,2, 27.

Lieblich, A. (1994). *Seasons of Captivity—The Inner World of POW's*. New York: New York University Press.

Lieblich, A. (1997). The POW Wife—Another Perspective on Heroism. *Women's Studies International Forum*, 20:5/6, 621–630.

Lev,Y. (1967, May 31). The Brigadier's Mother. *Ma'ariv*, 5. In Hebrew.

Manuel, G. (1999, November 1). Waking Up to the Baby Blues. *South China Morning Post*, 23.

Matchan, L. (1983, July 23). Women in Israel, Family Life Comes First. *Boston Globe*, 10–11.

Moore, D. (1988). Gender Identities and Social Action, Arab and Jewish Women in Israel. *The Journal of Applied Behavioral Science*, 34:1, 5–29.

Moore, D. (2000). Gender Identity, Nationalism, and Social Action Among Jewish and Arab Women in Israel, Redefining the Social Order? *Gender Issues*, 18:2, 3.

Ofer, T. (1972, March 19). The Unknown Servicewomen. *Ma'ariv*. In Hebrew.

Oppenheim Mason, K. (1997). Explaining Fertility Transitions. *Demography*, 34:4, 443–454.

Padan Eisenstark, D. (1973). Are Israeli Women Equal? Trends and Patterns of Israeli Women's Labor Force Participation, A Comparative Analysis. *Journal of Marriage and the Family,* 35:3, 538–45.

Parker, A., Russo, M, Sommer, D. & Yaeger, P. (Eds.). (1992). *Nationalisms and Sexualities*. New York: Routledge.

Peck, E. & Senderowitz, J. (1974). *Pronatalism: the Myth of Mom & Apple Pie*. New York: Thomas Y. Crowell Company.

Rapoport, T. (1988). Socialization Patterns in the Family, the School, and the Youth Movement. *Youth and Society*, 20, 159–179.

Rapoport T. & El-Or, T. (1997). Cultures of Womanhood in Israel, Social Agencies and Gender Production. *Women's Studies International Forum,* 20:5/6, 573–580.

Remarks at a Dinner Hosted by Prime Minister Netanyahu in Jerusalem. (1998, Dec. 13). *Weekly Compilation of Presidential Documents*. Washington D.C.: U.S. Government Printing Office, 34:2483–2485.

Remennick, L. (2000). Childless in the Land of Imperative Motherhood: Stigma and Coping Among Infertile Israeli Women. *Sex Roles*, 43: 11/12, 821–841.

Safir, M., Nevo, J. & Swirski, B. (1994). The Interface of Feminism and Women's Studies in Israel. *Women's Studies Quarterly,* 3&4, 116–131.

Safir, M. P. (1991). Religion, Tradition and Public Policy Give Family First Priority. In Swirski, B & Safir, M. P. (Eds.), *Calling the Equality Bluff, Women in Israel.* New York: Pergamon Press, 57–65.

Sered, S. (1999). Women Pilgrims and Women Saints: Gendered Icons and the Iconization of Gender at Israeli Shrines. *NWSA Journal*, 11:2, 48–72.

Sharoni, S. (1995a). Gendered Identities in Conflict, The Israeli-Palestinian Case and Beyond. *Women's Studies Quarterly,* 3 & 4, 117–135.

Sharoni, S. (1995b). *Gender and the Israeli-Palestinian Conflict, The Politics of Women's Resistance.* Syracuse: Syracuse University Press.

Solomon, A. (1991). Anything for a Baby, Reproductive Technology in Israel. In Swirski, B. & Safir, M. P. (Eds.), *Calling the Equality Bluff, Women in Israel.* New York: Pergamon Press, 102–7.

Swirski, B. & Safir, M. (Eds.). (1993). *Calling the Equality Bluff, Women in Israel.* New York: Teachers College Press.

Tora, B. (1967, September-October). Natality in the World and in Israel. *Dvar Hapoelet*, 309. In Hebrew.

United Nations. (1996). Department for Economic and Social Information and Policy Analysis. *Global Policy Data Base, 1995.* New York: United Nations.

Van Creveld, M. (1992, Fall). Women of Valor: Why Israel Doesn't Send Women Into Combat. *Policy Review*, 62, 65–68.

Weiss, S. & Yishai, Y. (1980). Women Representation in Israeli Political Elites. *Jewish Social Studies,* 42:2, 165–76.

Wilshire, D. (1989). The Uses of Myth, Image, and the Female Body in Re-Visioning Knowledge. In Jaggar, A. M. & Bordo, S. R. (Eds.), *Gender/Body/Knowledge, Feminist Reconstructions of Being and Knowing* (pp.98–114). New Brunswick: Rutgers University Press, 92–114.

Yishai, Y. (1993). Public Ideas and Public Policy, Abortion Politics in Four Democracies. *Comparative Politics*, 25:2, 207–228.

Yuval-Davis, N. (1989). National Reproduction and 'the Demographic Race' in Israel. In Yuval-Davis, N. & Anthias, F. (Eds.), *Woman-Nation-State.* London: Macmillian, 92–109.

Yuval-Davis, N. (1997*). Gender and Nation*. London: Sage.

Chapter Three

An Examination of Intimate Danger: Verbal and Nonverbal Displays of Intimacy in Lesbian Relationships in Film

Catherine Gillotti

Three years ago I was teaching an undergraduate class on interpersonal communication. As an in-class exercise, I showed a scene from the film *When Night Is Falling*. In this provocative scene, one woman, Petra, makes an overt pass at another woman, Camille, who is struggling with her sexual identity. When Petra says, "Camille, I would love to see you in the moonlight with your head thrown back and your body on fire," Camille replies, "That was uncalled for." At this point, many of the men in the room began to cheer and the dialogue of the film was drowned out by their comments and laughter. Did I show the scene to reinforce the stereotypical male fantasy? No, I did not, but clearly that was the response from my class. Their reaction to the scene and their visible discomfort toward any meaningful discussion was a not a surprise, but still a disappointment. The point of the exercise was to educate the students on the notion of intimate danger and to demonstrate communicatively what happens when someone's image is threatened in conversation.

The outcome of the exercise reinforced the very essence of this chapter, which is an examination and demonstration of intimate danger (Carilli, 1998) through four scenes from four different films depicting women loving women. The films included in this analysis are *Basic Instinct*, *Bound*, *When Night is Falling*, and *High Art*. An infinite number of scenes from many films could have been utilized in this analysis. The first two films were chosen based upon their mainstream appeal and release, and both were directed by men. I selected the latter two, both directed by women, to demonstrate the authenticity of women in romantic relationships. The four scenes exemplify the media's power to create intimate danger and the subsequent implications of the meanings derived. I will examine these scenes by integrating Goffman's face concept with intimate danger.

INTIMATE DANGER

Intimate danger is defined as behavior which challenges the norms and values of both heterosexual and homosexual communities (Carilli, 1998). In other words, intimate danger suggests that the behavior that validates the world view of one group's existence ultimately threatens the other group. Between genuine, legitimate interpersonal interactions, lesbians challenge heteronormativity while inauthentic sexualized interactions between lesbians challenge lesbian identity. This unavoidable dichotomy challenges scholars to dissect the microscopic, interpersonal behaviors which carry multiple and sometimes conflicting meanings as we search to understand the dynamics of interpersonal relationships in both communities, and the impact of media-driven stereotypes on these relationships.

FACE CONCEPT

Goffman (1967) defined *face* as "the positive value a person effectively claims for himself by the lines others assume he has taken during a particular contact" (p. 5). In other words, face is the image we have of ourselves and wish others to have of us, and line is the means by which we communicate face. Goffman (1967) separates face concept into *positive face* and *negative face*. Our positive face is our need for affirmation and validation, while negative face constitutes our need for autonomy (Goffman, 1967). Importantly, Goffman argues that individuals must work to save face for themselves and others, and that each culture has its own rules for face-saving strategies. Goffman (1967) equates learning face-saving strategies with learning the "traffic rules" of interaction (p. 12).

What is unique about the study of face (identity) maintenance in interactions involving gay men and lesbians is that gay men and lesbians sometimes feel stigmatized by their sexual identity, which ultimately affects interaction (Goffman, 1963). Goffman (1963) defines categories of stigma, which include "abominations of the body," "blemishes of individual character," and "tribal stigma" (p. 4). Taking into account the publication date of this work, it seems logical that homosexuality would fall under the "blemishes of individual character" category (Goffman, 1963, p. 4). It logically follows that if face is the image we have of ourselves and wish others to have of us, stigmatized individuals bring that to bear in their presentation of self. Goffman was particularly interested in how the stigmatized person behaved in interaction with "*normals*," and he refers to these interactions as mixed contact (p. 5). He eloquently draws the distinction between parties knowing the "discrediting" features of the stigmatized prior to interaction and the times when interactants are unaware of the attributes in question (Goffman, 1963, p. 4). He suggests there is a burden on the stigmatized individual to decide whether to reveal or not and then deal with the consequences of possibly discrediting oneself. "The issue is not that of managing tension generated during social contacts, but rather that of managing information about his failing. To display or not to display; to tell or not to tell; to let on or not to let on; to lie or not to lie; and in each case, to whom, how, when, and where"(Goffman, 1963, p. 42). Thus, the presentation of self becomes of crucial importance and is sometimes thoughtfully planned and executed, and this active maintenance of face is known as impression management (Goffman, 1959).

Goffman (1959) essentially viewed interaction as dramaturgical performance with on-stage and off-stage behaviors. He argues that the complexities of interaction are contingent upon many factors, including the judgments others make of the individual in interaction. For instance, he details how an innocent act can be misconstrued, and the effect of that is a bad impression. Feeling that we have created a bad impression can lead to the creation of self-fulfilling prophecies that further confirm these "bad" impressions. The bottom line resides in the perceptions of others, which are formed from our overt behavior and management of their impression of us (Goffman, 1959). "Shared staging problems; concern for the way things appear; warranted and unwarranted feelings of shame; ambivalence about oneself and one's audience; these are some of the dramaturgical elements of the human situation" (Goffman, 1959, p. 237).

Goffman wrote about the power of interpersonal interactions to create impressions, but the media determines what interpersonal interactions or dramas will be displayed for the masses, upon which impressions of cultural groups will be made. Without direct interaction, audiences then rely on the media to inform their impressions of various groups. "The mass media play a major role in this process of social definition, and rarely a positive one. In the absence of adequate information in their immediate environment, most people, gay or straight, have little choice other than to accept the narrow and negative stereotypes they encounter as being representative of gay people" (Gross, 1991, p. 27).

The following four scenes exemplify how intimate danger is created in the interpersonal interactions between these fictional characters. Through the verbal and nonverbal communication of the characters, we witness the simultaneous perpetuation of negative stereotypes and the validation of authentic relationships between women.

Basic Instinct

Basic Instinct is a psychological thriller starring Sharon Stone and Michael Douglas. Stone's character, Catherine Tramell, is a bi-sexual fiction writer suspected of a string of murders. Douglas' character, Nick, is the chief detective investigating the most recent murder. Nick becomes intimately involved with Catherine as he investigates the case. The scene selected for analysis takes place in a gay dance club where Nick follows Catherine as part of his surveillance on the case.

Nick enters the dance club in pursuit of his suspect, Catherine Tramell. He locates Roxy, Catherine's lesbian lover, on the dance floor with another woman. She exits the dance floor and enters the men's restroom where she finds Catherine doing drugs in a stall with an unknown character. Nick follows Roxy to Catherine. Roxy seductively sits on Catherine's lap, and Catherine begins to rub Roxy's sides and hips. When Nick moves to enter the stall, Catherine slams the stall door shut. Obviously, this action powerfully communicates his out-of-group status. The scene returns with Nick throwing back a shot and watching Catherine and Roxy fondle each other on the dance floor. Catherine and Roxy kiss, and then Catherine turns her back to Roxy as she runs her hands up and down Catherine's breasts. Nick watches and waits. Catherine then moves over to dance with Nick.

The scene conveys great attention to impression management. Catherine clearly seduces Nick through his desire to watch. She communicates her sexual prowess and her high sensation-seeking behavior through the drug use and her obvious sexual interest in both men and women. Everything about Catherine's behavior in this scene is scripted and manipulative. While there is no dialogue, Catherine's nonverbal behavior and impression management telegraphs intimate danger. Genuine lesbian relationships are the casualties of this scene because the scene depicts "every man's fantasy," suggesting that women behave sexually with one another only for the seduction of men.

Bound

Bound stars Jennifer Tilly as Violet and Gina Gershon as Corky. Violet is a prostitute involved with a member of the mafia. Corky is the maintenance worker in the apartment building where Violet resides. Violet pursues Corky by requesting plumbing repairs for her apartment. She does this knowing the landlord will send Corky to do the repairs. The scene selected presents the seductive interplay between Violet and Corky and highlights the stereotypical images of lesbians representing the butch-femme dichotomy.

What characterizes this scene is the disingenuous dialogue between Violet and Corky. The entire scene is punctuated by stereotypes of extreme femme-butch behaviors. Violet offers Corky a drink for fixing the sink, asking, "What would you like?" Corky replies that she wants a beer, and Violet retorts, "Of course." Violet invites Corky to sit down. She then remarks on the fact that Corky seems uncomfortable. Corky denies being uncomfortable but admits being curious. Notably, Corky is sitting in a very masculine position with her legs open, resting her elbows on her knees as Violet sits on the arm of an adjacent chair in a very feminine manner. The sexual interplay of the scene escalates as Violet responds to Corky's curiosity by stating, "That's funny. I'm feeling a bit curious myself." They continue the conversation by discussing Corky's tattoo, located on her breast. The scene ends with Violet asking Corky whether or not she likes it.

The scene is disingenuous because the only face that these two acquaintances are attending to are the characterizations of sexual image. Typically, genuine escalation of sexual desire is approached with greater care given the risk involved in revealing one's desires, and in the case of lesbians and gay men, revealing one's orientation offers the potential for stigma. Conversely, these characters communicate no risk or apprehension. The scene comes off as a fraudulent representation of lesbian desire and thus creates intimate danger for the lesbian community.

When Night Is Falling

In contrast to the first two films, the second two clips represent genuine dialogue and greater attention on the part of the characters to maintain face. *When Night Is Falling* is a story about Camille, a Christian college teacher, and her coming out in a relationship with Petra, a circus performer. Petra meets Camille in a laundromat. In their first meeting, Petra comforts Camille when she finds out that Camille's dog has just died. Petra is moved by Camille and wishes further interaction, so she switches their laundry on purpose to insure a future meeting. The scene selected for analysis is their second interaction, where they meet at Petra's trailer on the circus lot to exchange their laundry. The scene highlights the nuances of impression management, threats to positive face, the concern for stigma, and conversational repair.

Walking on the circus lot where Petra works, Camille and Petra approach Petra's trailer to exchange laundry bags. As they enter the trailer, their conversation begins with phatic (superficial) communication about the decorations in Petra's trailer. Petra invites Camille to stay for a drink. Camille replies that she is not much of a drinker, but stays anyway. Camille breaks the ice by self-disclosing that she wore one of Petra's tops. Petra compliments her on how she must have looked, and Petra covertly inquires as to whether or not Camille is seeing anyone: "Your man must have liked it." Camille replies, "What man?" This exchange alone is characteristic of any conversation where the interactants subtly reduce the uncertainty about each other.

Petra continues to escalate the risk involved in the conversation by complimenting Camille: "You have an exquisite mouth, you know?" Seeming surprised, Camille replies, "I do?" Notable pauses between the verbal exchanges bring a genuineness to the interaction. Petra then self-discloses that she switched their laundry on purpose. Camille asks the reason, and Petra responds, "I don't know; you moved me." Camille reciprocates by stating how tender Petra was to her in the laundromat. At this point, Petra makes an overt, verbal pass at Camille. "Camille, I would love to see you in the moonlight with your head thrown back and your body on fire."

This is clearly a conversational violation—a threat to positive face—in Camille's eyes. She raises her hand to warn Petra to stop. Then she says, "That was uncalled for." Petra replies, "True, but if you wait for what is called for, usually nothing happens." Camille then responds, "I'm clearly out of my element here." This scene typifies a blatant face threat and then a series of statements of facework and conscious impression management to restore Camille's face. Camille denies her sexual identity by separating herself from Petra. It also demonstrates internalized homophobia. Petra proceeds to engage in protective facework (defending another's image) to repair the conversation, but the damage is done. She de-escalates the verbal exchange by trying to re-initiate the conversation regarding Camille's teaching. Camille does not respond to this but simply asks for her laundry and leaves.

Verbally and nonverbally, this scene represents genuine conversation and interpersonal relational escalation. Visible, nonverbal discomfort intensifies as both Petra and Camille slowly escalate the intimacy of their talk. Nonverbally, as the verbal intimacy escalates, the characters avert eye gaze and fidget. The genuineness of this scene creates intimate danger for the heterosexual community because it legitimizes relationships on the same levels of risk in intimacy that are found in all romantic relationships.

High Art

In *High Art*, Ally Sheedy plays a famous photographer named Lucy Berliner. Lucy struggles with a collapsed career and a drug habit. She meets her downstairs neighbor, Syd, who happens to be an assistant editor for a major photography magazine. Upon seeing Lucy's photographs in her apartment, Syd convinces Lucy to come out of retirement and work a photo shoot for the magazine. Motivated by her personal interest in Syd, Lucy agrees to do the work. The scene selected for analysis takes place in Lucy's car. The characters are on their way to spend the weekend together working on the shoot.

Lucy pulls the car over to the side of the road and begins to take her camera out of her bag. Syd looks into the bag as Lucy removes the camera and finds a vial of drugs. The following verbal exchange occurs.

Syd: I didn't know you were going to bring that.

Lucy: I wanted to get high with you.

Syd: I don't think I want to this weekend.

Lucy: No?

Syd: No.

Lucy: Okay.

Syd: I don't want to get high with you all the time.

Lucy: Alright.

Syd: I mean, I don't want that to be our only connection.

Lucy: It's not our only connection.

Syd: I mean, I don't want it to become like that.

At this point, Lucy becomes defensive, takes the drugs, and holds them out of the car window. She inquires whether that makes Syd feel better and then asks her what the point is. Syd replies that she does not have a point but that she does not want to be with Lucy "like that right now." Syd then leans over and kisses Lucy, but Lucy pulls back and does not fully return the kisses.

From an interpersonal perspective this scene demonstrates negotiation, meta-communication, and power in relationships. When Syd and Lucy talk about their connection, they are affirming for one another through meta-communication that they are connected beyond the drug use, thus supporting each other's positive face. Lucy is managing an impression that she is in control of the relationship by not returning Syd's kiss. Syd actually exerts power by initiating the physical contact, and Lucy does not want Syd to know how much she really loves her, so she withholds her affection.

The dialogue in this scene is coded and tentative as it was in *When Night is Falling*, again indicating the risk involved in disclosing interest in an intimate relationship in the early stages of relationship escalation. The authenticity of the dialogue and the corresponding nonverbal behaviors of the characters are what pose the intimate danger for the homophobic, heterosexual community. In contrast, the lack of meaningful dialogue, and the heavy-handed, stereotypical portrayals of the women in both *Basic Instinct* and *Bound* convey an appeal to a visually stimulated audience seeking to fulfill voyeuristic pleasures. The portrayals reinforce existing stereotypes about women as sex objects and create intimate danger for the lesbian community.

DISCUSSION

Intimate danger is about dialectically opposed values regarding sexual identity. Gross (1991) argues that the media is driven by social, political, and, especially, economic forces. These forces wield tremendous power for legitimizing or marginalizing various social groups. He continues that those with power do not seek representation, while those without power are not represented. "That is, while the holders of real power—the ruling class—do not require (or seek) mediated visibility, those who are at the bottom of the various power hierarchies will be kept in their places in part through their relative invisibility" (Gross, 1991, p. 21). The above literature review emphasizes that gay men and lesbians have been those who have been made invisible, and this invisibility comes with tremendous personal and political cost.

As Weeks (1991) stated, sexual identity is a "strange thing," and the communication of that identity is not to be taken lightly (p.79). The film industry has perpetuated stereotypes about gay men and lesbians that are far from accurate (Russo, 1987). The four film clips included in this analysis demonstrate the concept of intimate danger because they appeal to the polar ends of the sexual identity continuum.

The first two movies, *Basic Instinct* and *Bound,* align with many films reviewed by Russo (1987) that provide only stereotypical images of gay life and love. The mainstream release and appeal of these movies legitimize and reinforce a heterosexist value system where women may love women only in the context of male pleasure. The lack of meaningful discourse and relational substance between the characters creates intimate danger and threatens the legitimacy of lesbian relationships. Notably, Catherine Tramell and Violet sleep with both men and women. At face value these characters represent the fluidity of sexual identity. I argue, however, that this subtlety is lost in their stereotypical depictions. Instead, the films reinforce mass audiences' existing frame of reference regarding sexual identity. Thus, intimate danger is created for the lesbian community. The second two films, *When Night is Falling* and *High Art,* depict genuine and naturally occurring conversation and highlight the risk involved in the disclosure of the desire for intimacy. They thus threaten the homophobic heterosexual communities because they illustrate that gay relationships are as legitimate, as relational, and as beyond sexual as their own relationships. The latter films make it harder to dismiss same-sex love as nothing more than a sexual behavior.

Every interaction we have is a performance on Goffman's (1959) dramaturgical stage, and we make choices about the images we want to portray to others. Petra and Camille, and Syd and Lucy, were highly conscious of their impressions and attended to them in their interactions. This attention to and maintenance of one's own and the other's face is virtually absent from the first two films, leaving the audience with only stereotypes to form their impressions of the characters, and of gay men and lesbians in general.

The implications of intimate danger are profound when consideration is given to the power of the media to legitimize and mobilize masses of people with powerful and political agendas who write the cultural history of our times. At the interpersonal level, intimate danger has the potential to significantly affect the valuing or devaluing of one's sense of *self*. The fact that film makers create characters like Catherine, Roxy, Violet, and Corky and market them to "mainstream" audiences to portray normative lesbian relationships, while characters like Petra, Camille, Syd, and Lucy are virtually dismissed, is evidence that intimate danger continues to lurk in our midst.

REFERENCES

Boros, S., Lazar, A. (Producers), & Wachowski, A. & Wachowski, L. (Writers/Directors). (1996). *Bound* [Motion picture]. United States: Dino De Laurentiis Company.

Carilli, T. (1998). Intimate danger: Depictions of lesbian desire in mainstream films. Paper presented at the meeting of the Central States Communication Association, St. Louis, MO.

Goffman, E.(1959). The arts of impression management. *The presentation of self in everyday life*. (pp. 208–237). Bantam Doubleday Dell Publishing Group, Inc.

Goffman, E. (1963). *Stigma: Notes on the management of spoiled identity*. New York, NY: Simon & Schuster, Inc.

Goffman, E. (1967). *Interaction ritual: Essays on face-to-face behavior*. New York, NY: Pantheon Books.

Gross, L. (1991). Out of the mainstream: Sexual minorities and mass media. *Journal of Homosexuality, 21*, 19–46.

Hall, D., Levy-Hinte, J., Stover, S. (Producers), & Cholodenko (Writer/Director). (1998). *High Art* [Motion Picture]. United States: 391 Productions.

Marshall, A. (IV) (Producer), Eszterhas, J. (Writer), & Verhoeven, P. (Director). (1992). *Basic Instinct* [Motion picture]. United States: Carolco.

Russo, V. (1987). *The Celluloid Closet*. New York, NY: Harper & Row Publishers.

Tranter, B. (Producer), & Rozema, P. (Writer/Director). (1994). *When Night Is Falling* [Motion Picture]. Canada: Crucial Pictures.

Weeks, J. (1991). Sexual identity is a strange thing. In J. Weeks (Ed.), *Against nature: Essays on history, sexuality and identity* (pp. 79–85). London: Rivers Oram Press.

Chapter Four

Cuteness:
The Sexual Commodification
of Women in the Japanese Media

Kimiko Akita

Japanese pop-culture and cuteness have been studied by many Western scholars, but from Western perspectives. The Japanese fondness for cute goods is
often viewed as a 'cult of cuteness' (Schomer & Chang, 1995; McVeigh,
2000a). This cuteness is almost depicted as exotic (See Kinsella, 2000a;
Williams, 2000) by Western scholars. Cuteness is often considered a major
cultural trait of young women's collective behavior (Darling-Wolf, 2001;
Kinsella, 1995, 2000a, 2000b; Klippensteen, 2000; McVeigh 1996, 2000a,
2000b; Sato, 1998; White, 1993). However, these Western-oriented perspectives are based on dualistic/dichotomized constructs such as individualistic-
collectivistic, I-thou, and power-powerlessness underlying a Western subjectivity (free will), not a Japanese styled (allocentric and alteritic) subjectivity.
Oftentimes, what appears to be unusual or strange to Western eyes is depicted
as exotic and presented so as to appeal to Western audiences hungry for interesting oddities. Waldron and Mare (1998) argue "recent research indicates
that conceptions of the Japanese as a gendered society are, to some extent,
stereotypical and more representative of how Westerners perceive the Japanese to behave communicatively" (p. 181) rather than how the Japanese see
themselves from an insider or *emic* perspective.

Cuteness, taken as a masking or masquerade, "can be subversive (under-
mining male domination) but can also provoke critical praxis [analysis]" (Patel, 2001, p. xvi). "*Kawaii*" (cuteness) masquerades offer useful ways to understand structures of hegemony that have been generated over the years.
Because "the marginalized woman can effectively use masquerade to disrupt
patriarchal structures and 'speak' for herself and on her own terms" (p. xxv),
I wish to explore here the sexual commodification of women in relation to
cuteness in the Japanese media from a woman's insider perspective using an

autoethnographical approach. As a native Japanese who was once willing to objectify herself to become a commodity, I have become more sensitized to my own experiences. I have spent countless hours talking with *ganguro*[1] girls (darkened faces) and *Sailor Moon*[2] look-a-likes. I taught many such young girls at a women's junior college in the suburbs of Nagoya, Japan, between 1992 and 1998, as one of the few female full-time faculty. While I was a college teacher for ten years (1989–1998), the image of 'cuteness' was becoming idealized. I was intrigued by the prevalent image of cuteness everywhere, especially as artifactually represented and communicated among my students (i.e., through their clothing, accessories, and behaviors). At the same time, I was very interested in my students' ideologies. My students' voices as well as some of the surveys and interviews on 'cuteness' that I conducted will be woven throughout this text.

WHAT IS CUTE?

When I was a women's junior college teacher in Japan, what struck me most were my observations of supposedly mature students (aged 19–21) wearing "cute" childish outfits (e.g., mini skirts, *luuzu socks*[3], or *atsuzoko*[4] platform shoes), various Hello-Kitty[5] items (e.g., slippers with a big Hello-Kitty face, hair pins, bags, accessories), speaking in "cute," baby-like voices, and behaving with "cute" infantile manners and "puckish styling" (Goffman, 1979), such as fondling one's clothes and posing with pigeon toes. Those girls appeared to look like Sailor Moon or Hello Kitty, and I felt they came right out of *manga* (comics and animation) stories. Some students wore *ganguro* (darkened faces) style, bleached blonde or colored hair, glittering flakes on their cheeks, and blue contact lenses. Other students even spoke softly in an infantile manner to appear cute, and I had a hard time hearing and understanding their babyish voices. I observed infantile linguistic or communicative behaviors, such as unnecessary, incessant smiles and giggling, often used to avoid saying a full sentence; frequent onomatopoeias or cute body signs (e.g., showing and waving open palms) instead of completing a sentence; rounded writing styles; pop writing neologisms such as "I like English xx2" instead of "I like English very very much;" abbreviated verbal expressions such as "*Hage*" meaning "Haagen Dazs," "*Makudo*" meaning "McDonald's," and "*Ushi*" (cow) meaning "*Yoshinoya Gyudon*" (a popular beef restaurant); and use of their first names as the subjective "I" (i.e., Yukari herself says, "*Yukari did it!*" instead of "*I did it!*"). This manner of a girl addressing herself by her first name[6] is usually tolerated only for small children (aged 2–7) in Japan because children have not developed the concept of a subjective, "I," yet. Therefore, this was one of my most shocking observations.

The everyday lives of Japanese are hegemonically influenced by mass media, which actively promotes cute images. Cuteness is one of the most dominant pop-culture trends, creating a pervasive idealism for women in Japan (McVeigh, 1996, 1997, 2000a, 2000b). Japan is flooded with *kawaii* (cute) objects. *Kawaii* can refer to various things: clothes, accessories, manners, personalities, feelings, looks, smells, colors, tastes, etc. Babies, grandmothers, bald men, crooked faces/teeth, carelessness, dumbness, strawberry or other fruity sweet smells, flatulence, white and pinkish colors, ice cream, and candy were all considered as *kawaii* by Japanese college students in my survey[7] conducted in 2001.

Kawaii objects (i.e., artifacts) are often worn as extensions of one's body image, informing others of one's own charming nature and how one would like to be considered in the social world (McVeigh, 1996). *Kawaii* may be a mask, a "multi-toned masquerade, which can be both subversive and non-subversive, critical and non-critical, ambiguous and non-ambiguous, . . . [a *kawaii* mask that] is continually being redefined and modified as different political, social, and economic structures come into play" (Patel, 2001, p. xiv–xvi).

Discourses of cuteness carry gendered messages mediated through artifacts such as food, facial expression, clothing, and objects. Japanese women wearing cute clothes speak in a cute manner because "appropriate language has a similar function to appropriate attire in Japan" (Ide, 1997, p.48), and "there is a strong association between etiquette and ethics, external appearance and internal attitude, what one wears and one's character" (McVeigh, 1997, p. 125). For example, ice cream is considered cute food. A girl drinking black coffee looks masculine and appears intimidating in men's eyes, while a girl eating ice cream appears cute and fits within the patriarchal social norm. An example from my own personal experience can clarify this. Once, when I ordered black coffee, my ex-boyfriend changed my order to ice cream, saying, "Don't be like a man. Eat ice cream. I want you to look cute" (meaning: "You're wearing nice, feminine clothes and you're cute to me, so why don't you eat cute food, too?" and "I want you to be submissive, especially in public, to make me appear more manly").

Because of Japan's patriarchal social system, the country's economic situation is connected to the commodification of women. For instance, although more women than men get a higher education ("Higher Education Rate," 2001), men have better opportunities to secure jobs ("College Graduates' Employment Rate," 2000). While 40 percent of unmarried men would like their future wives to quit work upon having children, only some 20 percent of unmarried women want to be stay-at-home mothers (Kashiwagi, 2001). Increasingly, Japanese women are finding that the negative aspects of marriage outweigh the benefits, so they prefer maintaining their single status. Mothers continue to be solely responsible for managing all housekeeping duties, finances, and child-rearing functions in Japan. This means that more single young women are remaining jobless or working part-time, hoping to stay single and live with their parents. These women live at home free of charge ("Girl Power Hits Tokyo," 2000) as so-called "parasite singles" (" 'Parasite Singles': Problem or Victims?" 2000). As a result, the cute products have been targeted to young unmarried women (20 to 30 year olds) who have the most disposable income (their consumer spending accounts for 60% of consumer economic activity) ("Girl Power Hits Tokyo," 2000). However, as we shall see, the cute images help maintain a Japanese patriarchal socioeconomic system, perpetuating the expectation that women behave submissively to men. Cute products and cute manners clearly represent an unconscious hegemonic oppression of women in a Japanese patriarchal society.

TRANSITION IN THE MEANING OF KAWAII

The meaning of *kawaii* has evolved over many years. In Japanese literature, the word, *kawa-yui*[8], had been used frequently instead of *kawa-ii* until the mid-1950s when the *kawaii* image was first promoted by representing an ideal image for girls in Japanese girls' comic books. *Tomoko Matsushima*, a girl (aged seven to ten) with big, doll-like eyes and the first popular girl actress, appeared on the cover pages of girls' magazines (Yonezawa, 1999, pp. 38–39). From then on the *kawaii* image for girls became a face with large eyes like a doll. Many women had and still have surgery to enlarge their eyes or surgery to make their facial bone structure smaller so that their eyes appear larger. Women and teenagers apply mascara to change the downward slant of their eyes or to make their faces look smaller ("Kids Caught in Latest Cosmetics Fad," 2001).

Kawaii (kawa-ii) has been used to refer to small children, animals, or small objects, but it has never been proper to use *kawaii* to refer to adult men and women. The word *kawaii* has now come to have more versatile meanings. It became more popular among teenage girls particularly in the mid-1980s when people became materialistic, and young teenagers started to commodify themselves and others more by using the word. (Saito, 1999, p. 47). More and more *kawaii* products targeted at adults have been produced since the mid-1980s (when redesigned Hello-Kitty products came out). Saito notes that Japanese teenagers nowadays lack proper vocabularies and expressions (pp. 48–57). *Kawaii* now extends its meanings to delicious, cool, chic, exciting, fun, funny, dumb, fragile, vulnerable, smooth, obedient, accepting, ambiguous, neutral, cheap, soft, tender, glittering, pretty, colorful, easy, careless, forgetful.[9] At the same time, younger people are having trouble differentiating private spaces from public spaces because of the pop-cultural artifacts such as *keitai* (cellular phones) and Walkman (p. 48). *Kawaii* artifacts and the faddish expressions help young people identify with the people they want to be "camp" or super cool with, alienating themselves from other groups and creating their private spaces in public spaces (p. 61). For instance, *jibetarian*[10] (punned on vegetarian for *jibe;* "ground") became popular with the *ganguro* look and the *luuzu* socks. *Jibetarian* sit with their friends on the floor of a train or a platform talking loudly, which can annoy other passengers very much. Young women also may appear to be making a statement to express their transformed identities by wearing Sailor Moon-like clothes or those fashioned from popular *manga*, magazines, movies, and television.

Traditionally, women's intimacy and outspoken manners may be expressed in private spaces such as their homes. Presently, however, façades of infantile, cute manners (e.g., doing *jibetarian*) and artifactual communication can help them turn the public spaces into private ones. In other words, I argue that their artifacts work as Halloween masks emancipating and empowering them because "infantile manners and cute artifacts soothe and provide a release from adult responsibilities" (McVeigh, 1996, 2000b; Sato, 1998; White, 1993, p. 126). Their artifacts, or mediated material culture, help them feel free by "escaping from the real world, or at least from the high-pressured social world of Japan, creating a 'consumutopia'" (McVeigh, 2000b, p. 228) and by evading or delaying the adult imperative for self-control to maximize their freedom (Sato, 1998, p. 39). In a way, however, these women are turning their supposedly public spaces into private spaces through their artifacts so that the public gaze focuses on their artifacts, but not on them as authentic persons. Therefore, young girls' pretentious artifacts and *jibetarian* behaviors can help them construct their identities, making them feel as if they are backstage, Goffman's (1959) dramaturgical concept, when they are in fact on a public stage.

"Infantility, stupidity, rudeness, vulgarity are released or deliberately acted out in an intimate situation . . . . boisterousness, crying, postural indulgence such as lying on the floor . . . such violations of conventional norms are permitted or even endorsed in intimate interaction" (Lebra, 1976, p. 116). Although some young women may express their independent thoughts, thanks to their cute artifacts creating an imaginary backstage, they depend only on the rhetorical power of cuteness. However, in effect, this behavior continues to confine them to enacting the roles of vulnerable, submissive, and immature second class citizens.

Murase (2000) claims that *kawaii* is a hierarchical adjective because it was used only by older or superior people to negate younger or inferior people (including girls and immature-looking women) (pp. 216–217). Murase assumes that *kawaii* has rhetorical power to enable users to commodify and disempower others. For instance, suppose a girl calls a teacher, a dinosaur, or a monster "*kawaii*." She is transforming a scary object with power into an object without power by referencing that object as *kawaii*. *Kawaii* images used for pornography or *manga* can mask the hidden meaning: the sexual exploitation of women. Murase believes that *kawaii* is contributing to the reproduction of sexually exploitive social structures.

Once I was seriously speaking to a class, scolding my students for their misbehavior. One student suddenly said, "Teacher! Your earrings are so *kawaii*!" All my students laughed, and I had to stop my scolding. I was stunned by this unexpected, ill-mannered remark, but at the same time I learned about the rhetorical power of *kawaii* because it instantly turned a sullen atmosphere into a cheerful one. But the word *kawaii* only helped my students evade their adult responsibilities to listen to me as more mature young women should have. In support of Murase's idea, I think *kawaii* cannot solve the core problem of sexual commodification. It only helps to recreate hierarchical (e.g., teacher-student, adult-child, men-women) or gendered relationships (e.g., Men work "outside" to earn money, while women take care of children and homes, staying "inside").

GIRLS' MANGA AND WOMEN'S POWER

Cuteness has been projected in *manga*, especially through girls' comics. "Girls' *manga* are central to the contemporary medium, as indeed young women are to contemporary Japanese culture in general" (Kinsella, 2000, p. 138). When fighting girl characters like Sailor Moon came out in the 1990s, people thought women's liberation had begun. Although Murase agrees that fighting by young girls such as Sailor Moon meant social participation and self-identity, she argues that "fighting girl" characters are simply pleasing male TV or girl-comic audiences (Murase, 2000, p. 79). The femininity of Sailor Moon and other fighting girl characters is expressed by their big breasts, long hair, long eye lashes, high toned voices, and mini skirts, but their fertility and menstruation are completely eliminated (p. 78). Although the number of girl's comics featuring "fighting girls" is increasing in Japan, "fighting girl" comics appear to please primarily male publishers and audiences who wish to be reminded of male dominance. Moreover, these characters help sell pornographic stories that are even spicier (Murase, 2000, p. 220).

"Fighting girl" characters like Sailor Moon seem to have contradictory characteristics because they possess beauty, cuteness, and power (assertion and independence) (pp. 35–49). Murase contends that comics supercede novels in terms of the audience's perception of "beauty" (pp. 35–49). Thus, Sailor Moon may be portrayed as having power, even when she is submissively beautiful and cute at the same time. However, in giving the quality of cuteness to fighting girls, comic writers disempower fighting girls in order to subordinate them to the traditional male norms of the audience. "Women's power" represents a form of subjugation. Murase argues that girls especially are encouraged to become consumers in the sexually exploitative market system through media exposure, while these girls are hegemonically influenced to become women "happily exploited by men" (p. 218). When a girl first has sex, she is considered to have become a woman for the first time. Unlike in the West, sexuality has been men's arena, not women's.

JAPANESE WOMEN'S SUBJECTIVITY AND MEDIATED OBJECTIFICATION

On my last visit to Japan in July, 2001, I went to a bathhouse to relax and watch TV with other women in a sauna room. I noticed that most of the commercials projected cute images and used humor to capture the audience's attention, while motherhood, marriage, and women's domestic lives continued to be idealized. The obvious trend was that younger women were presented as sexual objects behaving in a cute, infantile, ignorant, and stupid manner. Women's bodies were presented as sexual and material objects. While women's bodies and their projected images were objectified (commodified), the women watching the same TV scenes with me were nonchalant and uncritical. *Akashiya Sanma* is one of the most popular male comedians in Japan. His program is called *"Appare Sanma-dai-sensei,"* or *"Sanma* the Great Teacher." On one of the evening programs for children, I saw *Sanma* jokingly uttering a sexual remark (i.e., "You're so cute! I feel like raping you!"[11]) to one of the little girls on the program. My jaw dropped! At the end of another weekly late hour program, *Sanma* appeared with a fake bat in a disguise, laughingly and abusively hitting a young woman's head. She had a *ganguro* face, wore very "cute" clothes, and was tied to a chair. He said, "You're dumb! Stupid!" I found *Sanma's* behavior sexually and physically abusive, but I was shocked to find that many of the women in the sauna room were laughing while watching *Sanma's* abuse. When I shared my critical opinions about these programs and TV commercials with other women in the sauna room, they admitted, "Oh, come to think of it, you're right!"

"I've never thought about this before."

One young woman said, however, "I like that scene where *Sanma* hits a woman's head every week because those women are very stupid anyway."

My experience in the bathhouse demonstrates the lack of critical thinking among Japanese women. I was just like them not too long ago. I could not think critically or analytically about social phenomena. When I heard the young viewer's nonchalant reaction, I wondered how Japanese women ever could be made to develop their autonomous subjectivity and critical thinking. I also wondered if the media's hegemony had influenced Japanese women to accept their objectification. Knowing that almost all Japanese mass media, companies, and bureaucracies were controlled by men, I began to feel that Japanese women were puppets, mediated through their artifacts, on a stage built by men to maintain the patriarchal social system.

In patriarchal discourse, the nature and social role of women are defined in relation to a norm created by men to meet individual men's needs. In Japan, women are highly vulnerable to male-controlled messages from the media. Due to communication technology, media access is extremely easy and powerful in Japan. Japanese women may wear cute technological artifacts or behave in cute ways while using communication technologies to project themselves as appealing objects/images/symbols to comply with men who control the media and the social system. This artifactual communication is the material culture. "Discursive practices are embedded in material power relations . . ." (Weedon, 1997, p. 103). As Foucault (1981) says, "the manner in which what is most material and most vital in them has been invested" (p. 152). Gender-relationships and sexuality exist in the discourses of gendered-artifacts and mediated sexuality in the material culture.

"By the average Japanese, individualism is understood as selfishness. It represents antisocial behaviour. . . . 'Human rights' and 'women's rights' may be common phrases in the West but are understood differently in Japan" (Morley, 1999, pp. 24–25). In Japan, women are expected to support others to maintain social harmony, *wa*, which is a norm created by men. "The demand upon a woman is not so much for self-focused coping as it is for other-focused caring" (Plath, 1980, p. 163). Kondo (1990) deconstructs the binary between subject and object and argues that selves and society are not separate identities in Japan, but that persons (especially allocentrically inclined women) are constituted in and through social relations and obligations to others (pp. 22–24). Japanese women may be willing to become objects/images/symbols (not persons or individuals with subjective free will) mediated through artifacts because it helps them project their subservient, allocentric, and supportive socio-cultural roles. This allocentric behavior is used to "*craft*" (Kondo, 1990) women's identity. Some of their crafting behaviors may be observed in their refusal to be subjective or to think critically. Other crafting may be observed in the artifactual communication in which women interact with one another. As a result, Japanese women appear eager to become objectified, stopping themselves from speaking up, adapting instead "a 'coercive consensus' that prevents open discussion of any sensitive issue" (Field, 1991, pp. 28–29).

Conscious of becoming ideal objects for the male gaze, women are driven to seek the latest information about fashion and goods from the various media. Within Japan's patriarchal material culture, I argue, "*common-sense*" thinking becomes a highly valued norm. Japanese women who seldom discuss issues among each other critically, analytically, and openly, gain their collective social experiences through media, which also helps them maintain social harmony, *wa*, among themselves. Statements in the media often support the value of common-sense knowledge, such as "*we all know that it is natural*" or "*everyone else is doing it!*" Weedon (1997) argues that common-sense thinking is a way of understanding social relations that denies history and the possibility of change (p. 5). The sources of common-sense knowledge are general education, the media, relatives, and friends (p. 73). This form of thinking puts pressure on individuals to accept these forms of knowledge (p. 74). In fact, for women to support the male norm deprives them of opportunities to develop critical thinking or autonomous, free-willed subjectivities. Instead, Japanese women's subjectivities are circumscribed, constructed, represented, and recrafted aesthetically through material culture.

SUMMARY

To wear masks . . doesn't always indicate masquerade. We wear masks to conceal; we masquerade to conceal and reveal. Through masquerade we enter new terrains, make new faces. . . To make face is to have face—dignity and self respect . . . It is through art and activism, and expression that masquerade displaces and replaces memories. It is through masquerade that we can understand and critique the world we live in. (Patel, 2001, p. 120).

As Rosaldo and Lamphere (1974) noted, women's status will be lowest in those societies where there is a firm differentiation between domestic and public spheres of activity. Japanese women construct their hegemonically subjugated identities and represent them aesthetically by wearing their *kawaii* masks (i.e., masquerades, artifacts). Their masks may reveal, conceal, reject male authority and social orders, and maintain their dignity and self-respect, although their masks may also commodify them, consume them, subjugate them, or sexually exploit them. What we see in their artifacts, material culture, in their maskings may actually be what we would see behind their masks: their authentic selves, however impoverished.

Japanese patriarchally repressive and sexually exploitive society itself may be presented in a cute, aesthetic, clean, and moralistic way, making it harder for women to think critically and search for the rhetorical meanings and power of their masquerades. Technology, media, the patriarchal capitalistic system, the material culture, and even culture itself are all interconnected in the commodification of Japanese women.

The key factors reflecting these conditions, and thereby perpetuating them, are the persistent objectifications of women in relation to the cultural desire for an aesthetic in the gaze of others, the cult of cuteness, the lack of a female subjectivity, and a consequent lack of critical thinking and behaviors. As Patel (2001) claims, "it is not possible to retrieve the subaltern woman's voice consciousness, for example, on its own terms when she is denied the position of subject" because women without subjectivities are overly conscious of the gaze of others and start to live and perform in the counter gaze (masks) of others (p. xxi). I cannot deny that the expectations from the people surrounding me did, indeed, influence me to dream of becoming a stewardess, their dream flower. A woman's critical thinking must develop before any resistance can occur to counteract what has been described in this article as a pervasive disrespect and mistrust of Japanese women's abilities, their inherent value, their right to exercise choice, and their independent freedoms.

NOTES

1. *Ganguro* girls (usually teenage girls) wear mini skirts, crop tops, *luuzu socks* (knee socks bunched up around their fat ankles), and *atsuzoko* ("Ganguro," 2001). They accentuate their orangish fake tans with pink (or white, silver) eye shadows, plucked eyebrows, blue contact lenses, white lipstick, sparkly makeup, bleached bright blonde hair and outrageous mock-'70s fashions. Darling-Wolf (2001) claims that Japan's Westernization hegemonized Japanese women to make efforts to have white skin. She means that Japanese women have admired Westerners' white-skinned faces and have tried to make their skin almost as light as white Western women. I think she may infer, presently, that the ganguro girls have given up this whitening attempt and are now trying to tan themselves like tanned, white Western women. However, it appears to me that Darling-Wolf's position is a colonialist view. The desire for white skin is not new and has been admired in Japan for centuries (even before the Meiji era). The kind of white skin Japanese women admire is not the same white skin some Western adult women have. Japanese women like to have *yuki-no youna shirosa* (as white as snow) with *suki-tooru youna hada* (baby-like, fine, pretty, succulent, transparent skin). As a result, ganguro faces, bleached blonde hair, and blue colored contact lens seem to me to signify a creative fashionable fad and not some repressed

obsession. "It should not simply be evaluated as a sign of Western hegemony, but is part of a much larger process through which the occident is brought under control and opposed to Japanese uniqueness and homogeneity" (Creighton, 1995).

2. Sailor Moon was a popular character in Japanese comic books and TV programs in 1992–1993. Sailor Moon, *Usagi*, is about an ordinary, klutzy, cry-baby, 14 year old junior high school girl. She receives a special quest from a talking cat named, Luna, to fight evil and find "Moon Princess." She accomplishes all this by transforming into the sailor-suited "pretty soldier" Sailor Moon. Usagi is joined by some other girls to form a team of sailor-suited fighters (Takeuchi, 2001).

3. Women wear *luuzu socks* (loose socks), knee socks, around the bottom of their legs. In the 1940's, they were called "Bobby Socks" in the U.S.A. In the military, they can be called "Leggings," and sometimes they are called "Knee Socks," because they come up to just below the knee. Luuzu (bunched up) socks help girls hide their fat ankles (a common trait) to make them appear to have skinny pretty legs. To wear luuzu socks, girls feel they must wear mini-skirts in any weather.

4. *Atsuzoko* (thick sole) are bulky platform boots/shoes, six–inch high-heel boots, that have become the latest fashion rage among young Japanese women, because they believe *atsuzoko* are cute. Or, they feel good wearing atsuzoko because the level of their eyes is higher than the level of some arrogant middle-aged men's eyes in the office. There have been many traffic accidents and deaths reported in relation to wearing atsuzoko (Sims, 1999). Some girls twist their ankles badly. Walking is unnatural. Girls' feet can become deformed and girls can suffer medical problems. I believe this phenomenon is similar to 'foot binding' in China or wearing restrictive *kimono* in Japan in the old days when women's lives and movements were confining in order to serve men. But, then again, many short Japanese women desire to be tall in their cute masquerade, while naturally tall women are often intimidating to Japanese men who are often short.

5. Hello-Kitty, called "Kitty-chan" in Japanese, is a white kitten character, extremely popular merchandise from Sanrio Co. Kitty was born 25 years ago. In those days, Kitty was popular among small girls. After 15 years, the first generation of Kitty fans became mothers and began buying Kitty products for their children. Today, Kitty is popular not only among small girls, but also university students, young working women and mothers. The Kitty market is worth more than 300 billion yen a year, which covers 60% of Sanrio's business ("Hello Kitty," 1999). There are more than 15,000 Kitty items! Sanrio has 3,500 sales outlets in 40 countries and Kitty is becoming extremely popular in other Asian countries ("Kitty-chan's Popularity," 1999).

6. For the last three years, while studying at Ohio University, I have met at least three Japanese female students (22–28 years old) who addressed themselves by their first names instead of using "I." This was quite shocking not only to me but also to my other Japanese friends who study at my university. Since we tend to assume a student who studies overseas has a more independent mind, this infantile behavior was unexpected among more independent Japanese students.

7. I conducted a survey about *kawaii* with 12 Japanese college students (7 male; 5 female) who came to study English at Ohio University for the summer of 2001.

8. According to the Japanese *Kojien* Dictionary, *kawa-ii* means cute, lovely, small and beautiful, something which provokes our love, empathy and pity. *Kawayui*, the original adverb for *kawaii*, was commonly used in Japanese classical literature. While *kawaii* emphasizes the meaning of cuteness, *kawa-yui* emphasizes the meaning of empathy such as feeling shy, or showing pity, and compassion.

9. These are the results of a survey I conducted after I quit my teaching job. In total, I surveyed almost 250 junior college students between 1998 and 1999.

10. In 1990s, many young people (boys and girls in their 10s and 20s) were observed sitting on the ground, floors, and stairs, in public space. This shocked older generation Japanese who value endurance, believing that they should not show their laziness, shameful postural behaviors, and private intimate behaviors in public.

11. In Japanese, Sanma exactly said, *"Kawaii-neeee, anata"* [You're so *kawaii*!], *"Sonnani kawaii to 'okachichau'-zou!"* [If you're so *kawaii*, I am going to rape you!]. *Okasu* (meaning "rape"), extremely vulgar dirty expression, which may be used only by men, was seldom used in public such as in the media until recent years, but it is often uttered by men in various TV programs recently.

REFERENCES

Akita, K. (1994a). Nagoyan *omiai*. *Nagoya Avenues, 57*, 5–7.

—— (1994b). Nagoya-*joke town? Nagoya Avenues, 55*, 5–7.

—— (1995). A Nagoyan wedding. *Nagoya Avenues, 59*, 16–18.

—— (2001). *Keitai* use in Japan: A digital revolution and radical cultural change. *Human Communication: A Journal of the Pacific and Asian Communication Association, 4* (1), 31–42.

College graduates' employment rate. (2000). *Rodo-shou Shokugyou Anteikyoku Gyomu Chosei-ka* [Labor Ministry's Unemployment Office]. [On-line]. Available: http://www2.mhlw.go.jp/kisya/syokuan/20000512_02_sy/20000512_02_sy.html.

Creighton, M. (1995). Imagining the other in Japanese advertising campaigns. In J. G. Carrier (Ed.), *Occidentalism: Images of the West* (pp. 135–160). New York: Oxford University Press.

Darling-Wolf, F. (2001). Gender, beauty, and Western influence: Negotiated femininity in Japanese women's magazines. In E. L. Toth, & L. Aldoory (Eds.), *The gender challenge to media: Diverse voices from the field* (pp. 277–311). Cresskill, NJ: Hampton Press, Inc.

Field, N. (1991). *In the realm of a dying emperor: A portrait of Japan at century's end*. New York: Pantheon Books.

Foucault, M. (1981). *The history of sexuality, Volume one: An introduction*. Harmondsworth: Pelican.

Ganguro. (2001). *Live Music* [On-line]. Available: http://www.livemusicstudio.com/mac/pages/ganguro.html

Girl power hits Tokyo. (2000, March 30). *The Scotsman, p. 27.*

Goffman, E. (1959). *The presentation of self in everyday life*. New York: Doubleday.
—— (1979). *Gender advertisements*. New York: Harper Colophon Books.
Hello Kitty makes Sanrio a fat cat. (1999, May 9). *Asahi Newspaper*.
Higher education rate. (2001). *Foreign Ministry of Japan*. [On line]. Available in Japanese: http://www.mofa.go.jp/mofaj/world/ranking/shingaku.html
Kids caught in latest cosmetics fad. (2001, June 22). *The Japan Times*.
Kinsella, S. (1995). Cuties in Japan. In L. Skov & B. Moeran (Eds.), *Women media and consumption in Japan* (pp. 220–254). Honolulu: University of Hawai'i Press.
—— (2000a). Japanese high-school girl brand. In J. Pavitt (Ed.), *Brand.New* (pp. 104–105). Princeton, NJ: Princeton University Press.
—— (2000b). *Adult manga: Culture and power in contemporary Japanese society*. Honolulu: University of Hawai'i Press.
Kitty-chan's popularity. (1999, February 3). Broadcasted by *CNN News*.
Klippensteen, K. (2000). *Ganguro girls: The Japanese "black face,"* (With photographer: E. K. Brown). Budapest, Hungary: Koenemann Verlagsgesellschaft.
Kondo, D. K. (1990). *Crafting selves: Power, gender, and discourses of identity in a Japanese workplace*. Chicago: The University of Chicago.
Lebra, T. (1976). *Japanese patterns of behavior*. Honolulu: University of Hawai'i Press.
McVeigh, B. J. (1996). Commodifying affection, authority and gender in the everyday objects of Japan. *Journal of Material Culture, 1* (3), 291–312.
—— (1997). *Life in a Japanese women's college: Learning to be lady like*. New York: Routledge.
—— (2000a). *Wearing ideology: State, schooling and self-presentation in Japan*. New York: Oxford.
—— (2000b). How Hello Kitty commodifies the cute, cool and camp: 'Consumputopia' versus 'control' in Japan. *Journal of Material Culture, 5* (2), 225–245.
Morley, P. (1999). *The mountain is moving: Japanese women's lives*. Vancouver: University of British Columbia Press.
Murase, H. (2000). *Feminism-subculture: Hihansengen* [Declaration of criticism]. Tokyo: Shunjuu-Sha.
'Parasite singles': Problem or victims? (2000, April 7). *The Japan Times*.
Patel, N. S. (2001). Postcolonial masquerades: Culture and politics in literature, film, video, and photography. In W. E. Cain (Ed.), *Literary criticism and cultural theory: The interaction of text and society*. New York: Garland Publishing, Inc.
Plath, D. W. (1980). *Long engagements: Maturity in modern Japan*. Stanford, CA: Stanford University Press.
Rosaldo, M. Z., & Lamphere, L. (Eds.). (1974). *Woman, culture, and society*. Stanford, CA: Stanford University Press.
Saito, T. (1999). *Kodomo tachi wa naze kireruka* [Why do children get upset so easily?]. Tokyo, Japan: Chikuma Shobo.
Sato, R. S. (1998). What are girls made of?: Exploring the symbolic boundaries of femininity in two cultures. In S. A. Inness (Ed.), *Millennium girls: Today's girls around the world* (pp. 15–44). Lanham, MD: Rowman & Littlefield Publishers, Inc.

Schomer, K., & Chang, Y. (1995, August). The cult of cuteness. *Newsweek, 28*, 54–8.

Sims, C. (1999, November 26). Tokyo Journal; Be tall and chic as you wobble to the orthopedist. *The New York Times*, Section A, p. 4.

Takeuchi, N. (2001). *Bishoujo senshi* [Pretty girl fighters] *Sailor Moon*. [On line]. Available: http://www.tcp.com/doi/smoon/smoon.html, by Kodansha, TV-Asahi, & Toei Douga.

Waldron, V. R., & Mare, L. D. (1998). Gender as a culturally determined construct: Communication styles in Japan and the United States. In D. J. Canary & K. Dindia (Eds.), *Sex differences and similarities in communication: Critical essays and empirical investigations of sex and gender interaction* (pp. 179–202). Mahwah, NJ: Lawrence Erlbaum Associates, Inc.

Weedon, C. (1987/1997). *Feminist practice & poststructuralist theory* (2nd ed.). Cambridge, MA: Blackwell Publishers, Inc.

White, M. (1993). *The material child: Coming of age in Japan and America*. New York: The Free Press.

Williams, G. (2000). Hello Kitty. In J. Pavitt (Ed.), *Brand.New* (pp. 180–181). Princeton, NJ: Princeton University Press.

Yonezawa, Y. (Ed). (1999). Shojo *manga*'s world I: Children's Showa history, 1945–1962. Tokyo: Heibon.

Chapter Five

Gender, Class, and Suffering in the Argentinean *Telenovela Milagros*: an Italian Perspective

Giovanna Del Negro

In the mid-1990s an Argentinean *telenovela* (Spanish for soap opera) named *Milagros* (*Miracles*) was broadcast on network television in Italy. The show attracted a wide audience, and was particularly popular with the residents of Sasso,[1] a prosperous small town in the central Italian province of the Abruzzo. While a cross-section of Sasso's population was familiar with *Milagros*, its most ardent followers were older, working class women. A case study in the local reception of a transnational media product, this article explores the relationship between gender, class and religion in Sassani women's viewing of *Milagros*. Based on interviews with the women and fourteen months of participant observation fieldwork in Sasso, I hope to show how the use of traditional Catholic imagery allowed a televisual narrative from Latin America to resonate with conservative viewers from a forgotten segment of contemporary Italian society and help them make sense of their lives.[2]

WORKING CLASS WOMEN IN SASSO

To understand these dynamics, one must know something about Sasso and the predicament of working class women in the small town life of central Italy. The hilltop village of Sasso is located half an hour away from the Adriatic Sea and has a population of approximately three thousand people. Most Sassani work in factories in the town's industrial zone. This area has seen strong growth in the last twenty years because of tax incentives, cheap labor, and the government connections of local officials. Also present in the village is a small group of artisans and self-employed entrepreneurs. About 50 percent of the full-time wage earners own small plots of land in the surrounding countryside, and farming is a weekend or holiday activity that contributes to the family larder. In the local imagination, Sasso has often been viewed as a modern, cosmopolitan village with close affinities to the nearby coastal centers. The townsfolk affectionately call it *la piccola Parigi dell'Abruzzo* (the "little Paris" of the Abruzzo) and point to its attractive thoroughfare and well known *passeggiata* as a sign of the town's civility and enlightened modern spirit.

In the first part of the twentieth century, however, Italy was far from a modern nation and Sasso was not the prosperous small town it is today. Much of Italy, both rural and urban, was decimated by the Second World War, and electricity and indoor plumbing only became widely available in rural areas in the late 1960s. After the war, the country's economic devastation drove millions of Italians to emigrate abroad in search of better lives. In the late 1940s and early 1950s, fully half the population of Sasso left the town, many resettling in Canada, Belgium, Argentina, Australia, and the United States. The Italian construction boom of the 1960s, however, bolstered the national economy and brought about a period of affluence, and general prosperity helped pave the way for the emergence of large scale consumer capitalism in the Italy of the 1970s.

The central region of the Abruzzo profited greatly from this economic upsurge, and, in many ways, post-war Sasso is a case study in the modernization of rural Italy. In this period, corporate investment and economic development dramatically altered this once agricultural community into a local center of light industry. The former Sassani *contadini* (peasants) have now been transformed into the *impiegati* (wage earners) of the modern labor force. The town's former mayor held a number of posts in the national government, and his political connections have been partially responsible for Sasso's recent growth. Cheap labor and subsidies from *la Cassa del Mezzogiorno* (a national agency that earmarks funds for economically underdeveloped areas) not only paved the way for the development of the town's industrial base but supplied steady employment for the residents of Sasso and the surrounding towns.

It is within this broader context of intense economic development and rapid social change that we must ultimately understand the meanings that Sassani women bring to their interpretations of the Argentinean *telenovela Milagros*.

With varying degrees of acceptance and resistance, almost all of the older women of Sasso have been informed by traditional Catholic notions of womanhood. Born before World War II, they are too old to have taken advantage of the broadened gender roles and career opportunities that younger Sassani women enjoy. Whether they view the women of the postwar era with scorn or longing, those of the previous generation cannot fully share in the new found freedoms. Further, older working-class women have reaped the least economic benefit from Sasso's industrialization. While they have known the pleasures of child rearing and the domestic life, they look out at today's society and see images of gender and class progress that they know they will never directly experience. The term "modernization" is commonly used to refer to a group of closely related social changes—the development of an industrial economy and consumer capitalism, the growth of mass mediated popular entertainments, and the emergence of new gender roles. Although this term is not without its problems, "modernization" succinctly describes the kinds of sweeping transformations that struck Italy in the post-war period, and we may say that Sasso's working class women have found themselves to be doubly marginalized by modernity. Seeing their role as mothers and matriarchs devalued, but unable to enjoy professional careers or substantial upward mobility, these women are precariously perched between the present and the past.

MILAGROS

During my fieldwork in Sasso, I wanted to understand how working class women might deal with their situation, and I searched for a way to get closer to their experiences. Engaging with the everyday life of the community and making my daily rounds of Sassani shops and homes, I quickly learned that the Argentinean television series *Milagros* had a loyal following among this group. Every Wednesday evening, they tuned their televisions to Channel 4 and enjoyed this two-hour *telenovela*. At first, I believed that watching *Milagros* was a trivial pastime, and I had little enthusiasm for the hours which awaited me if one of my research participants invited me to spend a Wednesday evening at her home. It was only after several months that I realized the importance of this show for these women. *Milagros* was the entrance for which I had been looking.

The story, dubbed in Italian, is set in turn-of-the century South America and revolves around a young woman named Milagros who struggles to become reunited with her long lost mestizo lover. Throughout the series, Milagros becomes embroiled in a string of ill-fated events that test her honor, virtue, and perseverance. Despite her trials, Milagros remains steadfast in her female chastity, her Catholic faith, and her fidelity to her absent partner. Across the span of the series, she fends off her evil stepbrother's sexual advances and desperately tries to evade the unkind and malicious strangers who cross her path. In one episode she is duped into joining a brothel and is saved from a tragic end by a sympathetic prostitute.

The experience of watching *Milagros* in the Italian home is an active one. The performers in the series are well known in Italy, and families all over

Sasso discussed the episodes and bantered about the gyrations of the plot. The women with whom I watched the program identified with the protagonist's circumstances and shared a special kinship with her. A modern day Madonna figure, she was deeply admired for her courage and elicited an almost religious devotion from her fans. As we will see, this character's troubled life parallels the trials and tribulations of female Catholic martyrs. In the face of rapid social change, this pious vision of femininity valorizes suffering and provides a metaphor for understanding the social inequalities of class and gender. This traditional model of womanhood ultimately helps older, working-class Sassani women make sense of the social changes that they have experienced.

It is important to understand the differences between the American soap opera and the Latin American *novela* or *telenovela*. Discussing the *novela*, Ondine Fachel Leal and Ruben George Olinen (1988) explain that:

> they deviate from the basic melodramatic formula, incorporating elaborate outdoor stagings, up-to-the minute fashions, trends, and current events, and modern cinematic techniques. Irony, innuendo, and political content are important elements of their texts (Leal and Olinen, p. 85).

As a genre, *novelas* usually employ nationally recognized writers, directors, and performers (Leal and Olinen 1988, p. 85). Grecia Colmenaris, the actress who plays Milagros, has acted in a large number of both evening and daytime *telenovelas*. The leading man, Osvaldo Laport, a performer not unlike Fabio in appearance, is an established actor who also starred in a variety of equally successful shows.

These lavish shows are frequently co-produced and distributed by the private Finivest Corporation, which belongs to the Italian television mogul, Silvio Berlusconi. The first run of these programs in Italy usually garners high ratings and thus allows them to occupy premium time slots. These *telenovelas* enjoy a wide second-run syndication in markets such as Montreal, Toronto, and Buenos Aires—places with large Italian immigrant populations. After they run their course in Italy, they are often broadcast in these countries. Italian immigrants who, on their summer vacations in Italy, have seen the shows while visiting with relatives, often share the upcoming plot twists with their friends back home in Canada or the United States. Popular with Italians and a wide range of Latin Americans, the shows draw on longstanding Catholic images and ideas about gender. Distinct from American soap operas, they are part of an international, Pan-Catholic media culture.

The women with whom I watched *Milagros* greatly admired the actress who played the leading role. Light-skinned, with long, straight, auburn hair, a moon-shaped face, and an angelic smile, she bore an uncanny resemblance to Renaissance images of the Virgin Mary. This affinity was not lost on the

Sassani women who would reverentially say, *"Sembra una Madonna"* ("She looks like the Madonna"). The dramatic close-up shots of celestial adoration and despair often reminded me of the stylized portraits of *Maria Addolorata* (Maria of the Suffering), which I had seen in Italian churches throughout the country—including Sasso. In these depictions *Maria Addolarata* is almost always seen pleading, and her pain is clearly visible. This supplicating pose was frequently affected by the actress who played the lead role in *Milagros*.

CATHOLICISM

In Catholicism, beauty and suffering are often essential to the attributes of female saints and martyrs. The theme of the fair and dutiful daughter who endures great misery is a leitmotif in Catholic folk legends. In keeping with this tradition, Milagros undergoes various forms of humiliation before she can achieve salvation. As Kathy Figgen (1990) argues in *Miracles and Promises: Popular Religions, Cults, and Saints in Argentina*: "The physical subjection of the body to the pains and ordeals of ascetic discipline [is] an integral part of sanctity" (Figgen, p. 68). As the quintessential martyr, *Milagros* is continuously resisting rape and defending her chastity. The perils of sexual contact are omnipresent.

The Catholic pantheon is replete with the stories of victimized women who are praised for their courage and stamina in the face of adversity. In her book *One Hundred Towers*, anthropologist Lola Romanucci-Ross describes the popularity in central Italy of such a martyr as Santa Rita (1991). In the small town of Ascoli-Piceno, legend has it that after Santa Rita's abusive husband dies, she has a vision from God and enters a convent where she develops the gift to heal the sick and the infirm. The travails of Santa Rita are especially well known to the women of the town who hold her devotion to family and husband in high esteem.

In Argentina, one of the *telenovela* centers of the Spanish speaking world, writers have borrowed from the rich tradition of Catholic folk religion by adapting the stories of the saints for radio and television (Figgen 1990). Like *Milagros*, the popular folk legend *Defunta Correa* deals with a woman's search for her lost companion. Unlike *Milagros,* who is blissfully reunited with her partner, the Correa is found dead with her newborn infant sucking her lifeless breast (Figgen 1990, p. 172). In both accounts, the heroines are recognized for their ability to "triumph over the demeaning circumstances of the feminine role" (Romanucci-Ross 1991, p. 123). Their characters are, in fact, defined by their abiding sacrifice and submission. While these legends clearly endorse gender inequities by promoting female compliance, they also speak of freedom from bondage and servitude and celebrate the power of divine intervention to restore justice in the world.

CLASS

Class plays a prominent role in *Milagros*. The animosity between the landed aristocracy and the rural peasants in the show clearly resonated with many Sassani viewers. The women with whom I watched the *telenovela* identified with the character's humble origin; all of them were from modest, working-class backgrounds who themselves remember long hours of agricultural work. Crucial here is that, underneath her tattered clothes, Milagros is from a noble family. Unbeknownst to her mother, Milagros is switched at birth with her wicked aunt's illegitimate child. While she is raised by a poor but loving family of carnival entertainers, her cousin enjoys the benefits of affluence and respectability.

The ambiguity that we find in Milagros' class status is echoed in her Native American love interest. Of Spanish and Indian background, Catriel also betrays his fine pedigree. Both noble savage and urban sophisticate intellectual, he writes popular novels under a pseudonym but is disqualified from enjoying the privileges of class and wealth by his racial background. While his marginal status excludes him from the world of comfort and power, it also frees him from the racist confines of the white man's world. Like *Milagros*, Catriel seeks the higher goals of truth and justice.

This theme of dual identity is crucial to the *telenovela*. The protagonist is not really a downtrodden peasant girl but a member of the upper echelons of society; her boyfriend is not the savage society believes him to be but the child of a misbegotten love affair between a wealthy white man and a common Indian woman. Milagros and Catriel have a hidden virtue that their assigned roles obscure and are larger and more complex than the labels society has placed upon them. Their commitment to honor and justice is the only outward sign of the nobility they hold within.

CONCLUSION

What is it about Milagros that resonated so deeply with my informants? Employing powerful imagery from the Catholic tradition, the *Milagros telenovela* allows Sassani women to make sense of the difficulties in their lives. They identified with Milagros's experiences of gender and class-based oppression, and her ultimate triumph gives them hope. The protagonist is a genteel aristocrat who appears to be a peasant; identifying with *Milagros*, the women ultimately transform their female and working-class status from a marker of social disadvantage into an almost mystical sign of inner nobility. Even the smallest indignity of everyday life becomes a reminder of hidden grace and a promise of eventual redemption.

It is not surprising then that these older Sassani women preferred the Latin based *telenovelas* to the America style soap operas such as *The Bold and the Beautiful* (broadcast in Italy under the English title *Beautiful*). The viewers of *Milagros* found little solace in the machinations of rich people who work in lavish corporate offices and commit adultery. The travails of a humble peasant girl vividly speak to these women's memories of the devastating effects of World War II and the oppressive class barriers of their youth. Identifying with Milagros, the women see her story as a confirmation of the values of nurturance, sexual chastity, and self-sacrifice—values whose transgression is the main theme of America's soap operas.

In sum, the soaps from the New World celebrate a decadent American modernity, while *Milagros* valorizes the tenets of traditional Catholic culture. If Sasso's older women do indeed look out at today's society and see images of gender and class progress that they know they will never enjoy, they also see pitfalls which they are glad they will never have to face. While they may envy the opportunities that young women have and the wealth of Italy's postwar middle class, they also see consumerism as shallow and the search for individual fulfillment as self-centered. Alienated from the benefits of modernity, they are both attracted to and repelled from this modern world that they constantly see but cannot possess. Ironically, it is *Milagros*—a product of the transnational, pan-Catholic media culture—that offers an alternative. *Milagros* celebrates a traditional Catholic ideology and provides a critique of modern society that both validates the women's experiences and gives meaning to their suffering.

Beyond the lives of women in the small town of Sasso, this work suggest the value of studies of popular culture that focus on the reception of the mass media. By exploring how women interact with and interpret television images, we can discover neglected and often surprising understandings of gender in contemporary culture.

NOTES

1. Because of the political nature of related research, the name of the town has been obscured.

2. For more on the community of Sasso please see Giovanna P. Del Negro's *The Passeggiata and Popular Culture in an Italian Town: Folklore and the Performance of Modernity* (McGill-Queen's University Press, 2004).

REFERENCES

Del Negro, G. P. (2004). *The Passeggiata and popular culture in an Italian town: Folklore and the performance of modernity*. Montreal: McGill-Queen's University Press.

Figgen, K. L. (1990). *Miracles and promises: Popular religious cults and saints in Argentina*. Unpublished doctoral dissertation, Indiana University, Bloomington.

Leal, O. F. and G. R. Olinen (1988). Class interpretation of soap opera narrative: The case of the Brazilian novela, *Summer Sun. Theory, Culture, and Society* 5: 51–99.

Milagros. 1994. Co-produced with Silvio Berlusconi Communications (Italia). Director Omar Romay.

Romanucci-Ross, L. (1991). *One Hundred Towers: An Italian Odyssey of Cultural Survival*. New York: Bergin and Garvey.

AUTHOR'S NOTE

A different version of "Gender, Class, and Suffering in the Argentinean *Telenovela Milagros*: An Italian Perspective" first appeared in *Global Media Journal,* Volume 1, Issue 2.

Chapter Six

Images of Gender in Super Bowl Advertising: A Content Analysis

Barbara King

At the dawn of a new century, we live, some scholars claim, in the age of advertising. Jhally (1995) likens advertising to "the air that we breathe as we live our daily lives" (p. 79). Twitchell (1996) argues that advertising is the central institution in American culture, as it pervades every aspect of our lives and shapes how we make sense of our world. As a key meaning-making system, advertising constructs notions of self, other and society. Advertising, says Twitchell, "is language not just about objects to be consumed but about the consumers of objects" (p. 13).

Few events underscore the centrality of advertising in American culture like the Super Bowl. Commercial time on the Super Bowl is the most expensive in the world. The cost of a 30-second spot aired during Super Bowl XXXIV, played January 30, 2000, averaged $2.2 million, with some advertisers paying up to $3 million (Wells, 2000; Zito, 2000). In 1999, Fox Broadcasting charged an average of $1.6 million for a 30-second spot on Super Bowl XXXIII (Beatty, 1999). A year later, ABC, which broadcast Super Bowl XXXIV, took in more than $130 million in advertising revenue, a 38% increase over Fox's take in 1999 (Hajewski, 2000).

Commercial time on the Super Bowl is not only the most expensive but also the most hyped. The news media feature stories about the Super Bowl commercials in the weeks preceding the game. *USA TODAY* sponsors a game-day poll where viewers vote for their favorite Super Bowl commercials; the newspaper publishes the poll results the following day. The Super Bowl has become as well known as an advertising event as it has a sporting event (McAllister, 1996).

A huge audience attracts advertisers to the Super Bowl, which is consistently the most watched event on U.S. television (Caulfield, 2000). Nielsen

Media Research estimated that 130.7 million people tuned into at least some of Super Bowl XXXIV, which was the fifth most-watched telecast in U.S. history and whose rating of 43.3 marked a 7% increase over the 1999 game (5th-largest, 2000). The majority of the Super Bowl's television audience is male, but the game attracts a sizable number of female viewers as well. Historically, the Super Bowl audience hovers at 56% male and 44% female (Kiska, 1999). Long regarded by advertisers as a principle vehicle for reaching men aged 18–45 (Twitchell, 1996), the Super Bowl also offers an effective means of reaching adult female consumers.

Much of the previous scholarship on Super Bowl advertising has taken an experimental approach, examining the effects of viewing the commercials on recall of those ads and consumption of advertised products (Eastman, Newton & Pack,1996; Pavelchak, Antil & Munch, 1988). I could locate only one study, however, that describes what this advertising looks like. My study, then, attempts to fill a gap in the scholarly literature by presenting a content analysis of Super Bowl advertising. It explores the kinds of images that advertisers are presenting to the largest television audience of the year. Of course, Super Bowl advertising is not representative of television advertising as a whole, because it is the most expensive commercial time in the world and is supposed to represent the best of what the advertising industry has to offer. Still, Super Bowl advertising merits scholarly attention, given the sheer size of the Super Bowl audience and advertising's ability to create and transmit cultural meaning. A content analysis of Super Bowl advertising pairs what Twitchell (1996) calls "the dominant meaning-making system of modern life" (p. 253) with the highest rated television show of the year, thereby shedding some light on key meanings that shape our culture.

METHOD

Data for this study were generated from the coding of television commercials broadcast during Super Bowl XXXIV, played on January 30, 2000. One-hundred and three commercials, aired on ABC's Milwaukee affiliate WISN between the coin toss and the last play of the game, were videotaped. Consistent with other analyses of television advertising content, duplicate commercials, local ads, and network programming promotions were excluded from the analysis, leaving 65 commercials to code.

Two coders—one male and one female—independently coded commercials using booklets containing specific categories of analysis. Most of these categories have been widely used in previous research, thus allowing comparisons of this study's results with findings of other studies. The coding booklet, which included operational definitions of variables, was pretested on both coders on four of the commercials. Slight adjustments were made to obtain the final version of the coding booklet, designed to examine two separate units of analysis: the commercial itself and the central characters in the commercial.

For each commercial, the type of product advertised, the gender of the primary narrator (coded as male, female, or no narrator) and the types of characters depicted in the ad (human, real animal, animated character, any combination of these, or no character) were coded. The product categories used by Bretl and Cantor (1988) were adopted with slight modification for the present study. Product categories were food and non-alcoholic beverages, personal care/cosmetics, household items, pet-related items, toys, medications, travel, restaurants, banking/finance/insurance, electronics/communications, magazines/newspapers, sporting goods, clothing and shoes (non-athletic), automobile/auto-related, alcoholic beverages, and other. The primary narrator was defined as "the voice, not attributable to any on-screen character, which is heard for the longest time" (Craig, 1992, p. 201). If the commercial had no central character, the primary setting of the commercial was coded; otherwise, setting was coded for each central character. Setting categories, borrowed from Taylor and Stern (1997), were home, business, outdoors/natural scenery (away from home), social setting outside home, other (which includes artificial settings or specially built backgrounds), and unable to determine.

For each central character, gender, race, age, physical allure, and setting were coded. Coding of central character's race, age, allure, and setting was performed to provide a richer context in which to understand the images of gender. A central character was defined as one who plays "a major role in a commercial by virtue of either speaking or having prominent visual exposure" (McArthur & Resko, 1975, p. 211). Coders were instructed to designate a character as a central character if the commercial's basic nature would be changed if this character did not appear. Gender was coded as male, female, or unable to determine, while categories used to code the race of central characters were borrowed from the 2000 U.S. Census report (Population Reference Bureau). Consistent with the research of Signiorelli, McLeod, and Healy (1994), coders assessed age by designating the character's stage in the life cycle (ranging from infancy to old age). Physical allure was included as a coding category in order to enable comparisons between the findings of this study and those of other content analyses of commercials in men's sports telecasts, as such ads have been found to rely considerably on the provocative portrayal of women as a persuasive appeal (Craig, 1992). Characters were coded as obviously alluring, meaning the character's physical appearance was "used to create viewer liking (or purchase intention) for the product" (Lin, 1997, p. 242), or other, in which the character's physical appearance was not used as part of the sales appeal.

Coders' responses were compared after commercials had been coded. Where discrepancies existed, the commercial was viewed again, discussed, and a consensus was reached. Percentages, rounded to the nearest whole number, were calculated on all variables to determine the overall look of Super Bowl commercials. Chi-square tests were used in instances where cell frequencies supported a valid assessment of differences between categories.

FINDINGS

Analysis by Commercial

Product Category

The product category scheme adopted from Bretl and Cantor (1988) proved largely unsuitable for the coding of Super Bowl commercials in that a sizeable percentage of the ads (22%) fell into the "other" category. Refinement of the category scheme showed 28% of commercials in the Internet companies category, 15% in automobile/auto-related, 11% in alcoholic beverages, 9% in electronics/non-Internet communications, 8% in food/non-alcoholic beverages, 8% in motion pictures, 6% in banking/finance/insurance, 5% in professional sports organizations, 3% in public service announcements, 2% in medications, and 6% in other. Super Bowl XXXIV did not contain any commercials for personal care/cosmetics, household items, pet-related items, restaurants, travel, toys, sporting goods, or clothing/shoes (non-athletic).

Commercials for Internet companies accounted for more than one-quarter of all Super Bowl XXXIV ads, when just one year earlier, Super Bowl XXXIII featured only three dot.com ads. In light of their proliferation, dot.com commercials were subject to further analysis. Fifty-six percent of these ads featured human characters only, while 17% featured humans and real animals, 11% humans and animated characters, 11% no characters, and 6% humans, real animals, and animated characters. Seventeen percent of dot.com commercials featured animated characters, making these ads nearly three times more likely than ads for other products combined to contain animated characters. Seventy-two percent of dot.com commercials featured a narrator. Males narrated 77% and females 23% of these commercials. Women were nearly four times more likely to narrate dot.com commercials than commercials for other products combined, although the difference between dot.com commercials and commercials for other products combined with respect to narrator gender was not statistically significant (perhaps due to small cell sizes).

Dot.com commercials featured 58 central characters. In cases where gender, race, and age of central characters were evident, characters were overwhelmingly male (79%), White (80%) and adult (89%). The gender of central characters did not differ significantly between dot.com commercials and commercials for other products combined. Nor was there a significant difference between dot.com ads and other ads with respect to the frequency of White versus non-White central characters. However, central characters in non-dot.com ads were nearly twice as likely as central characters in dot.com ads to be an age other than adult (i.e., infant, child, teen or older adult). No central character in a dot.com commercial was coded as obviously alluring. Finally, central characters in dot.com commercials appeared in significantly different settings than central characters in ads for other products combined ($?^2 = 14.4$, n $= 164$, df $= 4$, p $< .01$). Most central characters in dot.com commercials (34%) were depicted in an outdoor setting. Compared to central characters in ads for other products combined, central characters in dot.com commercials were over three times more likely to appear in a business setting and over two times less likely to appear in a setting coded as "other."

While Internet companies as a whole bought the most advertising time during Super Bowl XXXIV, the event's largest single advertiser was Anheuser-Busch. In fact, the brewing company was the only national beer advertiser in the broadcast (Wells, 2000). Given their prevalence in televised sports programming (Madden and Grube, 1994) and their contribution to the sex-object image of women (Finn & Strickland, 1982; Hall & Crum, 1994), commercials for alcoholic beverages were also singled out for additional analysis. All seven alcoholic beverage commercials were for Anheuser-Busch brands of beer (Budweiser and Bud Light). Seventy-one percent of beer ads featured humans and real animals, while 29% featured humans only. Beer commercials were over three times more likely than commercials for other products combined to feature real animals, a significant difference ($X^2 = 8.33$, n $= 65$, df $= 1$, p $< .01$). Further, beer ads were significantly less likely than ads for other products combined to feature a narrator ($X^2 = 5.49$, n $= 65$, df $= 1$, p $< .025$). No beer commercial featured a female narrator.

All beer commercials contained central characters. In those beer commercials where gender, race, and age of central characters were evident or applicable, central characters were overwhelmingly male (82%), White (70%), and adult (95%). African Americans were the only racial minority group depicted in beer commercials. Five of the six African American central characters in these commercials appeared in a single commercial—the Budweiser spot that popularized the expression, "Whazzup?" Surprisingly, none of the central characters—male or female—was coded as obviously alluring. Also unexpected was the finding that central characters in beer commercials were nearly four times more likely than central characters in commercials for other products combined to appear in a home setting (55% to 14%, respectively). Further, no central characters in a beer commercial appeared in an outdoor setting, while most central characters in commercials for other products (34%) appeared outdoors. Overall, central characters in beer commercials appeared in significantly different settings than central characters in spots for other products combined ($X^2 = 23.92$, n $= 164$, df $= 4$, p $< .001$). Chi-square analysis showed no significant differences between beer commercials and commercials for other products combined with respect to gender, race (White vs. non-White), age (adult vs. non-adult), and allure of central character.

Gender of Narrator

Of the commercials having narrators (68%), 89% of the narrators were male, and 11% were female. Chi-square analysis showed this difference to be highly significant ($X^2 = 26.27$, n $= 44$, df $= 1$, p $< .0001$). Of the five commercials featuring female narrators, three advertised Internet companies, one advertised automobile/auto-related products, and one displayed a public service announcement discouraging youth smoking. Of the 39 commercials featuring male narrators, 10 were for Internet companies, six for electronics/non-Internet communications, five for motion pictures, four each for banking/finance/insurance, automobile/auto-related and other, three for professional sports organizations, two for alcoholic beverages, and one for food/non-alcoholic beverages. When product categories were grouped by value (high vs. low), chi-square analysis revealed that males and females were equally likely to narrate commercials for high value products.[1]

Type of Character

Of all 65 commercials, 60% contained human characters only; 23% humans and real animals; 5% humans and animated characters; 3% humans, real animals, and animated characters; 2% animated characters only; and 8% no characters. No commercial contained real animals only or real animals and animated characters. Just over 9% of all commercials contained animated characters. Males were more likely than females to appear as central characters in Super Bowl commercials. Of the 47 commercials featuring male and/or female central characters, 89% contained male central characters, depicted alone or with female central characters, and 51% contained female central characters, depicted alone or with male central characters. More

specifically, 35% of Super Bowl commercials depicted male central characters only, 29% male and female central characters together, 17% no central
characters, and 8% female central characters only. Eleven percent of commercials contained at least one central character of indeterminate gender.

Analysis by Central Character

Commercials broadcast during Super Bowl XXXIV contained 172 central
characters. In a number of cases, coders were unable to determine the gender,
race and/or age of a central character. Inability to code these physical characteristics stemmed mainly from cases of real animals or animated characters,
where gender, race, or age was either not apparent or not applicable. Data
analysis showed central characters in Super Bowl commercials to be overwhelmingly male, White, adult, unalluring and most often depicted in an outdoor setting. Table 6.1 summarizes the findings on central characters.

Of the 165 central characters whose gender was determinable, males were
significantly more likely than females to appear as central characters in

**Table 6.1.   Central Characters in Commercials, by Gender, Race, Age, Allure,
and Setting**

	N	% (Rounded to nearest whole number)
Female	40	24
Male	125	76
White	120	75
African American	31	19
Latino	1	1
Asian	7	4
American Indian	0	0
Infant	1	1
Child	3	2
Teenager	15	9
Adult	135	83
Older Adult	9	6
Obviously Alluring	2	1
Not Alluring/Other	172	99
Home	32	20
Business	22	13
Outdoors	48	29
Social	27	16
Other	35	21

Note: Cases in which a variable was coded "unable to determine" or "does not apply" were excluded from
analysis.

Super Bowl commercials, outnumbering females over 3 to 1 ($X^2 = 43.79$, n = 165, df = 1, p < .0001). Males as well as females appeared as central characters most frequently in commercials for Internet companies. Thirty percent of female central characters appeared in dot.com commercials, 15% in public service announcements, 10% each in ads for food/non-alcoholic beverages, electronics/non-Internet communications, and alcoholic beverages, 8% each in ads for automobile/auto-related and motion pictures, 5% in professional sports organizations, and 3% each for banking/finance/insurance and other. Thirty-five percent of male central characters appeared in commercials for Internet companies, 14% for alcoholic beverages, 11% for motion pictures, 10% for food/non-alcoholic beverages, 6% each for banking/finance/insurance, auto, and public service, 5% for electronics/non-Internet communications, 4% for other, 2% for professional sports organizations, and 1% for medications. A 2 (gender) by 11 (product category) chi-square analysis showed no significant difference between male and female central characters with respect to product category promoted. When product categories were grouped by value (high vs. low), statistical analysis showed males and females equally likely to appear as central characters in ads for high value products.

Of the 159 human central characters whose race was evident, 75% were White, 19% African American, 4% Asian (including Asian Indian, as defined by the U.S. Census Bureau), and 1% Latino. A chi-square goodness of fit test showed that Super Bowl commercials paint a lopsided picture of racial representation in the United States ($X^2 = 30.7$, n = 159, df = 5, p < .0001). African Americans, who comprise approximately 12% of the U.S. population, were most overrepresented as central characters in Super Bowl commercials, while Whites, 69% of the population, were also overrepresented. American Indians, who make up approximately 1% of the population, were slightly underrepresented, and Latinos, at over 12% of the population, were drastically underrepresented.[2]

Of the 120 male central characters whose race was evident, 76% were White, 20% African American, 3% Asian, and 1% Latino. No commercials featured American Indians as central characters. A similar portrait of race emerged for the 38 female central characters whose race was apparent; 76% were White, 18% African American, and 5% Asian.

Of the 163 central characters whose age was evident, 83% were adults, 9% teenagers, 6% older adults, 2% children, and 1% infants. Coders were unable to determine the age of four male central characters, leaving 121 for analysis. Eighty-eight percent of male characters were adults, 6% teenagers, 5% older adults, and 2% children. No commercial featured a male infant as a central character. Similarly, most female central characters (73%) were adults. Eighteen percent were teenagers, 8% older adults, and 3% children. No commercials featured a female infant as a central character. A 2 (gender) by 2 (adult vs. non-adult) chi-square analysis revealed that male central characters were significantly more likely than female central characters to be adults ($X^2 = 5.06$, n = 161, df = 1, p < .025), with female central characters three times more likely than male central characters to be teenagers.

Physical allure figured minimally into the depiction of gender. Of the 40 female central characters, only 2 (5%)—one human and one animated—were coded as obviously alluring, while none of the 125 male central characters was considered alluring. The alluring human female appeared in a spot for the World Wrestling Federation (product category of professional sports organization) as a contestant in a beauty pageant. As she is crowned "Miss Congeniality," she is physically attacked by other contestants, all of whom look like glamorous models in their sequined gowns. In the ensuing fight for the crown, contestants employ a variety of all-star wrestling moves against each other. The winner, whose dress is ripped away in the fight, revealing skimpy undergarments, eventually re-claims the crown, but at the expense of some lost teeth, mussed hair, and torn clothing. The commercial ends with the tag, "WWF Entertainment. It ain't pretty."

The alluring animated female appeared in a spot for M&M candies (product category of food/non-alcoholic beverages). The spot, featuring Jimi Hendrix's song, "Foxy Lady," opens with a man standing on a city sidewalk, calling to an off-camera passer-by, "Baby, you are looking sweet!" Eight more men make similar comments or turn to stare as this character walks down the sidewalk. Even a dog licks its chops. The "Foxy Lady" is finally revealed as a green M&M with plump lips and long, curled eyelashes. "Men," she mutters, as she struts down the sidewalk in white, high-heeled fashion boots. Next, she is admired by four women, one of whom sighs, "I'd like to get my hands on that." The commercial ends with the M&M shouting in an annoyed tone, "Go buy a bag!" to someone who has whistled at her.

While these two commercials comprise only a tiny fraction of Super Bowl XXXIV spots, they clearly support the stereotypical notion of women as sex objects. The WWF suggests in its commercial that "catfights" involving beautiful, scantily clad women are part of the "entertainment" that it offers to its largely male audience, while the M&M commercial literally depicts the sexy female as a snack—an object to be consumed—and subtly condones sexual harassment. This depiction is consistent with the findings of Craig's (1992) study of advertising in men's sports telecasts.

In terms of the setting in which male and female central characters were depicted, both genders appeared most frequently in an outdoor/natural setting, although females were significantly more likely than males to appear in this setting than some other setting ($X^2 = 4.09$, n $= 157$, df $= 1$, p $< .05$). Also, males were more than twice as likely as females to appear in a social setting (20% to 8%). For male central characters, 26% appeared outdoors, 18% appeared at home, 13% in a business setting, and 23% in some other setting, whereas 43% of female central characters appeared outdoors, 19% at home, 16% in a business setting, and 14% in some other setting.

DISCUSSION

Had you tuned into Super Bowl XXXIV for only one commercial, chances are this ad would have promoted an Internet company, been narrated by a male, and contained a male or male central character(s) only. The male central character in this commercial most likely would have been a White adult depicted in an outdoor setting. On the remote chance that the central character was female, she most likely would have been a White adult depicted in an outdoor setting and promoting a high value product.

Three product categories—Internet companies, automobiles/auto-related, and alcoholic beverages—accounted for more than half of the commercial time of Super Bowl XXXIV. This finding is consistent with other research that shows commercials for alcoholic beverages and automotive products to be prevalent during televised sports programming. The newest product category—Internet companies—showed some sign of breaking gender stereotypes by employing females as narrators at a higher rate than other product categories combined. On the whole, however, males were much more likely than females to narrate Super Bowl commercials, supporting the notion suggested in previous research that the voice of authority in television commercials is male.

Another sign that advertisers are eschewing gender stereotypes is the virtual absence of alluring females in Super Bowl XXXIV commercials. Particularly surprising was the finding that beer commercials, long criticized for their sex-object portrayal of women, contained no alluring female central characters. Data from this study suggest that beer advertisers are replacing sexy women with furry animals, as beer commercials were significantly more likely than commercials for other products combined to feature real animals. On its face, this move seems like a step in the right direction by beer advertisers, unless one considers that real animals appeal considerably to young people (Tarlach, 2001). Thus, while Anheuser-Busch, the lone beer advertiser in Super Bowl XXXIV, could be applauded for not reproducing a gender stereotype, it could also be condemned for relying so heavily on a tactic that may encourage underage drinking.

Consistent with previous studies of advertising in men's sports telecasts, this study showed the overwhelming majority of central characters in Super

Bowl commercials to be male, despite the fact that over 40% of the Super Bowl's television audience is female (Kiska, 1999). The significant under-representation of females as central characters even held true for commercials in the latest product category—Internet companies. Super Bowl commercials further marginalized females by depicting them as children and teenagers at a rate nearly three times higher than that at which males were depicted similarly. This portrayal of females positions them as less powerful than males.

In light of advertising's status as a primary meaning-making system of modern life and the Super Bowl's status as the premiere advertising event, Super Bowl advertising shapes our interpretations of people as well as products. Consistent with decades of content analyses of television advertising, this study shows Super Bowl commercials in sheer number of central characters alone to elevate male over female, White over non-White, and young over old. Through their use of narrators and central characters, these commercials suggest to viewers that White males are figures of status and authority in American culture, while females and people of color are less powerful and influential. In reinforcing the symbolic power of White males, Super Bowl commercials play a role in the maintenance of the social hierarchy.

On the other hand, Super Bowl commercials suggest that meanings of gender may be shifting somewhat. This analysis, unlike many previous analyses, showed most female central characters promoting high value product categories that are not stereotypically feminine (e.g., Internet companies and electronics) in out-of-home settings. Considering product category and setting as subtle indices of power, results point to some progress in achieving a more balanced portrayal of gender.

Still, findings indicate that Super Bowl commercials could do much better at fairly and accurately representing gender. Results point to a need for longitudinal research on the content of Super Bowl commercials. Longitudinal studies of Super Bowl advertising could identify trends in the depiction of gender and determine whether or not the commercials with the widest reach, and thus considerable potential to shape meaning, are consistently presenting stereotypical images and reinscribing difference. After all, the real losers of the Super Bowl should not be America's females.

NOTES

1. Product categories designated as "high value" include products typically priced at $100 or more, such as electronics, Internet, automobile, and banking/finance/insurance. Product categories designated as "low value" include products priced at less than $100, such as food/non-alcoholic beverages, medications, alcoholic beverages,

motion pictures, professional sports organizations, public service announcements, and other. Internet companies were designated as a high value product because a consumer needs expensive computer hardware to access a dot.com. Pricing parameters were borrowed from the research of Licata and Biswas (1993).

2. U.S. population data for 2000 were reported by the U.S. Census Bureau on www.prb.org.

REFERENCES

Beatty, S. (1999, February 2). Ratings, viewers for Super Bowl slipped from '98. *Wall Street Journal* (Eastern ed.), p. B7.

Bretl, D. J., & Cantor, J. (1988). The portrayal of men and women in U.S. television commercials: A recent content analysis and trends over 15 years. *Sex Roles, 18*, 595–609.

Caulfield, B. (2000, January 1). Dot-com Super Bowl? *Internet World, 6*, 35.

Craig, R. S. (1992). The effect of television day part on gender portrayals in television commercials: A content analysis. *Sex Roles, 26*, 197–211.

Eastman, S. T., Newton, G. D., & Pack, L. (1996). Promoting prime-time programs in megasporting events. *Journal of Broadcasting & Electronic Media, 40*, 366–388.

5th-largest audience watched Super Bowl. (2000, February 2). *Arizona Republic*, p. E8.

Finn, T. A., & Strickland, D. E. (1982). A content analysis of beverage alcohol advertising. *Journal of Studies on Alcohol, 43*, 964–989.

Hajewski, D. (2000, January 26). Dot.coms to square off in Super Bowl. *Milwaukee Journal Sentinel*, pp. D1–D2.

Hall, C. C. I., & Crum, J. J. (1994). Women and "body-isms" in television beer commercials. *Sex Roles, 31*, 329–337.

Jhally, S. (1995). Image-based culture: Advertising and popular culture. In G. Dines & J. M. Humez (Eds.), *Gender, race and class in media: A text-reader* (pp. 77–87). Thousand Oaks, CA: Sage.

Kiska, T. (1999, January 30). Super Bowl advertisers get a good female crowd. *Detroit News*, p. C1.

Lin, C. A. (1997). Beefcake versus cheesecake in the 1990s: Sexist portrayals of both genders in television commercials. *The Howard Journal of Communications, 8*, 237–249.

Madden, P. A., & Grube, J. W. (1994). The frequency and nature of alcohol and tobacco advertising in televised sports, 1990 through 1992. *American Journal of Public Health, 84*, 297–299.

McAllister, M. P. (1996). *The commercialization of American culture: New advertising, control and democracy*. Thousand Oaks, CA: Sage.

McArthur, L. Z., & Resko, B. G. (1975). The portrayal of men and women in American television commercials. *Journal of Social Psychology, 97*, 209–220.

Pavelchak, M. A., Antil, J. H., & Munch, J. M. (1988). The Super Bowl: An investigation into the relationship among program context, emotional experience, and ad recall. *Journal of Consumer Research, 15*, 360–367.

Population Reference Bureau. (2001). *U.S. population: The basics*. [On-line]. Retrieved from http://www.prb.org.

Signorielli, N., McLeod, D., & Healy, E. (1994). Gender stereotypes in MTV commercials: The beat goes on. *Journal of Broadcasting & Electronic Media, 38*, 91–102.

Tarlach, G. (2001, February 19). When people attack animals: Wild kingdom draws more viewers to ads. *Milwaukee Journal Sentinel*, pp. 1E, 3E.

Taylor, C. R., & Stern. B. B. (1997). Asian-Americans: Television advertising and the "model minority" stereotype. *Journal of Advertising, 26*, 47–61.

Twitchell, J. B. (1996). *Adcult USA: The triumph of advertising in American culture*. New York: Columbia University.

Wells, M. (2000, January 24). Hey Bud, what's it to ya? *Forbes*, 70.

Zito, K. (2000, February 1). Dot-com companies score during Super Bowl with TV ads. *San Francisco Chronicle* (Final ed.), p. C1.

Chapter Seven

Locating Italianita in Nancy Savoca's *True Love* and Penny Marshall's *Riding in Cars with Boys*

Theresa Carilli

In her first book of poetry, *Italian Women and Other Tragedies,* Canadian Italian poet Gianna Patriarca (1994) describes Italian women with these opening lines: "these are the women / who were born to give birth / they breathe only leftover air and speak only / when deeper voices have fallen asleep" (9). With these lines, Patriarca captures the essence of southern Italian women's lives—women who are sacrificial and subservient, religious and pious, quiet and gentle. Patriarca creates a world where women are voiceless, invisible, and deferential.

The entertainer Madonna, however, presents a sharp contrast to this world of sacrificial, subservient women. With a series of outrageous personae, Madonna has challenged the American value system. Whether dancing suggestively on stage wearing a crucifix or rolling around to a music video with male and female lovers of various races and ethnicities, Madonna has unleashed the righteous chains of sexual fantasy and demonstrated that sexuality is positive. In her brash, outspoken manner, Madonna continues to challenge the limiting ways Americans see themselves and their lives. Like Patriarca, Madonna has Italian American roots.

Cultural Studies critic and theorist Camille Paglia once said that there would never be an Italian American woman of any importance. Paglia, an Italian American herself, rested her assertion on the self deprecation and the history of Italian American women who have seemingly accomplished little in American society. For Paglia, Italian American women are much like those depicted in Patriarca's poem. Yet, Paglia, like Madonna, has that tough exterior.

As an Italian American woman, I have tried to make sense of these two diametrically opposed worlds. The world of silence and self deprecation collides with the predominant image of Italian American women in film. This woman, usually an uneducated, foul-mouthed, oversexed East Coast Italian American female with no ambitions other than marriage and the re-creation of the Sicilian village in her hometown, has earned her infamous place in American popular culture. Often, she appears as the lead in romantic comedies or tragedies. This recurring image appears in *Saturday Night Fever* (1977), *Moonstruck* (1987), *True Love* (1989), *Jungle Fever* (1991), *My Cousin Vinny* (1992), *Household Saints* (1993), *Angie* (1994), *Gia* (1998), and *Riding in Cars with Boys* (2001). I contend that these images are based on culturally specific codes of behavior known as *italianita* which originate in Italy and are modified in America. I believe that misinterpretation of these codes perpetuates the image of Italian American women as substandard, trashy, and incapable of ever achieving professional or economic success. In this article, I will locate *italianita* in two movies directed by Italian American women, Nancy Savoca and Penny Marshall. I hope to show just how important depictions of ethnicity can be in the creation, perception, and perpetuation of ethnic stereotyping and how more opportunities for dialogue and discussion can broaden the American consciousness with respect to race and ethnicity.

ITALIANITA

In his 1972 book, *The Rise of the Unmeltable Ethnics,* Michael Novak declares honorary membership in a group he calls "PIGS." Novak writes:

> I am born of PIGS—those Poles, Italians, Greeks, and Slavs, those non-English-speaking immigrants numbered so heavily among the workingmen [sic] of this nation. Not particularly liberal or radical; born into a history not white Anglo-Saxon and not Jewish; born outside what, in America, is considered the intellectual mainstream—and thus privy to neither power nor status nor intellectual voice. (p. 53)

Even though Novak's book was written over 30 years ago, his unique observations about White ethnics are still timely. Novak explores how those of us who are among the *PIGS,* or White ethnic groups, have been silenced and discouraged from examining our assimilation into White American mainstream culture. While recognizing that many White ethnic Americans do not see themselves as part of White America, Novak maintains that White ethnics have been sidelined in favor of seemingly more important discussions about race. Since most Americans cannot distinguish between "White ethnic" groups and White mainstream or Anglo-Saxon groups, all individuals who are labeled "White" have been grouped together. While multi-culturalists have carefully argued against grouping together all Latinos or Asians, White people are often grouped together. For example, when Spike Lee's movie *Jungle Fever* (1991) was released, it was depicted as a film about an interracial relationship between a Black man and a White woman. By ignoring that the woman was an Italian American, this rendering omits the larger context of the struggle between African Americans and Italian Americans in New York. Of course, White skin privilege does exist to a large degree; however, some White ethnic groups such as Italian Americans have specific cultural behaviors which distinguish them among White ethnic groups. My argument does not deny the existence of White skin privilege.

In *Italian Signs, American Streets,* Fred Gardaphe (1996) describes the culturally specific behavior known as *italianita,* which he traces through several Italian American novels. According to Gardaphe, *italianita*, or the existence of elements which signify Italian culture, consists of two primary cultural codes: "*omerta,* the code of silence that governs what is spoken or not spoken about in public, and *bella figura,* the code of proper presence or social behavior that governs an individual's public presence" (p. 20).

Omerta, the code of silence, has roots in Sicilian history: various countries invaded Sicily and attempted to infiltrate and overthrow its government. As a protective measure, Sicilians learned to keep silent and created a familial government so that allegiance was only to other Sicilians and to the family. The effects of *omerta* on Italian and Italian American women are best described by anthropologist Ann Cornelisen in *Women in the Shadows* (1976) and writer Helen Barolini in *The Dream Book* (1985). While attempting to interview women who worked in the fields in southern Italy, Cornelisen encountered *omerta* when women refused to trust her and resisted telling her about their lives. In 1985, Barolini explored the absence of Italian American women writers, an absence she attributed to *omerta*. Literary critic Mary Jo Bona argues in *Claiming a Tradition: Italian American Women Writers* (1999) that Italian American women are beginning to break this code of silence with their stories rendering the Italian American family:

> *Omerta*—has peculiar resonance for women of Italian origins and for women who want to write. Perhaps the codes informing the southern Italian family were considered inviolate in Italy, but they were subject to an authority closer to home in America: the wife, the mother, the sister, the daughter. That Italian American writers have chosen to use their family as the focus of their novels, to write of the family and tell its secrets, is a profoundly courageous act of autonomy. (p. 14)

While *omerta* serves as a guideline for what might or might not be an appropriate topic for conversation, *bella figura* centers around the presentation of self in public situations.

In her ethnography of a Chicago Italian Ladies Club, Gloria Nardini (1999) defines *bella figura*:

> My contention is that *bella figura* is a central metaphor of Italian life, admittedly an extremely complicated one. It is a construct that refers to face, looking good, putting on the dog, style, appearance, flair, showing off, ornamentation, etiquette, keeping up with the Joneses, image, illusion, esteem, social status, reputation—in short, self presentation and identity, performance and display. (p. 7)

For women in particular, Nardini explains, *bella figura* entails "gentility, grace, thinking about others" (p. 11). Nardini continues by discussing *bella figura* as an integral part of Italian identity that "depends upon public performance for its reification" (p. 20).

Hospitality, warmth, and openness are ways in which *bella figura* operates in Italian American culture. This cultural code of manners dictates that Italians or Italian Americans, particularly women, must engage in generous and courteous ways.

Both *omerta* and *bella figura* are performative behaviors that I contend are key to understanding the Italian American persona. I call these performative behaviors because they are acts of identity which take shape through language and movement and are dependent upon audience response. Italian American performers such as Frank Sinatra, Dean Martin, Tony Bennett, Marlon Brando, and Sophia Loren masterfully used *omerta* or *bella figura* to seduce their audiences. With a sharp audience awareness and a charismatic presence, these performers have all learned to use their ethnicity to mesmerize audiences.

Omerta and *bella figura* have been examined in Italian and Italian American literature (Bona, 1999; Gardaphe, 1996; Tamburri, 1998) or in Italian and Italian American ethnographies (Cornelisan, 1976; Nardini, 1999). They have not been studied as performative behaviors which appear in Italian American films that are not about the Mafia (where depictions of *omerta* are obvious and heavy handed). For this reason, I would like to speculate on what acts of identity demonstrate *omerta* or *bella figura,* key components of *italianita*. To perform *italianita* means that the individual is behaving in a manner to highlight secrecy and self-presentation. By secrecy, I mean that the individuals are engaging in some behavior which cannot be openly discussed. Meanwhile displays of self-presentation under secrecy become overly dramatic, as though the individuals are attempting to conceal their true emotions. Furthermore, sometimes this self-presentation with its focus on audience awareness does not follow the precise rules of *bella figura.* For the sake of my argument, I refer to that component of *bella figura* which translates into the acute awareness that an audience is present and that one is performing behavior with that audience in mind.

In my examination of Nancy Savoca's *True Love* and Penny Marshall's *Riding in Cars With Boys*, I locate the performed behaviors of *italianita*. From this point of location, I demonstrate how ethnic sensibility plays an enormous role in films written and/or directed by members of that ethnic group.

NANCY SAVOCA'S *TRUE LOVE*

In writer/director Nancy Savoca's 1989 film *True Love,* the main characters, Donna (Annabella Sciorra) and Michael (Ron Eldard) prepare for their wedding. While the story focuses on their feelings of ambivalence and fear about marriage, the backdrop of the Italian American Bronx neighborhood contextualizes the impending wedding. Italian American family and friends demonstrate a limited cultural world with specific rules that cannot be broken. At its core, *True Love* is about entrapment and the process of accepting cultural rules and values.

While the audience witnesses wedding preparations such as selecting the wedding rings, the tuxedo, and the reception meal, two key events, Michael's bachelor party and the actual wedding, demonstrate a cultural world where men and women live very separate lives. *Omerta* keeps these worlds intact. The characters are not allowed to interrupt the gendered, homo-erotic pact, where the most significant exchanges occur between members of the same sex. When Donna attempts to challenge this world by asking to partake in Michael's bachelor party, the following interaction ensues:

Michael: Its ridiculous. OK. Its fuckin' ridiculous. Who the hell ever heard of having your girlfriend at your bachelor party?

Donna: Oh, come on, Michael. I said after the party, after the party, we could get together.

Michael: No. After Uncle Benny's party, I gonna go out with my friends. It's gonna be my last night out. Don't you understand?

Donna: No. How many nights are you gonna have Michael?

Michael: Oh, I don't believe this. What do you want? I'm gonna be with you for the rest of my life.

In *True Love*, the interactions between Michael and his friends and Donna and her friends assert the connectedness among members of the same sex. Nancy Savoca takes a huge risk by demonstrating that an Italian American wedding, which should be the quintessential celebration of heterosexuality, is tainted by the rules governing same sex and opposite sex relationships. Savoca pushes this assertion at the wedding reception, when Michael and his friends, Kevin, Brian, and Dominick, meet for a champagne toast:

Kevin: To the men. (All toast.)

Dominick: To the real men.

Michael: This didn't turn out so bad, did it? You guys havin' a good time?

All: Hell, yeah.

Dominick: Listen, Mike. You know that speech I had to make before. I don't know if it came out right, but I really meant it. I mean that. I wish you two the best. You know if you ever need me for anything . . .

Michael: Dom, Dom, no. (He kisses him.)

Kevin: You guys gonna get married now? (Michael kisses Kevin.) I went for it.

Michael: What time is it?

Dominick: About 11:30 I guess. Why?

Michael: How about when this thing is over, we go to the bar, and we have a few drinks on me.

Dominick: Mikie, I don't think tonight.

Brian: No, Mike, when you get back, ok?

Michael: No. No. This thing is almost finished here. I don't gotta be anywhere until tomorrow.

As this scene continues, Michael tells Donna that he's planning to go out with his friends. Donna becomes very upset, and both characters end up in the women's restroom arguing about whether Michael can or cannot go out with his friends. The film ends with the two characters posing for wedding photographs. During the first pose, Michael and Donna stare away from each other with a troubling look as though Savoca were indicating that this pattern between males and females would continue, and the unhappiness it would create is just a part of Italian American life.

Savoca's focus on the interaction between same sex and opposite sex characters marks *True Love* as a unique and culturally specific rendering of Italian Americans. Savoca underscores this rendering with a depiction of the Italian American interaction, a form of *bella figura*. The lively, colorful, dramatic exchanges among the characters represent an Italian American communication aesthetic. While at times these exchanges seem crass and hostile, they are performed for an audience's appreciation. They serve as entertainment for all participants witnessing or engaging in the interaction. Here are several examples:

1. Michael's uncle has invited his friend Ernie, a jeweler, over to Michael's house to assist Michael and Donna in selecting wedding rings. After showing some of his best jewelery, Michael's uncle responds to Ernie: "Cut the shit, will you Ernie? Show him something plainer."
2. As Michael and Donna prepare to baby sit for Michael's niece, Michael's sister comments on her husband Tom who is preparing to go out: "You believe this? He's worse than a woman."
3. As Donna's friends discuss preparations for Donna's wedding, one friend says to the other: "Could you take a valium or something?"
4. Donna enters Michael's bedroom to give him his tuxedo for the wedding. She throws it on him and he responds: "That's a nice way to suffocate someone." She responds, "You know, you and your buddies are a fucken' waste."
5. On the day of the wedding, one of Donna's relatives remarks to another relative: "That pin does not go with that dress. I'm sorry. Take the pin off. Fran, she's wearing that Jesus pin again."

With these interactions, the characters engage in culturally specific performances which are intended to entertain the participants. For example, in the interaction between Donna and Michael, his remark "That's a nice way to suffocate someone" is his attempt to be humorous and to engage her through his humor. While her response, "You know, you and your buddies are a fuckin' waste" has a serious and angry edge, it also serves as a dramatic response to his remark. In this case, both characters are engaged in an entertaining and dramatic moment by the way they enact this scene. If they were not Italian Americans, the exchange might have been different. Michael might have asked Donna if she were angry, and Donna might have explained that she felt hurt about Michael's attention to his friends. Instead, Donna throws the tuxedo at Michael, Michaels responds to her with humor, and she responds back in a charged and dramatic manner. The communication is indirect and demonstrates the cultural codes of both *omerta* (not to be direct and honest) and *bella figura* (engaging and entertaining self presentation). Savoca depicts these cultural values throughout *True Love,* which was originally rejected for being "too ethnic" (p. 54). By showing the same sex/opposite sex tension in a world flavored with expressive language, Savoca gives an authentic rendering of Italian American culture. With this sensibility, however, Savoca also portrays a world of desperation and entrapment, where economic success or professional aspiration are not apparent. Those values sanctioned in an American world seem to be invisible in an Italian American world. The audience might be left with a stereotypical sense of Italian Americans as expressive, working class individuals who are a fringe group in American society.

PENNY MARSHALL'S *RIDING IN CARS WITH BOYS*

In *Riding in Cars with Boys* (2001), Italian American director Penny Marshall (whose real surname is Marscharelli) brings her audience into the world of an Italian American family as told through the eyes of Beverly Donofrio (Drew Barrymore). Based on D'onofrio's autobiographical novel *Riding in Cars with Boys*, the film captures the life of Bev, who becomes a teenage mother in the 1960's. Like *True Love*, *Riding in Cars with Boys* uses the Italian American family to contextualize these events in Bev's life. At the beginning of the movie, an 11-year-old Bev waits for her father, Leo (James Woods), a Wallingford, Connecticut, police officer who takes his daughter to buy a Christmas tree. As Bev waits, her uncle dances around the living room singing along with an Italian Christmas song, "Hee Haw Hee Haw Hee Haw/It's Dominick the donkey. Hee Haw Hee Haw Hee Haw/The Italian Christmas donkey . . ." This opening signifies that the Italian American family will be a major part of Bev's identity. When Bev's father asks her what she wants for Christmas, Bev pleads for a bra. As her father denies this plea, the audience learns of the conflict between them. From this very moment, Bev experiences a controlling father who wishes to ignore and squash his daughter's sexuality. This conflict between Bev and her father creates the dramatic tension throughout the movie. At the end of the movie, Bev's realization that the treatment she received from her father parallels her treatment towards her adult son brings closure to her trials as a teenage mother.

Many of the dramatic scenes are colorful and humorous, yet poignant. For example, when 15-year-old Bev learns that she is pregnant, her best friend and confidante Fay (Brittany Murphy) encourages her to "practice" how Bev will break this news to her parents. With this role play, Fay responds as though she is Bev's mother:

Fay: My daughter's a tramp. My daughter's a tramp. My daughter's a tramp. You're fifteen years old. How can you do this to me? You make me sick to my stomach. Why don't you just take my gun, take my gun and shoot me in the head with it, tramp. I wish you were never born.

While the scene is comedic, the exaggerated language creating a melodramatic effect, it prepares the audience for the actual scene when Bev's parents learn about her pregnancy through a letter she leaves in the mailbox.

Mother: (sighing) This is what we're gonna do. She's gonna go to school until she starts to show. And then, she'll get her high school equivalency, and then she'll get a great job as a secretary. And after they're married, they can move into the rec room with the baby.

Bev: Actually, that's not the plan I have in mind.

Mother: Oh.

Bev: I've decided what's best for my future is not getting married. As you can see from my letter, I may have a flair for writing, so my plan is to move . . .

Father: (interrupting) Plan. You have a plan. Plan. You have a plan. Well, I had a plan, too. I was gonna work hard, raise a good family, hold my head up proud. That plan's dead. You know what else I thought? (pause) No. I better not.

Bev: Go ahead, Pop, say whatever you want.

Father: You were special, and you ruined your life, and you broke my heart. (He puts his head down and cries.)

While the film takes place prior to Roe vs. Wade, when young women could not legally choose abortion, and the depiction of the traditional family values in the mid 1960's play a key role in the plot, Bev's relationship with her Italian American father add a dimension to her dilemma. Silently, Bev accepts her circumstances and marries Raymond (Steve Zahn) as a way to restore her relationship with her father and his community. By marrying Raymond, Bev attempts to salvage her father's reputation among his family and friends. At the wedding reception, her father makes a toast, demonstrating his feelings of shame for his daughter's actions:

Father: There are times in a man's life when there's cause to celebrate. And finding friends to celebrate with is easy. (pause) But then, there are times like this. And if there are still people by his side, then those are his real friends, his real family. We all know what brought us here, and the fact that you all still saw it in your hearts to come—well, you're in my heart forever. *Salud.*

Bev willingly sacrifices her dreams to insure that her family can return to enacting *bella figura.* She never discusses or argues with her father about these decisions because of the code of silence between men and women in the Italian American culture. The wedding is full of colorful interactions which uniquely characterize Italian Americans: As the photographer attempts to take the wedding photo, every family member moves so that the photo shows each individual looking in a different direction. At the reception, the band plays the song, *The Lady is A Tramp*, only to be hushed by Bev's father. When the band goes on break, Fay grabs the microphone and sings to her boyfriend. Bev and Fay are seated in the middle of the reception room, and no one will speak to either of them. To garner attention and recognition, Fay announces her pregnancy at the wedding reception.

During a five-year period in young Bev's life, she gives birth to her son, Jason and breaks up with Raymond, a substance abuser. *Riding in Cars with Boys* juxtaposes this five-year period with a sub-plot of a 35-year-old Bev with a 19-year-old Jason. An older Bev and a grown up Jason drive from New York to Connecticut to meet Raymond and ask him to sign away his rights to Bev's novel. The plot takes some rather intricate turns as we learn that Jason is about to ask his mother's permission to attend Indiana University versus New York University because he has gotten involved with Fay's daughter, Amelia, who attends Indiana University. Bev does not respond well to Jason's intentions, and their interaction is only exacerbated as Jason meets Raymond, who he has not seen since his childhood. Finally, Jason and Bev have a confrontation. Bev perhaps realizing that by being controlling she is passing on her father's legacy, allows Jason to leave her on a deserted Connecticut road and move to Indiana. In the final scene, Bev's father comes to pick her up on this road, and they drive off singing a famous 60s song, *Dream*. This song has a particular significance to both Bev and her father, who sing it in the opening scene as a bonding experience. Also, the song signifies the interruption imposed by her father on Bev's dream to become a writer. To Bev's father, marriage was the only option for a pregnant teenage girl. Bev had to abandon her hopes and dreams of having a future outside of her family dynamics.

Penny Marshall chose to dramatize *Riding in Cars with Boys* because like Dononfrio, she shares both a working class Italian American background and a teenage pregnancy. Her intention, much like Savoca's, is to render a world where men and women don't communicate, and women's lives have limited options. Marshall captures the Italian American characters' efforts to mask pain and silence through humorous and exaggerated interactions. The movie, however, perhaps because of its mainstream release, does not show us how Bev makes her way out of her circumstances. Dononfrio's novel, equally powerful, poignant, and comedic, spends more time explaining her triumph over adversity.

In excruciating detail, the novel focuses on how Bev receives an education and becomes a New York writer. Her descriptions of her teenage poverty and her family are comic, insightful, and moving. She has a tremendous ability to capture a person or place in just a few words. For instance, she describes Raymond by using his one favorite expression: "How Come Dat?" She refers to her young son Jason as her Italian American father. Her description of attending Wesleyan University as a working class Italian American is hilarious and painful:

> I was the oldest person there and the only one with a kid all right, but I was also the only one who noticed. Since I might as well be invisible, it was safe to take a look around, and what I saw were people cut from a different mold. The guys had overdeveloped heads and underdeveloped bodies, and the girls had frizzy hair, backpacks, and frozen faced expressions. I felt like the Student from Another Planet . . . then a tall lanky guy touched my shoulder and said, "Excuse me, is this the line for registration?" "I guess," I said. What else would it be? "Excuse me," he said to the girl behind me, "Is this the line for registration?" "Quite," she said. Quite? Who in the world said *quite*. Was this what I'd have to choose from for friends? Why had I been in such a hurry to transfer from community college when I could've stayed there another year before I made this flying leap to whitebreadsville. (pp. 158–159)

Marshall's choice not to depict Bev's rise to fame and success contributes to a stereotypical depiction of Italian American women, raising some key issues about rendering ethnicity in film.

AUTHENTICITY VERSUS STEREOTYPE:
THE ANGLO SAXON LENS

Both Nancy Savoca and Penny Marshall can be viewed as promoting stereotypes of Italian American women. The depictions created by Italian American women about Italian American women should fairly represent the culture. Yet, both filmmakers render women trapped in worlds that are culturally dictated, without a promising economic or professional future.

In this paper, I argue that Savoca and Marshall provide accurate, authentic depictions based on their experiential world. They demonstrate *italianita* in their films, remaining faithful to the rules and codes of conduct in the Italian American family and rendering an Italian American aesthetic full of lively, dramatic, humorous, painful, and melodramatic interactions.

As film consumers, the American public has been taught to discover and devour stereotypes, particularly ethnic stereotypes. Stereotypes often allow consumers to engage in upmanship, believing they are better than the individuals being presented/represented.

But a closer reading of films (like *True Love* and *Riding in Cars With Boys*) that display sensitive cultural rendering indicates that authentic cultural depictions conflict with the Anglo Saxon core value system implicit in American films. The American movie industry seems smitten with dozens of films depicting the American hero on his quest to fulfill the American dream, which often means overcoming strife through rugged individualism. Movies with communal cultural values where individuals demonstrate how their interactions with other cultural members deeply affect their identities are dismissed because they do not reinforce individualism. Movies created by women or with women as the protagonists are not as visible or as valued as movies created by men about men. Examining these characterizations through a patriarchal Anglo Saxon lens makes them seem sub-standard and stereotypical. Future articles that share how cultural members experience films created by other cultural members invite a dialogue about gender and ethnic sensibility.

REFERENCES

Badham, J. (Director), & Cohn, N. and Wexter, N. (Writers). (1977). *Saturday Night Fever* [Motion picture]. United States: Paramount Pictures.

Barolini, H. (Ed.) (1985). *The dream book*. New York: Schocken.

Bona, M.J. (1999). *Claiming a tradition: Italian American women writers*. Carbondale: Southern Illinois University press.

Coolidge (Director), & Wing, A. and Graff, T. (Writers). (1994). *Angie* [Motion picture]. Unites States: Buena Vista Pictures.

Cornelisen, A. (1976). *Women of the Shadows*. Boston: Little.

Cristofer, M. (Director), & McInerney, J. and Cristofer, M. (Writers). (1998). *Gia* [Motion picture]. United States: HBO.

Donofrio, B. (1990). *Riding in cars with boys*. New York: Penguin Putnam Inc.

Fausty, J. and Giunta, E. (2001). An interview with Nancy Savoca. *Voices in Italian Americana*, 12(2), 47–57.

Gardaphe, F. (1996). *Italian signs, American streets: The evolution of Italian American narrative*. Durham, N.C.: Duke University press.

Jewison, N. (Director), & Shanley, J.P. (Writer). (1987). *Moonstruck* [Motion picture]. United States: Metro-Goldwyn-Mayer.

Lee, S. (Director), & Lee, S. (Writer). (1991). *Jungle Fever* [Motion picture]. United States: 40 Acres and a Mule Filmworks and Universal Pictures.

Lynn, J. (Director) & Launer, D. (Writer). (1992). *My Cousin Vinny* [Motion picture]. United States: 20th Century Fox.

Marshall, P. (Director), & Beverly Donofrio and Morgan Ward (Writers). (2001). *Riding in cars with boys* [Motion picture]. United States: Columbia Pictures.

Nardini, G. (1999). *Che Bella Figura: The power of performance in an Italian ladies' club in Chicago*. Albany, N.Y.: State University of New York Press.

Novak, M. (1972). *The rise of the unmeltable ethnics*. New York: Macmillan.

Patriarca, G. (1994). *Italian women and other tragedies*. Toronto: Guernica Editions, Inc.

———, (1989). *True Love* [Motion picture]. United States: United Artists/Metro-Goldwyn-Mayer.

Savoca, N. (Director), & Savoca, N. and Guay R. (Writers). (1993). *Household Saints* [Motion picture]. United States: Fine Line Features.

Tamburri, A.J. (1998) *A semiotic of ethnicity: In (re) cognition of the Italian/American writer.* Albany, N.Y.: State University of New York press.

Chapter Eight

Embodying Deviance, Representing Women and Drugs in the 1990s: Lessons from *Losing Isaiah* to *New Jack City*

Michele Tracy Berger

INTRODUCTION

In November 1993, the *New York Times* reported a disturbing incident. Six teenagers had allegedly raped a thirty-one-year-old woman, a resident of East New York. They pulled her into an alley while she was on her way home from grocery shopping. They sodomized and raped her, at times using a metal pipe. Afterwards the young men boasted and bragged to others about the incident.

Even more disturbing than the incident were the responses to it from the community. There were no memorials or outcries as in the famous case of the Central Park jogger. Instead, there was serious debate among community members about whether or not the woman was a drug-using prostitute. At that time several drug-using prostitutes (primarily crack cocaine users) frequented the area, and many residents knew that teenagers often targeted these women with acts of cruelty and violence. Gonzalez and Pierre-Pierre, authors of the *New York Times* article, noted that

> [v]iolence is an occupational hazard that is to be expected as much from an emotionally unhinged john as from a pack of teenagers who make sport of showering them [prostitutes] with rocks and bottles (p. 39).

The response from the families of the alleged perpetrators was equally troubling. Thus, if she had been a prostitute, according to many in the community, her abuse was implicitly justified.

The young men were arrested and brought up on charges. One of the boys' grandfathers was quoted as saying about the alleged victim, "She's a whore and a crackhead." The mother of another of the accused said, "I don't think these young boys' lives should be wasted over a prostitute" (Gonzalez and Pierre-Pierre, 1993).

This story stands as a cautionary tale for the issues I discuss in this paper. First, it highlights the changing environment urban women (particularly African American women) confronted during the nineties. Urban women lived in environments that were often devastated by the sale and use of crack cocaine and widespread street prostitution. Indeed, the late eighties and early nineties witnessed the rise of crack cocaine as a major social phenomenon in every large American city, along with its by-product of increased illicit activities, including street-level sex work (Ratner, 1993).[1] Second, the story allows us to witness, in microcosm, the continuum of hostility and violence directed at women assumed or perceived to be involved in particular kinds of illicit activities.

Words like "crack ho" "crackhead" "skeezer" and "crack fiend" have become, if not common parlance, definitely identifiable images easily conjured up by the average American. This article asks: Besides the news media, where did those specific images come from? What forces helped shape popular opinion in regard to women, drugs, and sexuality? How does one make sense of an almost ubiquitous representation in popular culture, during the nineties, of a pariah image of African American women[2] as sexually degenerate crack cocaine/drug users?

A body of work has developed through various interdisciplinary movements and inquiries charting and examining Black women's sexual representation and the connection between punitive and oppressive social ideologies (Austin, 1992b, 1989; Crenshaw, 1989, 1997; Collins, 1990; DuCille, 1994; hooks, 1989, 1992, 1994; Jewell, 1993; Lubiano, 1993; Painter, 1993; Rose, 1998; Spillers, 1984; Wallace, 1990). Although there have been analyses of the "New Jack aesthetic" and the "gangsterization" of movies and the depiction of women in them, few analyses or close readings of texts tease out the relationship between consistent depictions of women as crack/sexual fiends and the potential to shape social ideologies (Jones, 1992, 1996; Wallace, 1992).

Adapting the theoretical framework of Patricia Hill Collins, I will discuss the image of the crack fiend within the framework of controlling images (Collins, 1990). I argue that the representation of a sexually deviant crack user can be understood as a modern day controlling image highlighting race, gender, and class inequalities. Specifically, I will examine two representational sites of this controlling image: sexuality and motherhood. I will discuss the movies *Sugar Hill, Menace II Society, Boyz 'n the Hood, New Jack City, Clockers*, and *Losing Isaiah* as central to the creation of this controlling image.

These movies were selected because of their prevalent themes of inner city drug use and prostitution. They were also widely attended by Black and White audiences and enjoyed commercial success. The majority of the films were directed by African American men.

Indeed, while many of these films were touted for their originality, ambition and authenticity, few film critics made mention of the deeper insidious patterns of female representation. This feminist rereading of these films contextualizes their possible role in contributing to a climate of hostility toward female drug users.

Through the analysis, the repetition of specific negative images illustrates the lack of compassionate or even commonsensical narratives about "deviance" and female behavior. These images help to reify ideas about uncontrollable lower-income women (particularly welfare mothers), ideas already manifest throughout society (Jewell, 1993; Rose, 1998). Through these controlling images, audiences can only imagine women who are drug users as tragic, deceitful, demoralized, and disgusting—women to be reviled and held responsible for the social chaos within their communities—possibly women to harm.

CONTROLLING IMAGES

Patricia Hill Collins, in *Black Feminist Thought*, provides us with a framework for examining the ways Black women have been externally defined and represented within dominant culture. She calls these pernicious images, promulgated outside Black communities, *controlling*. They are a legacy from the ideological justifications for control over Black women's bodies during slavery. Briefly, they are: The *mammy*, a faithful, asexual obedient servant, the *matriarch*, symbolizing the mother in Black homes, an overly aggressive and un-feminine woman; the *welfare mother*, lazy, and unable to properly instill morality in the family, and the *Jezebel*, a woman who is defined as lascivious and sexually aggressive (Collins, 1990). Through historical analysis, Collins discusses how each of these images has helped to control and shape external defining realities. Because these images have permeated every aspect of popular culture, they have informed discussions on policy and have justified discriminatory treatment of Black women in the workplace and other institutions (Collins, 1990; Jewell, 1993). Although Black women have resisted these images, they have provided an accepted hegemonic influence. Controlling images "provide ideological justifications" for race, gender, and class subordination and the interlocking ways they manifest throughout culture (Collins, 1990, p. 66).

In using this framework to analyze popular cultural trends of the nineties, I posit that the controlling image of the crack fiend is a collapsed and sinister collage of the Jezebel, matriarch, and welfare mother. The concentration of images in these films portrays an aggressive woman who displays both hyper and deviant sexuality, compounded by the relentless pursuit of drugs (an especially stigmatizing and deviant activity for women) and the lack of concern for children.[3] Indeed, in some films the women prey on children, further severing a connection to standard ideals of mothering. If the female characters are mothers, they are usually lazy and incompetent, and often their behaviors lead to the downfall of their sons (whether the depiction is crack cocaine or heroin). The female characters in many of these movies molest and disturb the daily lives of everyday people. Overall, the result of the fusion of these three images is a simultaneous expression of licentiousness, aggressiveness, and lack of responsibility (or interest) in the well-being of the women's children, their communities, or themselves. The political result of this cluster of representations in the late eighties and nineties was a seemingly recognizable social evil that both Democratic and Republican political camps could agree upon and denounce with punitive criminal policies and moral condemnation (Campbell, 2000; Maher, 1992; Reeves, 1994).

THE FILMS

As texts, these films contain a recurring theme or commentary on women, drugs, and prostitution, much of it unflattering. They are an outcome of several structural developments that included the rise and popularity of the "authentic" inner city Black film of the late eighties and early nineties which in the tradition of "realistic cinema" often purported to show Black life as "it really was."[4] A second, related, phenomenon was the emergence of Black male directors and producers coming of age and having a minimal authority in the Hollywood industry, including Spike Lee, the Hudlin Brothers, Matty Rich, and John Singleton.[5] A third phenomenon was the reassertion of Black masculine identity in response to demonized ideological representations of single headed female households (Jones, 1992; Wallace, 1992). Although these films span diverse subjects, they all share a common center: they depict the ravages of crack cocaine use, particularly within urban communities confronting multifaceted challenges (Jones, 1992; Wallace, 1990, 1992). As cultural products produced and aimed at Black audiences, these movies mirrored political trends and ideologies prevalent in the late eighties and early nineties, including vigilantism, nationalism and sexism (Jones, 1992).

SEXUALITY AND MOTHERHOOD

Sexuality

According to Michele Wallace (1992) and Jacquie Jones (1992), when films concern themselves with heterosexual Black masculinity (*Boyz 'n the Hood* and *Menace II Society*), female participation fluctuates between the poles of the "bitch and the ho." Wallace asserts: "Before *Boyz 'n the Hood*, there were two kinds of Black female characters in films—whores and good girls" (Wallace 1992, p. 124). Doughboy (Ice Cube) in *Boyz 'n the Hood* identifies the women that exist in their world: "bitches, hos, and "hoochies." This same set of distinctions casts a pallor across the majority of the films.

In these movies (with often an almost entirely male cast), usually one woman is the "good woman," typified as upwardly mobile, educated, and sexually virtuous. In fact, she is more desirable because she "knows" her worth and is chaste. This type of character usually bemoans the lack of "decent" men worthy of her time or interest. For example, in *Sugar Hill*, Theresa Randle's character (Melissa), exemplifying the "good woman," is utterly terrified of violence and gainfully employed. She does not do drugs or have promiscuous sex. She is the epitome of the good girl, waiting for the right man, and keeping her legs "shut" in the meantime. Nia Long's character, Brandi, also exemplifies this pattern in *Boyz 'n the Hood*. She is a good Catholic girl who wants to get married and wait until then to have sex. Although she makes reference to the challenges of surviving in a violent neighborhood, her main struggle throughout the movie is the dilemma of if and when to sleep with her long time neighbor and boyfriend Tre (Cuba Gooding, Jr.). By the end of the movie she crosses over the line. Ronnie (Jada Pinkett) is Caine's girlfriend in *Menace II Society*. She is also the "good girl," who is in turn protected by Caine. She acts as both Caine's conscience and the moral arbitrator between Caine's aspirations and those of his friends.

Throughout these movies male characters are generally on the prowl and on the make and regard women primarily as sexual objects, therefore as easy and expendable. In *Menace II Society* and *Boyz 'n the Hood,* packs of teenage girls roam around with the bad boys. They are pretty and silent except for laments and taunts about getting money from the men, or getting the men to buy them something. In *Menace II Society*, they witness gruesome murders and other crimes yet hardly ever raise their voices to challenge or condemn their male companions. As minor characters in these films, they simultaneously pursue pleasure and the acquisition of luxury items; yet they are passive and acted upon by the whims of the group of young men. Seemingly oblivious to the derogatory remarks made toward them, or to other women, either they know their place or stay in their place under the threat of being replaced by another better-looking "bitch." Women's worth is represented in male sanctioned and defined terms.

Women addicts are depicted as ravenous and uncontrollable in their sexuality, so much so that they engage in public sex without shame for the possibility of a hit on a pipe or a few dollars. In *Sugar Hill*, the male characters are often equally fascinated and repulsed by female drug users. It is as if these women are the signposts of nature gone awry. They are there to be experimented on and then degraded.

The act of oral sex is the most defining depiction of the female drug user's degradation in the majority of these films. Repeatedly, the request to perform oral sex, specifically fellatio, is portrayed. Oral sex is a trope that allows for the further stigmatization and marginalization of women in public and private space. In *New Jack City*, character G-Money (Allen Payne) typifies attitudes about oral sex and the women who provide it. He tells Tito (Wesley Snipes), a major drug dealer in the Bronx, about this new drug—rock cocaine and the unusual benefits that seem to come with it: "And the bitches—oh, Lord the bitches! The bitches they do anything for this man. I had my Jimmy waxed [slang for oral sex] every day several times last week. Do you understand?"

Menace II Society was produced by the Hughes brothers and is a graphic and nihilistic depiction of four young men of color growing up and becoming involved with crime. Set in Watts, California, in 1993, the narrative also draws on flashbacks to Watts in the 1960s. In this movie, the trope of oral sex is used in multiple ways. In the beginning we learn that a drug dealer father and heroin addicted mother raised Caine, the main character. At the beginning of the movie, a squabble during a card game devolves into violence. A man tells Samuel Jackson (Caine's father) to "suck his dick" and then gets violently killed. Later in the movie this trope gets repeated when a basehead (male equivalent of a woman crack cocaine user) in desperation asks one of the guys to "suck his dick" and is shot immediately. This scene depicts a treble taboo: the desperation, the oral sex, and the implied homosexuality. Implicitly, a woman can survive and indeed deserve a specific type of degradation because she engages in oral sex—a man deserves death. Oral sex then becomes a specific way of representing women drug users and general sexual deviance in these movies. Although male drug users in these films hustle, work odd jobs, and steal, the only consistent representation of female drug users is through hypersexuality. These representations of drug using women as uncontrollable and willing to "do anything" for a rock is inconsistent with the majority of research on drug using women (Berger, 2004; Maher, 1997).

Depictions about oral sex also convey ideas about disease. Dooky, a minor character in *Boyz 'n the Hood*, suggests what drug using women are good for:

"I don't be fucking dopeheads; I might let them suck my dick. I mean, they got AIDS and shit."

Motherhood

In these movies, the representation of motherhood as intertwined with sexuality is also a trope that contributes to the crack/drug fiend controlling image, albeit in a more complex way. In several of these films, a narrative link is made to an earlier version of the downfallen women, either the mother of one of the male characters, or his sister or a close female neighbor, who is usually a heroin user. This trope is employed in *Boyz 'n the Hood* and *Sugar Hill*. In *Boyz 'n the Hood, Sugar Hill,* and *Menace II Society*, the mothers of the primary male characters are drug users. These movies suggest that the cycle of female deviance is passed on to the boys through their mothers with terrible consequences. For example, in the beginning of *Sugar Hill,* Roemello's mother is introduced to drugs (by a man, a heroin addict) and becomes a heroin addict and neglectful parent. The brothers Roemello and Raynathan (Michael Wright) suggest that she has made them "crazy." This is a typical mother narrative alluded to in other films.

In *Boyz 'n The Hood*, there are actually three images of mothers: the upwardly mobile Reva (Angela Basset), who sends her son, Tre, away so that she can work on her Master's degree and he can be taught how to "be a man" by his father Furious (Lawrence Fishburne); the mean Mrs. Baker (Tyra Ferrell), who calls one of her sons a "fat fuck" and constantly berates him; and Cheryl, a neighbor of Tre's (Cuba Gooding, Jr.). In one scene a little baby is about to get run over by a car. Tre steps in to save it and then brings the child to the mother's (Cheryl's) door. When she opens it she is physically repulsive, dirty, smelly and unkempt. He yells at her: "Keep your baby out of the street!" Taking the baby she immediately responds: "You got some blow? I'll suck your dick." Cheryl continues her negligent behavior throughout the movie. Wallace suggests that *Boyz 'n the Hood* "is really about the threat of female or aberrant sexuality to traditional family values" and that it reifies dominant ideological "family values" (Wallace, 1992, p. 128). Depicting women in these ways contributes to the idea that lower income women cannot help but have kids and do drugs. This idea suggests that the state is right to ignore them or subject them to harsh punitive responses. It is also a condemnation and rejection of female-headed households. Wallace identifies the typical audience's response to these images:

> [w]hat also made me the most uneasy about the portrayal of these single Black mothers was how little we're told about them, how we, as viewers are encour-

aged, on the basis of visual cues, to come to stereotypical conclusions about these women (Wallace, 1992, p. 123).

Losing Isaiah is a film about interracial adoption that centers around the struggle between Khaila (Halle Berry), a former crack addict, and Vivian (Jessica Lange), a nurse, over the adoption of Khaila's son, whom she has abandoned. Although this film is complex and tries to speak to the realities of women and drug use, it often lapses into the stereotypical, controlling image. Within the first five minutes of the movie we see that Khaila is living like an animal. In a crazed moment she puts her son in a garbage can and then leaves to solicit someone for her drugs. She feels some shame and loss, but throughout the movie her problems are individualized and not viewed as part of endemic social problems. How she got the child, what her previous conditions were, where the father of the child is, are questions that are never answered for the audience.[6] When Khaila enters drug treatment there is a scene in which other female addicts talk about their lives. With little context, they admit to the many offensive things they did while addicted to crack, mostly involving sex. Instead of developing empathy in this scene for Khaila or any of the women, the viewer is left feeling little.

Everyone has derision for the woman, *even* the people who are there to help and support her. Samuel Jackson portrays a megalomaniacal lawyer who simultaneously represents and condemns Khaila. Because he is against putting Black children in White homes, he agrees to take her case. He feels he has a right to control how she dresses and whom she sees romantically. She tries to transform herself into the "good girl," though she never quite makes it stick, even without drug use. Although Vivian is a nurse, with no real understanding of Khaila's situation, she acts as a judge and moral authority. In this film rarely does Khaila have a chance to speak for herself, except at the very end of the movie where she gives her child to Vivian even though she won her court case. There is a subtle message that even if "bad" (read, Black) mothers get off drugs, their children are really better off in other environments.

Clockers is based on a novel by Richard Price. The main theme revolves around the tension between several young Black men (some of whom are drug dealers) and the local police. Strike (Mekhi Phifer) is a small time drug dealer who dreams of leaving the inner city and has a passion for trains. The movie follows the plot and characterization of the novel closely except for several scenes that stand out prominently in contrast with the novel. These are all scenes where pregnant women are admonished for using drugs. The drug dealers chastise the pregnant women yet sell them drugs anyway. Through these scenes, drug-using women are blamed for their deviance, blamed for being bad mothers, and held responsible for the problems embedded in the community.[7] The penalization of drug-using mothers has been intense and severe, mostly affecting women of color. One study found that although 15.4 percent of White women and 14.1 percent of African American women used drugs during pregnancy, African American women were 10 times more likely than White women to be reported to the authorities (ACLU, 2000). Punitive policies with regard to drug use during pregnancy act as deterrents against women effectively participating in drug treatment programs.

CONCLUSION

Admittedly, this essay raises more questions about the relationship between the images of Black women who are crack cocaine users circulated during the nineties and public attitudes toward them that it answers. I have unearthed a potentially fruitful line of inquiry about how the dominant image of the "crack fiend" could be viewed as a collapsed version of older, long-standing images of African American women. Although I have not tried to pose a causal analysis of how these images might have been interpreted by the public, I would argue that such images reinforced an ideological context of punitive responses to female substance users. Many of the portrayals discussed offer easy answers to complex situations that might have been better settled through collective, public engagement than through narratives of individual blame.

In this chapter I shifted the focus from Collins' early examination of controlling images circulated by outsiders to the area of Black popular culture and the internal politics of representation. Another set of unsettling questions the chapter raises are about the role of several African American male filmmakers in their creation and use of these images. In the 1990s, many African American male filmmakers found themselves in an historic role—being sought after by the mainstream Hollywood industry. What understandings of women and drugs were they trying to convey to their audiences? I would argue that these images contributed to what Zerai and Banks identify as "dehumanizing discourse" (2002). They argue that such discourse is "potentially the most powerful weapon of those who wish to dehumanize African American women struggling with addition to crack" (p. 142). They document a hostile public climate for women who use drugs encouraged by "media hysteria around 'crack moms,' the publication of research findings driven by conservative political agendas, and anti-drug policies that reproduced the inequalities of race, class, and gender" (p. 37). By placing sole blame on women for their drug use, these movies ignore other important social factors during the 1980s and 1990s, including the significant withdrawal of resources from federal and state programs that helped the poor. Moreover, films that stigmatized African American female drug users ensured both a continued silence by middle class Blacks and Whites toward public policy and apathy at the ways in which all female drug users were targeted by the policymakers and others (Campbell, 2000; Zerai & Banks, 2002). Whatever the filmmakers' reasons, we are left with the fallout of these images that in part serve to distance us from the everyday complex lives of female drug users.

NOTES

1. The term sex work is a fluid concept, one that can denote the exchange of sexual services for food, clothing, money, drugs, or other primarily tangible items. Sex workers and feminist theorists have argued that these transactions are part of women and men's labor (See generally Bell 1987; Bell 1994; Delacoste and Alexander 1987; Jenness 1993; Nagle 1997).
2. Though the ravages of crack cocaine have affected many different types of women, I specifically focus on African American women in this analysis. Dominant representations of African American women figure prominently in the films discussed. More importantly, the incarceration rate for crack cocaine use and other illicit activities and policies targeting pregnant female drug users disproportionately affected Black women during the nineties (Maher 1997; Zerai & Banks, 2002).
3. Both Murphy (2000) and Campbell (2000) provide compelling historical insight about the stigmatization of women who use drugs.
4. There are also geographic distinctions between these films. There was a tension between East and West coasts in the depiction of Black inner city life. The West Coast movies include *Boyz 'n the Hood; Menace II Society. Fresh, Sugar Hill, Jungle Fever, Clockers* are from the East Coast. *Losing Isaiah* was set in Chicago.
5. There were other African American male filmmakers who struggled in getting recognition for their films, often because their subject matter was not about guns or violence (i.e., Robert Townsend and Charles Burnett).
6. There is a brief throwaway line by Khaila to a neighbor's son about "learning how to be invisible", which suggests that Khaila might have been the child of a drug user. But, her past history is never made explicit.
7. It is beyond the scope of this paper to speculate about of all the possible choices for representing verisimilitude in the urban setting and why specifically focusing on pregnant users would make it seem "real and authentic."

REFERENCES

ACLU (2000). *ACLU Supreme Court Preview: 2000 Term, Ferguson V. City of Charleston.*

Angelou, M. (Director). (1998). *Down in the Delta*. [Film]. Miramax.

Austin, R. (1992). Black women, sisterhood, and the difference/deviance divide. *New England Law Review,* 26, 877–87.

Austin, R. (1989). Sapphire Bound! *Wisconsin Law Review,* 54, 539–78.

Bell, L. (1987) (Ed.), *Good Girls/Bad Girls: Feminists and Sex Trade Workers Face to Face.* Toronto: Seal Press.

Bell, S. (1994). *Reading, Writing, and Rewriting the Prostititue Body.* Bloomington: Indiana University Press.

Berger, M. (2004). *Workable sisterhood: The political journey of stigmatized women with HIV/AIDS.* New Jersey: Princeton University Press.

Campbell, N.D. (2000). *Using Women: Gender, Drug Policy, and Social Justice.* New York: Routledge.

Collins, P. (1990). *Black Feminist Thought.* (1st ed.) Boston: Unwin Hyman.

Corblau, Gerard. (Director). (1995). *Losing Isaiah* [Film]. Sony Pictures.

Crenshaw, K. (1997). Beyond Racism and Misogyny: Black Feminisms and 2 Live Crew. In C. Cohen & J Tronto (Eds), *Women Transforming Politics: An Alternative Reader* (pp. 109–126). New York: New York University Press, 1997.

Crenshaw, K. (1989). Demarginalizing the Intersection of Race and Sex: A Black Feminist Critique of Antidiscrimination Doctrine, Feminist Theory, and Antiracist Politics. *University of Chicago Legal Forum* 3, 139–67.

Delecoste, F. & P. Alexander (Eds). (1987). *Sex work: Writings by women in the sex industry.* Pittsburgh: Cleis Press.

DuCille, A. (1994). Occult of the True Black Womanhood: Critical Demeanor and Black Feminist Studies. *Callaloo* 19, 591–629.

Gray, F. (Director). (1996). *Set It Off.* [Film]. 20th Century Fox.

Hooks, b. (1994). *Outlaw Culture.* New York: Routledge,

Hooks, b. (1992). *Black Looks: Race and Representation.* Boston: South End Press.

Hooks, b. (1989). *Talking Back: Thinking Feminist, Thinking Black.* Boston: South End Press.

Hughes A. & A. (Directors). (1993). *Menace II Society.* [Film] New Line Cinema.

Ichaso, L. (Director). (1994). *Sugar Hill* [Film]. 20th Century Fox.

Jenness, V. (1993). *Making It Work: The Prostitute's Right Movement in Perspective.* New York: Aldin de Gruyter.

Jewell, S. K. (1993). *From Mammy to Miss America and Beyond: Cultural Images and the Shaping of U.S. Social Policy.* New York: Routledge.

Jones, J. (1996). The Ghetto Aesthetic. In V. T. Berry & C. Manning-Miller (Eds.),*Mediated Messages and African American Culture: Contemporary Issues* (pp. 40–51). Thousand Oaks, CA: Sage Publications.

Jones, J. (1992). The Accusatory Space. In G. Dent(Ed.), *Black Popular Culture*, (pp. 94–98). Seattle: Bay Press.

Lee, S. (Director). (1995). *Clockers [Film].*Universal Pictures.

Lee, S. (Director). (1991). *Jungle Fever.*[Film]. Universal Pictures.

Lubiano, W. (1993). "Black Ladies, Welfare Queens and State Minstrels: Ideological Warfare by Narrative Means." In T. Morrison (Ed). *Race-Ing Justice, En-Gendering*

Power: Essays on Anita Hill, Clarence Thomas and the Construction of Social Reality. (pp 104–115). London: Chatto and Windus, 1993.

Maher, L. (1997) *Sexed Work: Gender, Race, and Resistance in a Brooklyn Drug Market.* (2nd ed.) Oxford: Clarendon Press, 1997.

Maher, L. (1992). Reconstructing the Female Criminal: Women and "Crack Cocaine." *Southern California Review of Law and Women's Studies,* 2, 131–54.

Nagle, J. (1997). (Ed.), *Whores and Other Feminists.* New York: Routledge.

Painter, N. I. (1993). Hill, Thomas and the Use of Racial Stereotype. In T. Morrison *Race-Ing Justice, Engendering Power: Essays on Anita Hill, Clarence Thomas, and the Social Construction of Reality,* (pp 200–14). New York: Pantheon.

Peebles, M. (Director). (1991). *New Jack City.* Columbia Pictures.

Ratner, M (1993). (Ed)., *Crack Pipe as Pimp.* New York: Lexington Books.

Reeves, J. L. & R Campbell. (1994). *Cracked Coverage: Television News, the Anti-Cocaine Crusade, and the Reagan Legacy.* Durham: Duke University Press.

Rose, T. (1998). Race, Class and the Pleasure/Danger Dialectic: Rewriting Black Female Teenage Sexuality in the Popular Imagination. *Black Renaissance/Renaissance Noire,* 3, 171–86.

Singleton, J. (Director). (1991). *Boyz 'n the Hood.* [Film]. Columbia Pictures.

Spillers, H. (1984). Interstices: A Small Drama of Words. In C. Vance (Ed), *Pleasure and Danger: Exploring Female Sexuality* (pp.73–100). New York: Routledge.

Wallace, M. (1992). Boyz 'n the Hood and Jungle Fever. In G. Dent (Ed.), *Black Popular Culture* (pp 123–131). Seattle: Bay Press.

Wallace, M.(1990). *Invisibility Blues: From Pop to Theory.* New York: Verso.

Yakin, B. (Director). (1994). *Fresh* [Film]. Miramax.

Zerai, A. & R. Banks (2002. *Dehumanizing discourse, anti-drug law, and policy in America: A "crack mother's" nightmare.* Burlington, VT: Ashgate Publishing.

Chapter Nine

Men Change, Women Stay the Same: Images in Ads Targeted Toward Young and Mature Adults

Tom Reichert

INTRODUCTION

Americans are awash in a sea of advertising images. Estimates vary, but by most accounts the average person is exposed to hundreds of promotional messages each day (Tynan, 1994). Consumer advertising contains images of idealized others involved with, or cheerfully experiencing, the benefits of the brand. These images of others are important because research has shown that viewers use them for social comparison purposes, for instructional purposes, and to help them know what behaviors are appropriate, and, for that matter, inappropriate (Gerbner, Gross, Morgan, 1994; Richins, 1991). Research has also shown that media images contribute to sex role socialization and sex role stereotyping throughout the lifespan (Signorielli, 1993). Essentially, media images are important because they contribute to the construction of what it means to be a woman or a man.

For these reasons, researchers across a wide-array of disciplines are concerned with the content and effects of gender images in advertising. The vast majority of assessments have either examined sex role portrayals over time (Allan & Coltrane, 1996) or at a single point in time (Belknap & Leonard, 1991; Bretl & Cantor, 1988). Research has also examined the variety of sex role images represented in media segmented by gender consumption (Craig, 1992; Klassen, Jasper, & Schwartz, 1993). Unfortunately, little is known about the variability of sex role images targeted toward adult audiences of different ages.

This study seeks to address this inadequacy and extend sex role research by assessing the variability of sex role portrayals of both women and men by (1) age-group and (2) gendered readership categories. It is hoped that this analysis will provide support for public policy debate, stimulate critical discussion related to sex role portrayal in advertising, and reveal how gender identity can be reinforced and perpetuated by media. Social Learning Theory is utilized as a conceptual framework to illuminate how people learn sex role stereotyping and to aid in the interpretation of the results of the present research.

SOCIAL LEARNING THEORY

Social Learning Theory (Bandura, 1977, 1986) is one of several theories used to explain how people are socialized into their respective sex roles. More important for the purposes of this research, social learning also explains how people learn appropriate gender behavior from mediated images of others.

The primary tenet of social learning holds that through observation, individuals form conceptual ideas regarding the performance of behavior (Bandura, 1977). Those conceptions ultimately serve to steer individual behavior. Research supports the suggestion that behaviors are learned via media exposure (DiBlasio, 1986, 1987; DiBlasio & Benda, 1990; Signorielli, 1993), and that behavioral approval expressed by peer groups and additional socializing agents serve to reinforce the learned behavior, thereby increasing the likelihood that the observer continually performs the behavior (Bandura, 1969; Woodarski & Bagarozzi, 1979).

Similarly, social learning has been extended to explain how images of others in the media contribute to sex role behavior and sex role stereotypes through identification and internalization. There is abundant research indicating that children learn sex role attitudes from the media (Signorielli, 1993), and although sex role attitudes become more resilient as people get older (i.e., less susceptible to media influence), media images can still reinforce or modify sex role stereotypes after exposure (Garst & Bodenhausen, 1997; MacKay & Covell, 1997; Morgan, 1982). Hearold's (1986) synthesis of media effects studies provides convincing evidence that media has a significant effect on role stereotyping. The following statement by Signorielli (1993) succinctly describes the role of media in socialization:

> Socialization is an ongoing process; we are socialized and resocialized throughout the life cycle . . . [and] over the past 25 years . . . numerous studies have revealed that the mass media play a very important role in the socialization process for both children and adults (p. 230).

Indeed, an assumption of social learning is that the source of sex typing is largely shaped by the social environment, of which images in the media are an important component. As such, social learning provides a useful explanation to help understand the influence of sex role images targeted toward different audience segments through advertising.

RESEARCH QUESTIONS

First, it is important to compare how sex role portrayals of women and men vary by readership age group. As previously mentioned, other studies have not distinguished between adult readership age groups (Lazier-Smith, 1989). These studies provide evidence of sex role portrayal across magazines, but it is important to extend these findings to determine what sex role images are available to adults of different ages. Second, the present analysis examines images of women and men, which offers the opportunity to compare sex role images and readership age group. Overall, it is expected that a higher proportion of women will be portrayed decoratively compared to men (Hall & Crum, 1994).

There is, however, little research to suggest if this pattern will be consistent across readership age groups. For example, sex role portrayals in ads targeted toward older adults may be less likely to be decorative, especially when compared to ads targeted toward younger adults. In addition, women and men may be portrayed differently if advertisers are targeting younger or more mature adults. Neimark (1994) suggests that recent shifts in gender roles are "turning men into objects of desire—much as women have traditionally been" (p. 32). If this is true, men may be portrayed more decoratively in ads targeted toward young adults. Because previous research sheds little light on this particular question, the following research question is posed:

> RQ1: To what degree do sex role images of women and men vary in ads appearing in magazines read by younger (20s) and mature adults (40s)?

In addition, it is important to consider differences in readership gender (magazines targeted toward men, women, or both men and women), if any, on sex role portrayal. Prior research shows that sex role portrayals of women and men differ depending on the gender of a magazine's readership. For example, ads in men's magazines have been found to portray women more decoratively than other types of magazines (Lazier-Smith, 1989; Skelly & Lundstrom, 1981), while ads in women's magazines portray both men and women decoratively (Busby & Leichty, 1993). In addition, there is a lower proportion of decorative portrayals of either gender in general interest magazines relative to female and male-oriented magazines (Busby & Leichty, 1993; Skelly & Lundstrom, 1981). It is assumed that ads in magazines differ depending on the target audience of the magazine. Verifying past research and extending it to determine if portrayals differ by readership is another research goal.

> RQ2: To what degree do sex role images of women and men vary in magazine ads stratified by readership gender (men's, women's, and general-interest)?

METHOD

As an overview, 2,863 full-page ads in three issues of six consumer magazines from both 1992 and 1998 were coded for sex role portrayal (decorative/traditional/progressive) and sex of the model (female/male). The magazines were stratified by average readership age (20s/40s) and readership gender (women, men, general-interest). Decorative portrayals were of women or men shown with no functional relationship to the product or present merely to enhance the product. Traditional roles included typed roles for both sexes, while progressive depictions emphasized nonstereotypical roles. Following is a description of magazines sampled and sex role variables.

SAMPLE SELECTION

The 36 coded publications (three issues of six publications in 1992 and 1998) yielded a large sample frame of 2,863 full-page or larger ads. Within this frame, 758 female models and 751 male models were coded. As the unit of analysis, only discernible adult models were coded, thereby eliminating ads with only hands, feet, illustrations, or sketches.

The six magazines included in the analysis were selected based on circulation, reader gender, and reader age. Age groups were identified based on mean readership age. According to Mediamark Research Inc. (1992), young adults are 20–29, and mature adults are 40-49. Regarding reader gender, women's and men's magazines are primarily consumed by women or men, respectively, and general-interest magazines are read by a similar proportion of women and men. Young adult-male, female, and general-interest magazines included *Gentleman's Quarterly (GQ)*, *Mademoiselle*, and *Rolling Stone*. Mature adult-male, female, and general-interest magazines included *Forbes*, *Redbook*, and *Time*. As a means of increasing generalizability and to reflect advertising's seasonality, three issues of each magazine were analyzed each year (March, July, and November).

VARIABLES

For the purposes of this study, four variables were employed: (1) sex of the model (male/female), (2) magazine readership age group, (3) gender of magazine readership, and (4) sex role portrayal. The first three variables were discussed above. Following is a brief description of the sex role portrayal distinctions.

Female and male models within these ads were coded according to three categories adapted from the Pingree, Hawkins, Butler, & Paisley (1976) sex-role scale. If the model was present merely to enhance the attractiveness of the product, the model was categorized as being "decorative." These portrayals show women and men as having no true functional relationship to the product and typically as nothing more than a nonthinking, two-dimensional object. Often, these models were dressed in provocative clothing that accentuated their well-sculpted physiques. The second category was labeled "traditional" and generally featured women and men in stereotypically masculine and feminine roles (e.g., nurses, mothers, fathers, executives). Depictions of either gender as equal, as managing role reversals competently, or as "whole persons" rather than caricatures were coded as "progressive." While procedures exist for assessing sex-role portrayals in advertising (Goffman, 1979; Kolbe & Langefeld, 1993), this analysis utilized the adapted sexism scale for its clarity and use in similar contexts, such as magazine ads (Busby & Leichty, 1993; Lazier-Smith, 1989) and MTV music videos (Seidman, 1992). Sex role portrayal was determined by trained coders working independently. Because of the large sample size, half the sample was used to calculate agreement coefficients. Inter-coder agreement for sex role yielded good results for both female (.81) and male (.80) portrayals.

RESULTS

The first research question (RQ1) sought to determine if sex role portrayals varied when magazines were stratified by age. For this analysis, both sex role portrayal and magazine age group were considered ordinal variables. Controlling for sex of the model, a Spearman rank-order correlation was used to test the relationship between sex role and age group. For an alpha level of .05, there was no relationship between magazine readership age groups for female sex role portrayal, Spearman $r = .03, n = 758, p = .38$ (see Table 1). The finding suggests that the sex role portrayal of women does not vary across readership age group. On the other hand, there was a significant relationship for male sex role portrayals, Spearman $r = .25, n = 751, p < .001$. The finding suggests that men were portrayed less decoratively in the magazines read by older adults. The percentages for female and male portrayals by age group are displayed in Table 9.1.

The second research question (RQ2) sought to determine if female and male depictions varied when publications were stratified by readership gender (women's, men's, and general-interest). To answer this question, a chi-square test of independence was used to test the relationship between sex role portrayal and magazine type. For female models, there was a significant rela-

Table 9.1. Sex Role Portrayal by Sex of the Model and Age of Target Audience

	Female Models		Male Models	
	Young Adult Magazines	Mature Adult Magazines	Young Adult Magazines	Mature Adult Magazines
Decorative	74%	72%	58%	31%
Traditional	17%	17%	39%	62%
Progressive	8%	11%	3%	7%
	n = 459	*n* = 299	*n* = 547	*n* = 204

tionship, chi-square $(4, N = 758) = 94.39, p < .001$ (see Table 9.2 for percentages). For example, 82% of female models in women's magazines were decorative compared to 44% in men's magazines. Similarly, there was a significant relationship in men's sex role portrayals, chi-square $(4, N = 751) = 24.13, p < .001$. Male models were portrayed most decoratively in general-interest (64%) and women's magazines (56%) compare to men's magazines (45%). Overall, there was a higher percentage of traditional portrayals of men compared to women, while women were disproportionately portrayed at the decorative level.

DISCUSSION

The present research was designed to extend previous media-related sex role research by determining how depictions of women and men vary by readership age (young adult, 20s; mature adult, 40s) and gender (general interest, women's, men's) in magazine ads. Overall, sex role depictions do differ. Specifically, depictions of women are consistently decorative across age group categories, while depictions of men are less decorative as readership age increases. In addition, sex role portrayals vary by readership gender.

Table 9.2. Sex Role Portrayal by Sex of the Model and Magazine Readership Gender

	Female Models			Male Moels		
	Men's Magazine	Women's Magazine	General Interest Magazine	Men's Magazine	Women's Magazine	General Interest Magazine
Decorative	44%	82%	73%	45%	56%	64%
Traditional	41%	9%	22%	52%	39%	32%
Progressive	15%	9%	5%	3%	5%	4%
	n = 145	n = 492	n = 121	n = 474	n = 84	n = 193

Readership Age and Gender

The findings of the first analysis suggest two patterns of female sex role portrayal across age groups—female roles are consistent and decorative. As shown in Table 9.1, the sex role depictions of women are almost invariable across the two readership age groups, suggesting that female sex roles depicted in ads are relatively homogenous. Second, these portrayals are primarily decorative. The results suggest that the image of woman available for consumption by audiences of different ages is the alluring sex object whose purpose is to adorn and enhance the product. The finding is congruent with previous sex role research. For example, both Ferguson, Kreshel, and Tinkham (1990) and Busby and Leichty (1993) report a high proportion of female decorative portrayals in magazines ads.

The relationship between male sex role portrayal and readership age is very different. The findings are such that there is a trend toward less decorative portrayals and more traditional portrayals of men as readership age increases. In other words, adults in their 20s see more decorative male images (58%) than adults in their 40s (31%). The variation in male sex role portrayal suggests that men's roles, at least those portrayed in advertising, shift as male audiences get older. The findings also suggest that males can be sources of visual pleasure used to enhance the attractiveness of products, much the same manner women are portrayed, but only for younger audiences. As readers age, however, they see males portrayed in more traditional ways (e.g., executive, father). Neimark (1994) suggests that the saying, "men do, women are" is no longer a valid distinction between men and women, meaning that men's gender roles have shifted to a point where there is little distinction regarding male and female roles. The present analysis suggests that men both "do" and "are," but increasingly "do" as they get older.

Although there is little comparable empirical research, the present findings correspond with previous analyses of masculinity in the media. For example, Skelly and Lundstrom (1981) found a relatively high degree of male decorative sex role portrayals magazine ads in 1979 (55%). Similarly, Kervin (1990) and Wernick (1987) identified a trend of increasingly decorative men in magazine ads. The value of the present research is that it allows examination of the age groups where the "decorative" trend is manifesting itself—in ads targeted toward younger adults.

The second research question (RQ2) sought to determine the relationship, if any, between sex role portrayal and readership gender. The analyses strongly suggest that both women and men are portrayed differently depending on the sex of the reader. For example, women are portrayed most decoratively in women's magazines (82%). It is likely the decorative portrayals are present in cosmetic and clothing advertising—both of which are common in mainstream women's magazines. Surprisingly, almost as many women are portrayed in traditional roles as are portrayed decoratively in men's magazines. Compared to the other magazine types, men's magazines appear to at least present women in traditional roles compared to decorative objects. Alternately, two decorative images—one of a woman wearing cosmetics in a women's magazine and the other of a woman in a bikini in a men's magazine, while still decorative—can differ significantly in degree of objectification.

On the other hand, men are objectified most often in women's and general-interest magazines. For example, over half the men in women's magazines are portrayed decoratively. This finding may suggest that it is "okay" for women to gaze at men, as long as it is within the confines of a "woman's book," and as long as they can do it in private. The inclusion of *Rolling Stone* as a general-interest magazine contributed to the rather large percentage of decorative images, of both women and men. Further analysis reveals that two-thirds of coded images in the general-interest category were from *Rolling Stone*, and those images are overwhelmingly decorative of both women and men. Apart from being an anomaly, these findings may represent the prevalence of decorative images in magazines read by large numbers of young adults.

Social Learning Theory

As previously mentioned, social learning places the source of sex typing in the socializing community. An influential socializing factor within the community is media. The first set of findings suggest that media audiences of different ages (adults, in this case), are not only exposed to different sex role portrayals of women and men, but that these sex role images diverge as a function of magazine age group. Consumers that consistently see decorative images of women may come to view women's role as functional only to the degree of looking desirable. According to social learning, people have the capacity to learn vicariously by watching others rewarded or punished for behaving in certain ways. Seeing women behaving decoratively, and being rewarded for it, has the capacity to teach viewers how women should behave and what about women is valued. For example, Then (1994) found that 61% of male Stanford MBA students reported wanting real women to more closely resemble female models in ads—primarily by getting thinner and enlarging their breasts. Taken together, it is evident that most audiences see women rewarded for being objects of visual pleasure (sexual, beautiful, and slender). The findings also suggest that audiences in their forties are exposed to images which perpetuate the impression that a woman's value and worth is located in her outward physical appearance.

On the other hand, the image of men available for observation varies as a function of audience age. Men are portrayed decoratively in ads targeted toward younger adults, but the images available to older audiences are increasingly traditional (e.g., father, manager, executive). The switch may communicate to audiences that it is acceptable for men to be portrayed for physical attributes when young, but that more functional roles are appropriate as men age.

The findings related to sex role portrayal and readership gender are important from a social learning perspective as well. An integral component of social learning is that people identify and subsequently imitate those that are similar to them. Social learning posits that women and men learn to behave and hold attitudes that are congruent with images of similar others they wish to identify with. For example, Then (1994) found that men engage in identification with male images. About 57% of Then's male sample reported that they compared their bodies to those of male models in magazines. Men, as well as women, learn vicariously that people who strive to look like models might be rewarded with positive social rewards, such as love, wealth, and happiness. Indeed, as men seek to be valued in ways traditionally reserved for women, there has been a corresponding rise in male body image disorders (Neimark, 1994).

Limitations and Directions for Future Research

Although the present research is formative, several limitations must be taken into consideration when interpreting the results. First, whereas this study sought to sample magazines representing readership variables of interest, namely gender and age group, the magazines are not fully representative of the magazine universe. Consequently, generalizations to magazines beyond those used in this study should be made with caution.

Second, although mean readership age for each of the respective magazine age groups was within the 20s and 40s age group, there is likely to be some crossover readership within these categories. For example, men in their 40s may read *GQ*. The same is true for gender readership. In one survey, 89% of men reported reading women's magazines and 88% regularly read the *Victoria's Secret* catalog (Then, 1994). Future studies should take these considerations into account. Future research should also extend age group analysis of sex role portrayal to other media (e.g., commercials shown during programs targeted toward audiences of different ages) to see if a similar pattern of sex role stereotyping exists. Craig (1992) found variations in gender roles in television commercials when dayparts were segmented by gender viewership.

Another direction for future research would be to extend the findings to male sex role portrayal over time. In this study, men were portrayed decoratively in young adult magazines but were portrayed more traditionally as readership age increased. Future research should seek to determine if this pattern of portrayal is a recent trend, or if young adult magazines have always portrayed men in decorative ways (Soley & Reid, 1988). In addition, research should examine the sex role stereotypes held by audiences to see how closely they correlate with sex role portrayals. For example, do sex role stereotypes of those in their 40s correspond to the pattern of male and female sex roles discovered in this study? This type of research may corroborate the effects of varying sex role images given social learning theory.

CONCLUSION

In sum, this analysis extends previous media sex role research by providing information about the patterns of advertising portrayals of women and men by magazine readership age group (20s, 40s) and readership gender (women's, men's, and general-interest magazines). Prior research has documented the variation of sex role stereotypes in the mainstream media by analyzing program, editorial, and advertising content. This study, in conjunction with previous studies, provides valuable indicators of the ways in which women and men are portrayed in advertising. The results of this content analysis show male sex-role portrayal to be varied across age groups (i.e., decorative portrayals are most prevalent in young adult magazines compared to more traditional portrayals in older adult magazines). Conversely, female sex-role portrayal is primarily decorative, remaining constant across readership age groups. Interestingly, most decorative images of women and men appeared in women's magazines. These findings are an important addition to what is known about media sex role portrayal and sex role stereotyping. The findings of this study are especially informative when viewed from a social learning perspective because the results provide indications of sex role images available for continued sex role socialization by audiences of various ages.

REFERENCES

Allan, K., & Coltrane, S. (1996). Gender displaying television commercials: A comparative study of television commercials in the 1950s and 1980s. *Sex Roles, 35*(3/4), 185–204.

Bandura, A. (1977). *Social learning theory.* Englewood Cliffs, NJ: Prentice Hall.

Bandura, A. (1986). *Social foundations of thought and action: A social cognitive theory.* Englewood Cliffs, NJ: Prentice-Hall.

Belknap, P., & Leonard, W. M. (1991). A conceptual replication and extension of Erving Goffman's study of gender advertisements. *Sex Roles, 25*(August), 103–118.

Bretl, D., & Cantor, J. (1988). The portrayal of men and women in U.S. television commercials: A recent content analysis and trends over 15 years. *Sex roles, 18*(May), 595–609.

Busby, L. J., & Leichty, G. (1993). Feminism and advertising in traditional and nontraditional women's magazines 1950s-1980s. *Journalism Quarterly, 70*(2), 247–264.

Craig, R. S. (1992). The effect of television day part on gender portrayals in television commercials: A content analysis. *Sex Roles, 26*(5/6), 197–211.

DiBlasio, F. A. (1987). Predriving riders and drinking drivers. *Journal of Studies on Alcohol, 49*, 11–15.

DiBlasio, F. A. & Benda, B. B. (1990). Adolescent sexual behavior: Multivariate analysis of a social learning model. *Journal of Adolescent Research, 5*, 449–466.

Durkin, K. (1987). Sex roles and the mass media. In D. J. Hargreaves & A. M. Colley (Eds.), *The psychology of sex roles* (pp. 201–214). New York: Hemisphere.

Ferguson, J. H., Kreshel, P. J., & Tinkham, S. F. (1990). In the pages of *Ms.*: Sex role portrayals of women in advertising. *Journal of Advertising, 19*(1), 40-51.

Garst, J., & Bodenhausen, G. V. (1997). Advertising's effects on men's gender role attitudes. *Sex Roles, 36*(9/10), 551–572.

Gerbner, G., Gross, L., Morgan, M., & Signorielli, N. (1994). Growing up with television: The cultivation perspective. In J. Bryant & D. Zillman (Eds.), *Media Effects: Advances in Theory and Research*. Hillsdale, NJ: Erlbaum.

Goffman, E. (1979). *Gender advertisements*. Cambridge, MA: Harvard University Press.

Hall, C. C., & Crum, M. J. (1994). Women and "body-isms" in television beer commercials. *Sex Roles, 31*(5/6), 329–337.

Hearold, S. (1986). A synthesis of 1043 effects of television on social behavior. In G. Comstock (Ed.), *Public communication and behavior* (pp. 136–174). Orlando, FL: Academic Press.

Kervin, D. (1990). Advertising masculinity: The representation of males in *Esquire* advertisements. *Journal of Communication Inquiry, 14*(2), 51–69.

Klassen, M. L., Jasper, C. R., & Schwartz, A. M. (1993). Men and women: Images of their relationships in magazine advertisements. *Journal of Advertising Research, 33*(2), 30-39.

Kolbe, R. H., & Langefeld, C. D. (1993). Appraising gender role portrayals in TV commercials. *Sex Roles, 28*(7/8), 393–416.

Lafky, S., Duffy, M., Steinmaus, M., & Berkowitz, D. (1996). Looking through gendered lenses: Female stereotyping in advertisements and gender role expectations. *Journal of Mass Communication Quarterly, 73*(2), 379–389.

Lazier-Smith, L. (1989). Advertising: Women's place and image. In P. J. Creedon (Ed.), *Women in Mass Communication: Challenging Gender Values* (pp. 247–262). Newbury Park, CA: Sage.

MacKay, N. J., & Covell, K. (1997). The impact of women in advertisements on attitudes toward women. *Sex Roles, 36*(9/10), 573–583.

Mediamark Research Inc. (1992, Spring). *Magazine Total Audiences Report* (M-1).

Morgan, M. (1982). Television and adolescents' sex-role stereotypes: A longitudinal study. *Journal of Personality and Social Psychology, 43*(5), 947–955.

Neimark, J. (1994, November). The beefcaking of America. *Psychology today, 26*, 32–42.

Pingree, S., Hawkins, R. P., Butler, M., & Paisley, W. (1976). A scale for sexism. *Journal of Communication, 26*(4), 193–200.

Richins, M. L. (1991). Social comparison and the idealized images of advertising. *Journal of Consumer Research, 18*(1), 71–83.

Seidman, S. A. (1992). An investigation of sex-role stereotyping in music videos. *Journal of Broadcasting & Electronic Media, 36*(2), 209–216.

Signorielli N. (1985) (Ed.). *Role portrayal and stereotyping on television: An annotated bibliography of studies relating to women, minorities, aging, sexual behavior, health and handicaps.* Westport, CT: Greenwood Press.

Signiorelli, N. (1993). Television, the portrayal of women, and children's attitudes. In G. L. Berry & J. K. Asamen (Eds.), *Children and television: Images in a changing sociocultural world* (pp. 229–242). Newbury Park, CA: Sage.

Skelly, G. U., & Lundstrom, W. J. (1981). Male sex roles in magazine advertising, 1959–1979. *Journal of Communication, 31*(4), 52–57.

Soley, L., & Reid, L. (1988). Taking it off: Are models in magazine ads wearing less? *Journalism Quarterly, 65*(Winter), 960-966.

Sullivan, G. L., & O'Connor, P. J. (1988). Women's role portrayals in magazine advertising: 1958–1983. *Sex Roles, 18*(3/4), 181–188.

Then, D. (1994). *Men's magazines: The facts and the fantasies.* Paper presented at the 102nd annual convention of the American Psychological Association, Los Angeles.

Tynan, K. B. (1994). *Multi-channel marketing: Maximizing market share with an integrated marketing strategy.* Chicago, IL: Probus.

Wernick, A. (1987). From voyeur to narcissist: Images of men in contemporary advertising. In M. Kaufman (Ed.), *Beyond patriarchy: Essays by men on pleasure, power, and change* (pp. 227–297). Toronto: Oxford University Press.

Woodarski, J., & Bagarozzi, D. (1979). *Behavioral social work.* New York: Human Science Press.

Part Two

STEREOTYPICAL DEPICTIONS

Chapter Ten

Safety and Restriction: The Construction of Black Women's Sexuality in *Essence* Magazine

Gloria Gadsden

Some feminist scholars have proposed that people with power in America control Black women's sexuality in various ways (Carby, 1992, Collins, 1990, hooks, 1992, Mayall, and Russell, 1990, Spillers, 1984). Historical examinations led scholars to recognize at least two images used to control Black women: the oversexed Black woman (Jezebel) and the asexual mammy (Campbell, 1986, Collins, 1990). Today, these controlling sexual images saturate rap videos, Hollywood films, television sitcoms, and pornography (hooks, 1992, Mayall, and Russell, 1990, Perry, 1995, Rose, 1994). The elite members of society who produce, distribute, and otherwise influence these media images are typically White, male, middle and upper-middle class, and heterosexual (Gross, 1991).

Mass media images of Black women as asexual mammies and Jezebels permit members of other social groups to continually gaze upon them, policing their behavior. This project explores this 'elite gaze' by examining textual images of Black women's sexuality in a woman's magazine, a sphere governed by Black women but influenced by more powerful groups. The article attempts to disclose the unremitting pervasiveness of the elite social gaze in America by denoting the existence of the mammy and Jezebel images in recent issues of *Essence* Magazine.

IMAGES OF BLACK WOMEN'S SEXUALITY

The sexual behavior and bodies of Black women remain ever present in media. Media, manifestations of the elite gaze, permit the social policing of Black women's sexuality. "[The subjects'] visibility assures the hold of the power that is exercised over them" (Foucault, 1978, 187). This social gaze is clearly articulated in current public policy and critical debates as expressed in a variety of scholarly journals, texts, newspapers, and magazines. These debates examine Black women's early initiation of sexual activity, high teenage pregnancy rates, (single) motherhood, exchange of sex for drugs, welfare dependence, and rates of HIV/AIDS infections. These aspects of Black women's sexuality (both oversexed and undersexed images) are often placed at the opposite end of a dichotomy that typically highlights "good" sexuality as the sexuality of middle-class White women (Wyatt, Newcomb, and Riederle, 1993). In other words, these aspects of Black women's sexuality are typically classified as deviant.

The ability to categorize behavior as 'normal' or 'deviant' reflects power — the power to determine the social status of a social group (Becker, 1973). Categorizing Black women's sexuality as deviant potentially prohibits Black women from creating their own images and re-defining their position as the surveyed group. Scholars have revealed only one public sphere in which Black women have had some ability to construct themselves sexually — music (Carby, 1992, Harrison, 1988, hooks, 1992).

Blues music in the early 20th century addressed a variety of issues including Black women's economic and sexual independence and self-reliance. Music provided (and continues to provide to some extent) a location where Black women could, potentially, define themselves with some success (Harrison, 1988). Yet, even this domain ultimately belonged (and still belongs) to privileged groups (i.e., few recording companies are owned by Black women). Because this medium was (and is) controlled by people from powerful groups who are invested in maintaining dominant ideologies, self-definitions of Black women's sexuality became lodged in a sphere that perpetuates the elite social gaze, creating a web of safety (i.e., Black women defining themselves) and restriction (i.e., Black women continually defined in accordance with notions of the mammy and Jezebel).

Missing thus far from examinations of Black women's sexuality is a contemporary in-depth exploration of a medium, other than music, that serves as a purveyor of information to Black women in the late 20th century. Also missing is an exploration of a "realistic" medium (i.e., a medium not dominated by fictional imagery). "Images of reality in [media] set the limits on who in the world we think we are and what in the world we think we are doing . . . by regulating the flow of 'who' and 'what' pass through the public information gates . . . [images of reality in] media hold enormous power" (Bennett, 1996, 26–28). This missing analysis of 'realistic' media prohibits scholars from fully deconstructing the elite gaze centered on the sexual, social, political, and economic lives of Black women. This project begins this analysis by examining a contemporary, realistic medium that is central in the lives of many Black women.

ABOUT *ESSENCE* MAGAZINE

Essence is the only magazine read predominantly by Black women that has a circulation of more than one million. Established in 1970, it is the oldest Black women's magazine in existence (Carmody, 1995). Ninety-one percent of all *Essence* readers are Black women. Sixty-seven percent of all Black women, ages 18–49, in the U.S. read *Essence*.[1]

Essence offers a social space in which Black female editors, writers, and readers contribute to definitions of Black women's sexuality.[2] Yet, as noted by McMahon (1990), contributions made by groups more powerful than the magazine's Black female constituency (i.e., White advertisers and Black male owners) are also abundant. Consequently, *Essence* Magazine offers Black women a space to construct themselves in a public medium while simultaneously reflecting the opinions of more powerful groups (i.e., the elite social gaze).

This study does not propose that *Essence* is the only influence on Black women's understandings of sexuality. According to de Lauretis, "at any one time there are several competing, even contradictory, discourses on sexuality— rather than a single, all-encompassing or monolithic, ideology" (1987, 16). It is likely that other magazines, music, movies, television, and public discourses define the sexual lives of Black women in multiple ways. But unlike music or fiction, as stated previously, some realms of media are understood (or assumed) to reflect reality more accurately than others. Therefore, this work's goal is to examine the textual imagery of one 'realistic' public medium and its possible contribution to the surveillance of Black women's sexuality.

RESEARCH DESIGN

The data for this study come from a ten-year textual analysis of *Essence Magazine*. According to McNay (1992), textual analyses explore the ways in which power operates at a micro-social level in order to produce images. In addition to exploring written images, textual analyses provide an opportunity to explore how meanings, particularly representations of sexuality, gender, and race, produce and reproduce asymmetrical relations among people.

This textual analysis encompassed every issue of *Essence Magazine* spanning ten years (January 1986 through December 1995). From these 120 issues, all feature articles, advice column questions, and advice column answers discussing relationships and sexuality were coded (in total 1034 feature articles, advice column questions and advice column answers). A single coding instrument was utilized in an attempt to standardize findings. An independent researcher coded a random sample of the material to ensure reliability and guard against interpreter bias.

The coding topics, derived from the magazine's content, were divided into four broad categories: discussions of pleasure and desire, discussions with no reference to sexuality, discussions of biological and/or medical topics (e.g., sexually transmitted diseases), and discussions about objectification and/or exploitation (e.g., child abuse or rape). The first category is of greatest importance to this research. The first two coding categories, which determined whether or not an article addressed sexual activity, desire and/or pleasure, were mutually exclusive. Additional topics, also derived from the magazine's content, were added during the coding process (see Table 10.1 and Table 10.2 below). All of the material was ultimately coded for these secondary coding categories. These secondary coding categories were not mutually exclusive.

FINDINGS

Advice Columns

There were 918 advice column question and advice column answers in *Essence.* As shown in Figure 10.1, approximately 22 percent of these units focused on sexual pleasure and desire.

The results of the coding of advice columns addressing Black women's sexual pleasure and desire is shown in Table 10.1. Sixty-five percent of the articles focused exclusively on heterosexuality and two percent focused exclusively on homosexuality.

Feature Articles

One hundred and sixteen feature articles discussed female sexuality. Each of these articles discussed relationships in some manner. The articles addressed

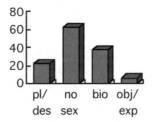

Figure 10.1.   Percentage of Advice Columns In Specific Categories.[3]

Table 10.1. Sexual Pleasure and Desire in Advice Columns

Discussions about sexual problems	14%
Discussions about Pregnancy and conception	12%
Tips on how to have better sex	8%
Discussions about STDs and/or AIDS	8%
Discussions about infidelity	6%
Discussions about non-traditional sexual practices	3%
Discussions about orgasms	2%
Discussions about masturbation	1.5%
Discussions about virginity	1%
Discussions about pornography	0.2%

a variety of topics reflecting women's sexual pleasure and desire (see Table 10.2). As noted in Figure 10.2, approximately 56 percent of these articles focused on sexual pleasure and desire.

Eighty-four percent of the articles focused exclusively on heterosexuality, and 15 percent focused exclusively on homosexuality.

Table 10.2. Sexual Pleasure and Desire in Feature Articles (page 237)

Discussions about infidelity	13%
Discussions about STDs and/or AIDS	10%
Discussions about sexual problems	7%
Discussions about virginity	6%
Discussions about pregnancy and/or conception	5%
Discussions about Non-traditional sexual practices	5%
Tips on how to have better sex	4%
Discussions about orgasms	3%
Discussions about masturbation	3%
Discussions about pornography	0.9%

DISCUSSION

Essence as a Sexual Safe Haven

Essence magazine provided a space where Black women—the vast majority of its readers—could explore sexual pleasure and desire. This aspect of the magazine reflects the ability of Black women, as editors, writers, and readers,

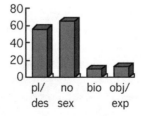

Figure 10.2. Percentage of Feature Articles in Specific Categories.

to construct their sexual selves. Many of the feature articles and advice column entries discussed various aspects of Black women's sexual lives. Overall, there was little evidence of at least one sexually controlling image—the mammy.

There was evidence in *Essence* that Black women engaged in sexual activity, debunking the myth of the asexual mammy. Approximately 50 percent of the women writing in to the advice columns expressed a need for sexual pleasure. For example, in the advice columns, readers sought ways to better enjoy sex (e.g., "to help him keep his erection, I must always be on top and my legs become very fatigued . . . can you suggest another position?" [1988]). Readers also wondered if they should sacrifice their own pleasure for that of their partners (e.g., "during intercourse I always reach climax before my fiancé. I get tired and uncomfortable waiting for him to have an orgasm . . . what can I do?" [1989]). Some readers who lacked sexual desire wondered if they were normal (e.g., "I am a 35-year-old mother of a 5-year-old. I am never in the mood for sex, although I love my husband. What's wrong with me?" [1990]). *Essence* offered these women a space to ask these questions as well as a place to get answers with little judgment passed.

Many of the messages in the magazine advocated that Black women should seek and receive sexual pleasure. In 1988, an advice columnist suggested:

Your sexual experiences should be pleasurable to both you and your husband.
Try to discover various positions that please both of you . . .

In 1992, another advice columnist stated "it is natural to desire sex that is satisfying to you." According to the author of the feature article "Am I The Last Virgin?":

Women are beginning to stand up and demand satisfaction from sex. . . . My girlfriends are now talking about orgasms and masturbation. Women are discovering their own bodies and letting brothers know it's not just about men getting theirs. They're touching themselves and demanding that brothers touch them too (1994).

Overall, *Essence* advocated sexual pleasure and desire as normal and healthy.

According to *Essence*, receiving sexual pleasure was important because it improved relationships, solved women's frustration, eased resentment between partners, and enhanced the bond between two (heterosexual) people. The magazine advised that Black women should become "pleasure claimers" instead of sexual objects. Pleasure claimers are, as noted in an advice column, "women who know what they need and go after it" (1992). *Essence* actively created a safe sexual space for Black women. Absent were the assumptions that Black women do not enjoy sex or are receptacles for men. The magazine also gave Black women ammunition for rejecting the notion that sexual pleasure and desire are "not ladylike." *Essence* sustained an ideological framework that promoted Black women's empowerment, including the fulfillment of their sexual desires. Seeking (heterosexual) sexual pleasure was not deemed immoral. The magazine did not label Black women deviant because they acknowledged and explored their sexual pleasure and desire.

Essence As Restrictor

At the same time that *Essence* liberated Black women's sexuality (as discussed above), it restricted them by offering a limited set of contexts in which readers could appropriately express their sexual pleasure and desire. Additionally, the magazine clearly delineated the situations in which sexual pleasure and desire were appropriate for Black women. And finally, *Essence* stipulated a need for Black women to control their sexuality. This section explores how these three categories of restriction in *Essence* demonstrate the ways in which the magazine endorsed the notion of Black women's possible oversexuality, yet simultaneously warns readers away from this "overtly" or "deviant" sexual existence. The restrictive nature of *Essence*, therefore, potentially reinforces the image of the oversexed Jezebel, and legitimizes the elite social gaze, by acknowledging that excessive amounts, or specific types, of Black female sexuality can be detrimental for Black women. *Essence* identifies these notions of oversexuality and ultimately provides an alternate, conservative social script for Black women.

The Image of the Legitimate Couple

Foucault (1978) located legitimate sexual pleasure and desire in the context of a specific relationship: a married, heterosexual, middle or upper class White couple. Empowered members of society approve of sexual pleasure and desire between this couple if they remain in the private sphere and if these couples produce children that can reproduce the system (Foucault, 1978). In *Essence*, legitimate or "safe" sexual pleasure and desire were located within the realm of a similar type of couple. The magazine's text revealed that this couple was monogamous and heterosexual. *Essence* also integrated notions of maturity and emotional intimacy into their construction of the "legitimate couple."

As noted earlier, 65 percent of the advice columns and 84 percent of the feature articles in *Essence* addressed heterosexuality.[4] Most of the textual messages examined provided suggestions to maintain heterosexual relationships (see Figure 10.3).

The legitimate couple practiced monogamy and postponed sex until an appropriate age. *Essence* further suggested that women in legitimate couples do not "really" want sex. They are seeking emotional intimacy instead. The following examples hail from various advice column answers:

Monogamy:

> Some women believe that they need two or more men to satisfy their emotional and sexual needs . . . [but] eventually this triangle will wear you out" (1991)
>
> "Casual encounters are not for the fainthearted . . . you may be physically satisfied (or not) and left dangling emotionally (1994).

Maturity:

> Most teenage girls do not enjoy sexual activity, but engage in it because of peer pressure (1990)

Emotional Intimacy:

> Deciding to remain a virgin until you have a relationship based on trust and intimacy is mature and sound. If at any time you have any doubt, say no. Unwanted sex leaves the reluctant partner (usually the woman) feeling used, angry, and insecure. Your boyfriend and you are making love when you and he are tender, kind, and responsible for each other . . . intercourse is not proof of love . . . (1987)

Finally, discussions of homosexuality remained relatively invisible, declining over time (see Figure 10.4).

In general, textual messages endorsed the notion of a particular kind of "legitimate" couple, one that was heterosexual, mature, and emotionally intimate.

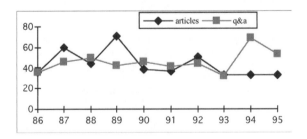

Figure 10.3. Percent of Units Promoting Maintenance of Heterosexual Relationships Over Time in *Essence*.

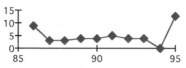

Figure 10.4.   Percent of Units Addressing Homosexuality Over Time.[4]

Pleasure and Desire Finish Last

In addition to sculpting an image of the legitimate couple, *Essence* dictated when, how, and in what way women should explore sexual desire and pleasure. After reading the magazine's text, a reader is left to conclude that she should, first, make sure her mate is 'appropriate' and interested in a committed relationship. Second, she should make sure she is protected from disease and pregnancy. And third, she should make sure she values emotionality over sexuality. Only after a strict adherence to these guidelines does the magazine endorse the exploration of sexual pleasure and desire. Below find examples of this script from *Essence's* advice column answers.

> There are fundamental differences in what men and women find sexually exciting. . . . Women respond more to the emotional aspects of sex . . . (1990)
>
> To meet 'Mr. Right', your sexual behavior should be oriented appropriately . . . [find] the man who will be stable enough to be the father of your children and provide you with a lifetime of romance and excitement (and great monogamous sex). (1991)
>
> It's okay to be sexy and sexual, but you have to 'do it' safely. (1992)
>
> Women tend to view sex as part of a committed relationship, whereas often when men have sex they're after sexual satisfaction. (1993)
>
> Saying yes to sex [first] is saying yes in the same instant to its potential consequences: disease, pregnancy . . . (1994)

This list is not necessarily invalid. Given the long history of Black women's sexual dominance, objectification, and exploitation, this list potentially contributes to the maintenance of healthy sexual lives. But in *Essence* this list appears as a mandate, not an option. *Essence* placed pleasure and desire last on their list and labeled women who wanted to satisfy their sexual desires first "desperadoes" (1989). The magazine suggested women must be cautious and not give in too quickly. They must be "smart women [who come] up with their own system of checks and balances" (1994). Even if these mandates actually reflect what Black women want, there is little opportunity in the magazine to explore alternatives. As this script reflects, *Essence* dictated what was good and bad for Black women, in effect regulating their sexual behavior.

Pleasure, Desire, and Control

Finally, *Essence* warned Black women to control their pleasure and desire in order to protect themselves from danger. Approximately one third of the feature articles and advice columns discussed the need to control sexual desire. In 1990, a columnist told a reader "it's fine to feel desire, but don't transform your sex drive into feelings of desperation." In 1994, a columnist stated "we all have a sexual drive, but you, not your libido, must take control of your steering wheel." In a feature article titled "Hooked On Love" (1988), a therapist described how women could become "love addicts" who experience the same compulsion, panic, and withdrawal as drug addicts. She discussed at length how women's desires could become so uncontrollable that they could result in physical violence.

According to *Essence*, Black women must control their sexuality, or they could find themselves in dangerous, compromising situations (e.g., ruined reputations, sexually transmitted diseases). According to *Essence* writers and columnists, Black women must police their sexual desire and pleasure in order to maintain their safety and attain what they really want (e.g., an appropriate mate). Therefore, they must strive to be part of a legitimate couple, follow the advocated script, and regulate their sexual desire (i.e., refute the image of the Jezebel).

CONCLUSION

Essence serves as a realistic purveyor of information to Black women in a society that has not traditionally portrayed Black women's sexuality positively or realistically. In *Essence*, Black women are constructed as sexual beings, not asexual mammies. *Essence* provides a sphere of safety in which Black female editors, writers, and readers encourage and support Black women's sexual empowerment. The magazine provides Black women with a relatively non-threatening environment in which they are encouraged to explore sexual pleasure and desire. It eliminates the controlling image of the asexual mammy, challenging this aspect of the elite social gaze.

Yet *Essence* also operates as a sphere of restriction, exclusively addressing 'safe' issues that attempt to steer Black women away from perverse or sexually loose behavior. The magazine reifies the ideology of the legitimate couple, promoting heterosexuality and monogamy. To remain safe, the magazine purports that women must find appropriate mates, avoid pregnancy and disease, and control their sexual pleasure and desire. It is likely, therefore, that Black female editors and writers have not forgotten the image of the oversexed Jezebel, and attempt to prevent Black women from continually being labeled as such by policing their sexual behavior and perpetuating the panoptic aspect of the elite social gaze.

So, while *Essence* encourages Black women to reject the image of the mammy, it does not enable Black women to embrace all sexual behaviors, ostensibly for fear they may still be seen as oversexed (i.e., Jezebels) or acquire other deviant labels (e.g., the lesbian). And while this may not be the intent of the magazine, these editorial choices have repressive effects. *Essence* does enable Black women to construct their own visible sexuality, but simultaneously determines that Black women must denounce "deviant" categories until they are no longer governed by the elite social gaze which continually scrutinizes their potentially "oversexed" sexual activity. This dichotomy—*Essence* as a social institution in which Black women manipulate their own images and *Essence* as a reflection of society's elite gaze that contributes to the subordination and marginalization of Black women—reflects the simultaneous safe and bounded nature of this magazine as well as the double-bind Black women face in America as a general rule.

ADDENDUM: TEXTUAL IMAGES IN *ESSENCE* SINCE 1995

My original research examined *Essence* from January 1986 to December of 1995. Below I provide a descriptive analysis of the magazine from January 1996 to March 2002. For this section, I examined quarterly issues of *Essence* over the course of six years.[5] There were a total of 128 advice column questions and answers for this time period.[6] These advice column questions and answers concentrated on many of the topics listed above, including (but not limited to) female sexual pleasure and desire, marriage, co-habitation, drug use, teen pregnancy, infidelity, homosexuality, tubal ligations, and pornography. Additionally, there were 153 articles listed under "feature articles" during the six years. Twenty-two of these articles (approximately 14 percent) discussed issues pertaining to female sexual pleasure and desire.

Have the textual messages in *Essence* addressing female sexual pleasure and desire changed in a significant manner over time? The answer is no. This conclusion is best summarized by a popular Southern saying, "it's the same old warmed over soup with a few new ingredients."[7] As previous findings revealed, the simultaneous safe and restrictive nature of Black women sexual lives, continually confined to the social space between the sexually loose Jezebel and the asexual mammy images, is clearly reflected on the pages of *Essence*.

Essence as a Sexual Safe Haven (January 1996—March 2002)

Essence continued to provide a space where Black women could acknowledge and accept their sexuality. Some advice column entries and feature articles encouraged women to embrace and/or reconstruct their sexual selves,
continually debunking the myth of the asexual mammy. For example, in 1996
a reader asked about initiating sexual activity with her husband. A columnist
responded: "you must realize that you are human, and you have a right to be
sexual." And when a reader expressed frustrated because her boyfriend did
not engage in pre-marital sex, a columnist replied: "if having sexual intercourse is really that important to you, you must be honest with him. You
might say, 'I need deeper physical intimacy in our relationship . . .'" (1998).

The magazine also helped women resolve various sexual problems. A
reader's question about her husband's impotence (1996) gave birth to a
discussion about "nonsurgical methods for restoring erections," including a
vacuum-erection device, penile self-injection, and a penile implant. The
columnist concluded with the following advice: "to learn to further increase
your pleasure, you may want to ask your physician to recommend a sex coun-
selor." A woman expressing dismay because her boyfriend watched adult
films and masturbated instead of engaging in sexual relations with her read:
"[masturbation is] just one type of sexual response to stimuli, and sexologists
refute the idea that masturbation is antisocial behavior" (1997). This columnist encouraged the reader to "include nude dancing to create sexual drama"
in order to stimulate her sex life and concluded with the following: "try not
to worry if your partner continues to masturbate, as long as it does not interfere with your mutual [sexual] pleasure" (1997). A woman who remained sus-
picious of her new beau after ending a painful relationship was encouraged
"to deliver herself from old wounds." And in 2000, a columnist offered advice to a woman experiencing vaginal dryness, suggesting solutions to overcome her sexual troubles.

Over the course of the six years examined, *Essence* sustained discussions
about Black women's sex and sexuality. Readers were encouraged to wel-
come their sexuality, writers were granted the freedom to tackle sexual issues,
and editors printed (were able to print) critical sexual information. The magazine unremittingly created a safe public space that allowed Black women to
claim an essential aspect of themselves—their sex lives.

Essence as Restrictor (January 1996—March 2002)

Much like the years between 1986 and 1995, *Essence* continued to ward off
images of the asexual mammy. The aforementioned section explored the

ways in which the magazine attacked this charge. But the image of the over-sexed Black woman was ever-present. Discussions promoted the preservation of the legitimate heterosexual couple, encouraged women to select "appropriate" mates, and warned against the dangers of casual sex, implying that women's sexual behavior was still problematic enough to require the control of the "elite social gaze." Additionally, the magazine offered messages that would guide women onto the "right" (i.e., moral) path. Some textual messages in the magazine challenged this restrictive mantra (e.g., discussions about the "single life"), but most adhered to the conservative social script delineated in previous years.

The Image of the Legitimate Couple

From 1986–1995, women were unceasingly encouraged to enter into and/or maintain the "legitimate couple." Again, much like Foucault's couple (1978), this ideal couple was heterosexual, monogamous, and emotionally oriented. This script remained virtually identical for the most part, with the exception of the removal of maturity (i.e., the magazine no longer stipulated that partners must be mature before engaging in sexual activity).

The vast majority of the advice column question and answers, as well as the feature articles, were limited to images of heterosexuality. Female readers, who far outnumbered male readers, were encouraged to abandon casual sex (e.g., "it is a mistake to look for the answers in the arms of another man" [2000]) and seek out intimacy in its place (e.g., what we all do need can be summed up in two words: human touch. . . . You think you need intercourse, when what you need is a hug . . . [2000]).

Some textual messages, especially messages concerning homosexuality, could have challenged the assumption of heterosexuality but failed to do so. Instead, discussions about homosexuality were limited to notions of deception, invisibility, and danger. One feature article entitled "Still Friends" (1997) described the confusion, pain, and suffering a woman experienced after her husband admitted he was gay. And the only article about lesbians, "Mirror Images" (1998), began with the following: "Black lesbians . . . don whatever masks we feel will protect us in a doubly hostile world." This article went on to describe one lesbian's encounter with a deceitful, abusive woman. The dominant message about lesbianism readers encountered was one of caution: "for now the thought of being intimate with another Black woman gives me pause. And I know that, among Black lesbians, I am not alone in this feeling."

A small number of advice column entries and feature articles attempted to provide a different option—a lifestyle labeled the "single" life (i.e., the single, heterosexual life). One author stated, "Black women must learn that we have got to survive with and without men" (1999) and a columnist advised: "rid yourself of the labels others have placed on you. . . . Manless does not mean mindless" (2002). The "single life" was one possible alternative to the legitimate couple. However, images of the legitimate couple clearly prevailed.

PLEASURE AND DESIRE FINISH LAST

No longer was there a need to decipher this sexual script in the magazine's text. The once subtle messages mandating that one must first, locate an "appropriate" mate interested in commitment, second, make sure to protect oneself from disease and pregnancy and, third, make sure to value emotionality over sexuality before exploring sexual pleasure and desire, were now unconcealed. Suggestions that one protect oneself from disease were downplayed, but the remaining features of this script rang through loud and clear.

Regarding appropriate mates, an advice columnist (1998) cautioned "be sure to discuss your concerns, expectations and emotional needs before becoming sexually intimate . . . don't begin a sexual relationship until you get to know the person. . . ." The author of the feature article titled "Thug Passion" (2000) warned against dating an "inappropriate" man: "A roughneck, thug, gangsta, bad boy, hot boy, fine, fine irresistible man. You crave him like chocolate even though you know he's the last thing a nice girl like you should be getting into." Additionally, the author of "Mr. Right.Com" described the "appropriate mate" in her personal ad: "financially stable, confident, honest, attractive . . ."

Regarding pregnancy, the author of the feature article "Baby's Momma" (1997) stated: "understanding that any man I sleep with is potentially the father of my child has made me much more selective. Fine and nice are no longer enough to qualify; now I have to ask myself if the brother is emotionally, spiritually, and financially able to be a good father." And pertaining to emotionality, the author of "Hit Me On The Hip" (1997) strongly suggested women typically favor emotional ties: "forget beeper codes and getting all his numbers. When you and your man can cuddle over the kitchen counter and write sweet messages to each other, you're on the way to building something real."

The author of "Will I Ever Have Sex Again?" (2000) unabashedly included the script in her article: "having sex is easy. You can have self-sex through masturbation; you can have casual sex, freaky sex, thank-you sex. But what most of us who aren't having sex are holding out for is sex within an intimate, loving and compatible relationship. In other words, good sex." These textual images were transparent—women must find an appropriate man, avoid pregnancy, and attach importance to emotional ties before expressing, or experiencing, sexual pleasure and desire.

PLEASURE, DESIRE AND CONTROL

Finally, the script attempting to persuade women to control their sexuality was still imbedded in the magazine's text from 1996 to 2002. In the article "Who Is That Man?/Check Him Out" (1996), the author offered the following words of advice:

> Let's begin at the beginning. You're introduced to someone. Sparks fly, and you have butterflies in your stomach. He asks you out. When you come home from your first date, you call all your friends to let them know what a wonderful evening you had. You're floating on air . . . STOP! RED FLAG! WARNING . . . WARNING! Your radar should automatically kick in. You just met this person. It's obvious that he's handsome and sexy and knows where to take a woman on a date. Don't let that [man] make you lose all your good sense. Most guys are all right, but you've got to keep an eye out for the bad apples. Though having all these romantic feelings is nice, what do you actually know about him? In this society we are very careful about everything else that affects our daily lives, but we eagerly enter into relationships with people about whom we know next to nothing! Did you check him out prior to agreeing to your date? Are you prepared to check him out now? This is usually a very vulnerable time. That love button has been pushed, and you're off like a horse at the starting gate. . . . Whoa!

In the feature article "Hands Off!" (1997), a woman who sought solace from her boss after she engaged in a consensual affair with him was told "the fact that your relationship was initially consensual will definitely pose a credibility problem for you. . . . When you gave this man entree into your personal life through intimacy, you muddied the water . . ." And in 2000, when a sexually curious woman, currently in a committed relationship, asked about engaging in sex with other men, a columnist chastised her in the following manner: "you cannot discover your sacred sexual self if you're lost in adolescent fantasia." Overall, *Essence* did not detract from the notion that women should be careful not to allow their hormones to govern decisions about sex relations.

CONCLUSION—ADDENDUM

The messages in *Essence* did not change significantly over time. From January 1996 to March 2002, *Essence* continued to grapple with the controlling sexual images of the undersexed mammy and the oversexed Jezebel. The magazine did provide a safe public space for Black women's sexuality. However, it also reinforced the image of the oversexed Black woman by suggesting, yet again, that women must find and/or keep "appropriate" mates, control their sexuality, and locate themselves within the legitimate heterosexual couple. Instead of refuting asexual and oversexual controlling images, the magazine seemingly attempts to create a sexual space between the images. In "essence," the magazine confines Black female readers to this new restricted space while continually endeavoring to prevent Black women from acquiring additional deviant labels (e.g., the lesbian).

So, over the course of 16 years, readers are confronted with a different dichotomy—*Essence* as a social institution in which Black women control their own images and *Essence* as a reflection of society's elite gaze that contributes to the subordination and marginalization of Black women. This dichotomy, once again, reflects the simultaneous safe and restrictive nature of *Essence* as well as the double-bind Black women in America typically encounter in public spaces.

NOTES

1. These statistics were obtained from the 1994 and 1992 Simmons Study of Media and Markets, Simmons Market Research Bureau, Inc., USA.

2. A brief interview with Executive Editor Linda Villarosa revealed that most of the editors and contributing writers are Black women (1995).

3. The category "pl/des" contains discussions of pleasure and desire. The category "no sex" contains articles/advice columns that did not address sexuality at all. The category "bio" contains discussion of biological/medical topics (e.g., sexually transmitted diseases). The category "obj/exp" contains discussions about female objectification and exploitation.

4. In 1995, the magazine's coverage of homosexuality increased, but these messages generally focused on the dangers gay and/or bisexual men present to heterosexual women.

5. The following issues were examined: March, June, September, and December of 1996; February, May, August, and November of 1997; January, April, July and October of 1998; March, June, September, and December of 1999; February, May, August, and November of 2000; January, April, July and October of 2001; January, February, and March of 2002.

6. A new advice column, "Ask Iyanla", was added in January 2002, but of the three entries, only one dealt with female sexuality. In particular, this entry dealt with sexual violence (i.e., the aftermath of rape).

7. I'd like to thank B. Alridge for this insight.

REFERENCES

Becker, H. (1973). *Outsiders*. New York: Free Press.

Bennett, W. L. (1996). *News: The Politics of Illusion*. New York: Longman Press.

Campbell, J. (1986). *Mythic Black Fiction: The Transformation of History*. Knoxville: The University of Tennessee Press.

Carby, H. V. (1992). "Policing the Black Women's Body in an Urban Context." *Critical Inquiry* 18:738–755.

Carmody, D. (January 23, 1995). "An Enduring Voice of Black Women." *The New York Times*. D1+.

Collins, P. H. (1990). *Black Feminist Thought*. New York: Routledge.

de Lauretis, T. (1987). "The Technology of Gender." In *Technologies of Gender*. Bloomington: Indiana University Press.

Foucault, M. (1978). *The History of Sexuality: Volume 1: An Introduction*. New York: Vintage Books.

Gross, L. (1991). "Out of the Mainstream: Sexual Minorities and the Mass Media." In *Gay People, Sex and the Media*, eds. M. A. Wolf and A. P. Kielwassen. New York: Haworth Press.

Harrison, D. (1988). *Black Pearls: Blues Queens of the 1920s*. New Jersey: Rutgers University Press.

hooks, b. (1992). *Black Looks: Race and Representation*. Boston: South End Press.

Mayall, A & D. E. H. Russell. (1990). "Racism in Pornography." In *Making Violence Sexy*, ed. Diana E H. Russell. New York: Teacher's College Press.

McCracken, E. (1993). *Decoding Women's Magazines: From Mademoiselle to Ms.* London: MacMillian Press.

McMahon, K. (1990). "The Cosmopolitan Ideology and the Management of Desire." *The Journal of Sex Research* 27 (3): 381–396.

McNay, Lois. (1992). *Foucault and Feminism: Power, Gender, and the Self.* Boston: Northeastern University Press.

Perry, I. (1995). "It's My Thang and I'll Swing It the Way That I Feel: Sexuality and Black Women Rappers." In *Gender, Race and Class in Media: A Text Reader*, eds. G. Dines and J. M. Humez. Newbury Park: Sage Publications.

Rose, T. (1994). *Black Noise: Rap Music and Black Culture in Contemporary America*. New Hampshire: University Press of New England.

Spillers, H. (1984). "Interstices: A Small Drama of Words." In *Pleasure and Danger: Exploring Female Sexuality*, ed. C. Vance. New York: Routledge & Kegan.

Wyatt, G. E, M. D. Newcomb & M. H. Riederle. (1993). *Sexual Abuse and Consensual Sex: Women's Developmental Patterns and Outcomes*. Newbury Park: Sage Publications.

Chapter Eleven

Press Coverage and Awareness of Gender-Equality Issues in Japan

Reiko Ishiyama & Shinichi Saito

It is often argued that Japan is still a more male-dominated society in many respects than other industrial countries, like the U.S., although the situation has gradually improved in recent years. Various policies have been implemented to achieve a gender-equal society since the International Women's Year in 1975,[1] with some success. As numerous data indicate, however, equality of the sexes has not been achieved. The Gender Equality Bureau of the Cabinet Office defines a gender-equal society as "a society in which both men and women, as equal members, have the opportunity to participate in all kinds of social activities at will, equally enjoy political, economical and cultural benefits, and share responsibilities" (http://www.gender.go.jp/sorcial_e.html). In this sense, inequality between women and men still exists in many domains.

In the home, a division of labor based on gender still prevails. The combination of the husband as the economic provider and the wife as housekeeper is still found in more than one third of all Japanese households, although the proportion is decreasing. When both the husband and wife do housework, the husband spends only 26 minutes a day, while the wife works for 3 hours and 18 minutes (Inoue & Ehara, 2001).

In the labor market, the percentage of female workers has been around 40% for the past decade. According to the Ministry of Health, Labor, and Welfare, however, in the year 2000, nearly half of the female workers were part-time (54% were full-time), while about 88% of male workers were full-time. This situation is likely the main reason for the inequality of income between men and women; on average, women earn only 60% of what men earn (Inoue & Ehara, 2001).

In addition, the percentage of female managerial workers is less than 5%. This figure is far smaller than in many other industrial countries. Similarly, 17.1% of the members of the *Sangi-in* (House of Councillors—the Upper

House) are women, and 5% of the members of the *Shugi-in* (House of Representatives—the Lower House). The percentage of women members in local assemblies is also only 5.0% (Inoue & Ehara, 2001). Women appear to be underrepresented in the process of business and political decision-making.

The current situation does not indicate gender-equality. In addition, many Japanese do not feel the current circumstances to be gender equal. According to a public opinion survey conducted by the Prime Minister's Office (currently the Cabinet Office) in January 2000, nearly 80% of the respondents thought that men and women were not equal in terms of social status as a whole. The feeling of inequality was especially strong in the political domain and in social customs.

How can we overcome the existing inequality and achieve a gender-equal society? We believe that one of the crucial factors is the role of the mass media. In contemporary society, we depend on the media to a great extent for information. Without the media, we would not be aware of social developments.

Every day, many events occur both locally and globally. Needless to say, the media report only a fraction of these events, due to restricted newspaper space or limited TV time. Furthermore, the media does not report all events that it covers in the same way. Some receive substantial coverage, while others are dealt with superficially. As an inevitable consequence, the news media select only a small number of events and rank-order them for their coverage. This process of selection, exclusion, and emphasis of events significantly influences our perceptions of what is going on, what issues should be considered, and how to think about them, as agenda-setting and framing research demonstrates (McCombs & Shaw, 1972; Neuman *et al.*, 1992; Entman, 1993; Kosicki, 1993; Dearing & Rogers, 1996; Scheufele, 1999).

While agenda-setting or framing studies make significant contributions to our understanding of the cognitive effects of the mass media, some issues still remain to be investigated. One of the most important, but rarely argued, aspects of cognitive effects is that if a certain social problem gets insufficient media coverage, it is unlikely that most people will recognize its existence (Saito, 2001). It is important to note that before forming an attitude or taking action on a social problem, we need to be aware that the problem exists. In this article, we examine the relationship between media coverage and the public's awareness of social issues concerning a gender-equal society.

AWARENESS OF KEY ISSUES CONCERNING A GENDER-EQUAL SOCIETY

In the 2000 survey on a gender-equal society conducted by The Prime Minister's Office, respondents were asked whether they were familiar with the following seven key words or phrases concerning a gender-equal society: "Convention on the Elimination of all Forms of Discrimination against Women," "The Basic Law for a Gender-Equal Society," "Positive action," [2] "Gender," "Unpaid work," "The Beijing Platform for Action," [3] and "Reproductive health/rights."

Needless to say, the Convention on the Elimination of all Forms of Discrimination against Women (CEDAW) is one of the milestones in the advancement of women. The United Nations ratified CEDAW in 1979, and Japan enacted it in 1985.

The Basic Law for a Gender-Equal Society, which went into effect in June 1999, attempts "to comprehensively and systematically promote the formation of a gender-equal society by laying out the basic principles in regard to the formation of such a society, clarifying the responsibilities of the State and local governments and citizens, and also stipulating provisions to form the basis of policies related to the promotion of the formation of a gender-equal society" (Article 1 of Chapter 1 of the law).[4] The law is a milestone in the advancement of women in Japan.

The Beijing Platform for Action was adopted in September 1995 at the U.N. Fourth World Conference on Women (FWCW), held in Beijing, China. It addresses "key areas of concern to the advancement of women and suggests ways that governments, NGOs, the private sector, and community groups could incorporate the suggestions made" (Danner & Walsh, 1999, p. 66). The Platform for Action is also an indispensable concept in discussing a gender-equal society.

Unpaid work, positive action (affirmative action), and reproductive health/rights were important items on the agenda of the FWCW. Reproductive health/rights was also an important agenda item in the International Conference on Population and Development (ICPD), held in Cairo in September 1994.

These seven key words and phrases in a sense serve as the starting points for discussing a gender-equal society. Therefore, it is essential that people recognize them. However, the results of the survey demonstrate that they are not widely known. As shown in Figure 1, more than 40% of the respondents said that they had never heard of any of these seven words or phrases. The best-known word was CEDAW (37.2%), followed by The Basic Law for a Gender-Equal Society (24.7%). These were the only two that more than 20% of the respondents knew; the other five were known to less than 15% each: positive action (13.6%), gender (11.1%), unpaid work (7.1%), the platform for action (4.3%), and reproductive health/rights (3.4%). Considering the importance of these words in discussing a gender-equal society, the results raise some significant issues.

The Prime Minister's Office frequently conducts nationwide public opinion surveys and occasionally asks respondents whether they know key words or phrases that are regarded as important at the time of the survey. Surveys that were conducted between July 1999 and June 2000 (namely, within six months of the survey on a gender-equal society) included questions on the knowledge of key phrases. These included two that were comparable with the gender-related phrases: World Trade Organization (WTO) and "lifelong learning."[5] The results indicated that 74.0% of the respondents knew the term "lifelong learning," and 66.6% knew the term WTO. Compared with these two terms, the numbers who knew the key phrases regarding a gender-equal society were very low.

RESEARCH QUESTIONS

To what extent do the media refer to these words in their reporting, and is there any relationship between the amount of media coverage and the level of knowledge about these words? If the media seldom use these words, it seems reasonable to assume that the general public does not have much opportunity to learn them.

In this study, we examined how often these words are used in the news media in Japan and whether there is any relationship between the media coverage and the knowledge level. To do this, we focused on the role of newspapers for the following reasons: An inherent property of TV news is that it requires visual images in its reporting. Without pictures, events are rarely used as news stories. TV news also rarely reports the same issue for a long period. By contrast, newspapers are much more likely to report events or issues when there is no picture, and they often continue to cover important social problems for a relatively long period (*e.g.*, McClure & Patterson, 1976). It seems reasonable to think that topics or issues related to a gender-equal society are more suitable for newspapers than for TV news.

METHODS

To address the research questions, we searched for the above-mentioned key terms in news stories using a newspaper archive (the *G-Search* database) of articles from the *Asahi Shimbun*, *Yomiuri Shimbun*, and *Mainichi Shimbun*, the three most influential national newspapers. Each paper reaches a large number of readers across Japan. The *Yomiuri Shimbun* is the world's only newspaper, with a daily circulation exceeding 10 million copies. The Asahi

Shimbun, the second largest daily in the world, has a daily circulation of about 8.3 million, and the *Mainichi Shimbun* has a circulation of nearly 4 million (See Saito, 2000 for details).

We searched the newspaper archive back to January 1995 for the seven key phrases on a gender equal society, to October 1994 for "WTO," and to December 1994 for "lifelong learning," covering newspaper articles for five years.

First, we searched for news stories that contained the key phrases in the headline but found very few articles on the gender-related phrases. Therefore, we extended the search to full articles. This crude content analysis of just counting numbers of relevant articles is far from perfect, but it is an important indicator of how much importance newspapers place on the key words in their reporting.

After searching the newspaper articles, we examined whether there was any relationship between the amount of media coverage and the knowledge of each phrase.

RESULTS

Table 11.1(a) through 11.1(d) show the results of the search for newspaper articles that included the key phrases. As these tables clearly show, lifelong learning and WTO were referred to much more frequently in articles in all three newspapers than the seven key gender-related terms. Of the seven gender-related terms, "gender" was mentioned most often. The second most frequently used term was "The Basic Law for a Gender-Equal Society." The other five words appeared in the newspapers much less frequently.

From 26 January 1999 to 26 January 2000, the phrase "lifelong learning" appeared in 880 articles in the *Asahi Shimbun*, 753 in the *Yomiuri Shimbun*,

Table 11.1(a).   The Number of Articles Including Key Terms in The Asahi Shimbun

	One year	Three years	Five years
Lifelong Learning	880	2538	3782
WTO	519	1192	2131
Gender	158	342	407
The Basic Law for a Gender-Equal Society	54	69	69
Reproductive health/rights	0	2	7
Positive action	8	11	13
Unpaid work	2	24	36
CEDAW	3	9	20
The Beijing Platform for Action	0	1	2

Table 11.1(b).   The Number of Articles Including Key Terms in The Yomiuri Shimbun

	One year	Three years	Five years
Lifelong Learning	753	1011	1238
WTO	442	1131	2183
Gender	87	160	199
The Basic Law for a Gender-Equal Society	80	90	90
Reproductive health/rights	1	2	3
Positive action	14	19	31
Unpaid work	4	16	28
CEDAW	3	12	21
The Beijing Platform for Action	1	5	5

Table 11.1(c).   The Number of Articles Including Key Terms in The Mainichi Shimbun

	One year	Three years	Five years
Lifelong Learning	1222	3253	4286
WTO	565	1379	2317
Gender	153	350	403
The Basic Law for a Gender-Equal Society	67	91	91
Reproductive health/rights	26	30	46
Positive action	1	29	29
Unpaid work	11	33	38
CEDAW	1	6	14
The Beijing Platform for Action	0	6	1

Table 11.1(d).   The Number of Articles Including Key Terms in All Three Newspapers

	One year	Three years	Five years
Lifelong Learning	2855	6802	9306
WTO	1526	3702	6631
Gender	398	852	1009
The Basic Law for a Gender-Equal Society	201	250	250
Reproductive health/rights	27	34	56
Positive action	23	59	73
Unpaid work	17	73	102
CEDAW	7	27	55
The Beijing Platform for Action	1	6	8

and 1222 in the *Mainichi Shimbun*. WTO was mentioned in 519, 442, and 565 articles in the respective newspapers during the same period. Compared with the frequent appearance of these two phrases, the key gender-related terms were far less likely to be used in the three newspapers. Even the most often used word, "gender," only appeared in 158, 87, and 153 articles in the respective papers.

The number of articles that included the phrases "CEDAW" and "The Beijing Platform for Action" was especially low: only three articles each in the *Asahi Shimbun* and Yomiuri Shimbun and one in the *Mainichi Shimbun* for CEDAW, no articles in the *Asahi Shimbun* or *Mainichi Shimbun*, and just one in the Yomiuri Shimbun for the Platform for Action during the 12 months before the survey.

Even when we went back five years before the survey, few articles containing many of the gender-related phrases were retrieved from the three newspapers. This was especially true for CEDAW and the Platform for Action: only 55 for CEDAW and eight for the Platform for Action in total for all three papers.

Table 11.2 shows the Spearman's rank-order correlation coefficients among the three newspapers and across time. As this table shows, there was no remarkable difference in this tendency to report the phrases in terms of frequency. Despite the differences in newspapers and coverage periods, the rank-ordering among the nine phrases in terms of frequency was highly correlated.

Next, we examined whether there was any relationship between the amount of media coverage and the awareness of each key phrase. Figure 11.2 compares these two variables. This figure illustrates that the more frequently a phrase was mentioned in the newspapers, the more likely it was to be known by the public. Compared with the seven key phrases on a gender-equal society, the phrases "WTO" and "lifelong learning" have received much more substantial coverage and were correspondingly known by a majority of people. By contrast, the key gender-related phrases were rarely used in newspaper articles and, probably as a result, only a few people knew these phrases.

There were some exceptions. Clearly CEDAW is one. This term was known by slightly more than one third of the public, but it rarely appeared in newspapers from January 1995 to January 2000. On the contrary, compared

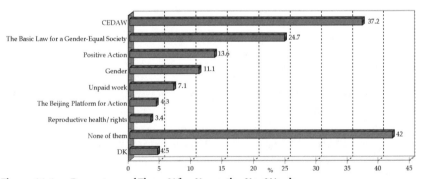

Figure 11.1. Percentage of Those Who Know the Key Words.

Table 11.2. **Correlations Between the Three Newspapers**

	Asahi Shimbun			Yomiuri Shimbun			Mainichi Shimbun		
	1 year	*3 years*	*5 years*	*1 year*	*3 years*	*5 years*	*1 year*	*3 years*	*5 years*
Asahi 1 year	—								
Asahi 3 years	.946***	—							
Asahi 5 years	.929***	.983***	—						
Yomiuri 1 year	.983***	.979***	.946***	—					
Yomiuri 3 years	.962***	.950***	.917**	.979***	—				
Yomiuri 5 years	.962***	.950***	.917**	.979***	1.00****	—			
Mainichi 1 year	.815**	.895**	.895**	.840**	.787*	.787*	—		
Mainichi 3 years	.828**	.937**	.912**	.887**	.845**	.845**	.971***	—	
Mainichi 5 years	.820**	.900**	.883**	.854**	.800*	.800*	.996***	.979***	—

*$p<.05$, **$p<.01$, ***$p<.00$.
The values are the Spearman's rank-order correlations.

with other gender-related words, the term "gender" was more likely to appear in the newspapers, but knowledge of this word was relatively low.

We then computed the Spearman's rank order correlation coefficients (rho) between the amount of media coverage of the key terms and the level of knowledge of them. The results are shown in Table 11.3. The amount of media coverage in the *Asahi Shimbun* and *Yomiuri Shimbun* was highly correlated with the level of knowledge of the words (rho ranged from .767 to .845, $p<.05$), while the correlations were lower for the *Mainichi Shimbun*.

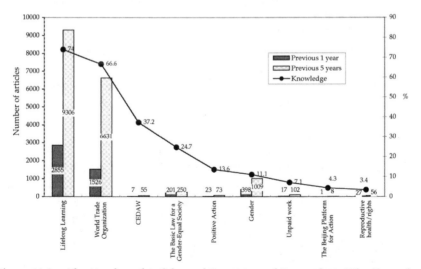

Figure 11.2. **The Number of Articles and Percentage of Respondents Who Know the Key Words.**

Table 11.3.   Rank-order Correlations Between the Amount of Newspaper Coverage and the Level of Knowledge

	With CEDAW	Without CEDAW
1 year (all three papers)	.567	.762*
3 years (all three papers)	.633 (p<.07)	.857**
5 years (all three papers)	.633 (p<.07)	.857**
Asahi 1 year	.845**	.922**
Asahi 3 years	.733*	.857**
Asahi 5 years	.767*	.857**
Yomiuri 1 year	.778*	.922**
Yomiuri 3 years	.767*	.905**
Yomiuri 5 years	.767*	.905**
Mainichi 1 year	.552	.714*
Mainichi 3 years	.527	.762*
Mainichi 5 years	.533	.714*

* $p<.05$, ** $p<.01$,
The values are the Spearman's rank-order correlations.

The rank order correlations between the amount of media coverage and the level of knowledge were higher when CEDAW was omitted. The correlations were especially high for the *Asahi Shimbun* and *Yomiuri Shimbun*, regardless of the period. When we combined the three papers into a simple variable, the rank order correlations were .762 ($p<.05$) when dating back one year and .857 ($p<.01$) when dating back three to five years.

This study provides evidence that there is a significant relationship between the amount of media coverage and the level of knowledge of key terms.

DISCUSSION

This study found that a lack of substantive coverage in the mainstream Japanese print media of the important terms related to a gender-equal society was correlated with a low level of knowledge of these terms. Several important points should be noted.

First, the study indicated that the phrase "Platform for Action" has been virtually ignored by the mainstream press. Our database search for five years found only eight articles mentioning this phrase. This raises a significant problem; several scholars have analyzed newspaper coverage of the FWCW, and found a negative tendency in the press reports (*e.g.*, Akahavan-Majid & Ramaprasad, 1998; Muramatsu & Fujiwara, 1998; Danner & Walsh, 1999). Likewise, the Platform for Action was one of the most important achievements of the FWCW, but we found that it was rarely discussed in the mainstream press in Japan. In an article discussing the media coverage of the

FWCW, Danner & Walsh (1999) pointed out that "if the media do not cover the conference, they do not have to acknowledge the existence of issues that are important to women" (p. 63). We endorse their conclusion.

Second, as previously mentioned, the UN ratified CEDAW in 1979, and Japan enacted it in 1985, so about 20 years have passed since this acronym came into existence. Therefore, it seems reasonable to assume that this acronym has already lost its current news value. This might partially explain why this word rarely appears in recent newspapers. Past public opinion surveys by The Prime Minister's Office also investigated the knowledge level of the term "CEDAW." In the 1991 survey, 39.3% of the respondents already knew the word. The knowledge level decreased to 27.8% in the 1995 survey, and rose to 37.2% in the 2000 survey. Although there has been some fluctuation, it is important to note that familiarity with the term has *not* increased over the past ten years. This might partially be attributable to the very infrequent appearance of CEDAW in mainstream newspapers.

As we pointed out earlier, if the media does not report on a certain social problem, its existence is highly unlikely to be perceived by the general public. The fact that people do not know key phrases that are important to a gender-equal society seems to indicate that they do not acknowledge the existence of the social problems that are represented by those key words, and consequently do not discuss the problems that should be solved.

We do not solely rely on the mass media to obtain information on what happens in society. There are interpersonal channels, such as conversations with family members or friends at school, work, or in community meetings. However, it is not too much to say that the media's role in constructing social reality is far more important than usually thought (Adoni & Mane, 1984). In order to achieve a truly gender-equal society, we should put more emphasis on the role of the media.

NOTES

1. To promote the formation of a gender-equal society, the Headquarters for the Promotion of Gender was set up within the Cabinet, and the Office for Gender Equality and the Council for Gender Equality were established by Cabinet Orders in 1994. Accompanying the reorganization of the Central Government in January 2001, the newly formed Council for Gender Equality and Gender Equality Bureau were established.

2. In Japan, the term "positive action" is used instead of "affirmative action".

3. Twelve critical areas of concern in the Platform for Action were (1) women and poverty, (2) education and training of women, (3) women and health, (4) violence against women, (5) women and armed conflict, (6) women and the economy, (7)

women in power and decision-making, (8) institutional mechanisms for the advancement of women, (9) human rights of women, (10) women and the media, (11) women and the environment, and (12) the girl-child.

4. A rough translation of the law into English is available at http://www.gender.go .jp/sorcial_e.html.

5. The acronym WTO was included in a survey conducted in October 1999, and "lifelong learning" was included in December 1999. Other surveys also asked for the level of knowledge of key words, but they were not directly comparable with the gender-related words, mainly due to differences in the wording of the questions.

REFERENCES

Adoni, H., and Mane, S. (1984). Media and the social construction of reality. *Communication Research, 11*, 323–340.

Akahavan-Majid & Ramaprasad (1998) Framing and ideology: A comparative analysis of U.S. and Chinese newspaper coverage of the fourth United Nations Conference on Women and the NGO forum. *Mass Communication and Society, 1(3/4)*, 131–152.

Danner, L., & Walsh, S. (1999) "Radical" feminists and "bickering" women: Backlash in U.S. media coverage of the United Nations Fourth World Conference on Women, *Critical Studies in Mass Communication, 16*, 63–84.

Dearing, J.W., & Rogers, E.M. (1996). *Agenda-Setting*. Thousand Oaks, CA: Sage.

Entman, R.M. (1993). Framing: Towards clarification of a fractured paradigm. *Journal of Communication, 43(4)*, 51–58.

Inoue, T., & Ehara, Y.(2001) *Databook on Women (in Japanese)*. Tokyo: Yuhikaku.

Kosicki, G.M. (1993) Problems and opportunities in agenda-setting research. *Journal of Communication, 43(2)*, 100–127.

McClure, R.D., & Patterson, T.E. (1976) Print vs. network news. *Journal of Communication, 26(2)*, 23–28.

McCombs, M.E., & Show, D.L. (1972). The agenda-setting function of mass media. *Public Opinion Quarterly, 36*, 176–187.

Muramatsu, Y. & Fujiwara, T. (1998) How did the media report the U.N. Fourth World Conference on Women? In K. Takana & T. Morohashi (Eds.)., *Analyzing newspapers from a gender perspective* (in Japanese). Tokyo: Kendai-shokan.

Neuman, W.R., Just, M.R., & Crigler, A.N. (1992) *Common Knowledge: News and the Construction of Political Meaning*. Chicago: University of Chicago Press.

Saito, S. (2000). Japan. In S.A. Gunaratne (Ed.), *Handbook of the Media in Asia: An overview*. Sage Publication: India.

—— (2001) Construction of social reality by the media. In Y. Kawakami (Ed). *Social Psychology of Information Behavior (in Japanese)*. Kyoto: Kitaooji.

Scheufele, D.A. (1999) Framing as a theory of media effects. *Journal of Communication, 49(1)*, 103–122.

Chapter Twelve

Women in Propaganda Posters in Post-Liberation China: Portrayals of Insidious Oppression

Xin-An (Lucian) Lu, Ph.D. & Linda Y. Devenish, Ph.D.

The portrayal of women in post-liberation Chinese posters presents illuminating comparisons and contrasts. Geographically, the portrayal gives a different status to women from that explained in Western feminist literature. Historically, the portrayal presents women in different images from those of women in pre-liberation Chinese history. Yet, paradoxically, the portrayal camouflages oppression of women behind a façade of emancipation, presenting an interesting case of what we identify as *insidious oppression*. Through analyses of a number of images of women, this essay uncovers their *insidious oppression* as contained in post-liberation Chinese posters.

This study moves beyond the research by Evans (1999) and Lee (1998) through a threefold comparison/contrast and a proposition of the concept of *insidious oppression*. Evans's work focuses directly on women's oppression depicted in post-liberation Chinese posters. This essay attempts to broaden Evans's work through geographical and historical contrast, and more importantly, by explicating the insidious or indirect nature of the oppression.

In addition, we believe that Lee's (1998) concept of emancipatory oppression does not uncover the nature of the oppression she attempted to address, because the phrase "emancipatory oppression" is semantically vague and misleading. The phrase is open to several interpretations: (1) some oppression is emancipatory; (2) the effort to emancipate may contain oppression; and (3) real oppression may be camouflaged under apparent emancipation. We propose the new concept of *insidious oppression* for better semantic clarity, and, more importantly, to help uncover the real nature of a more dangerous form of oppression.

We contend that *insidious oppression* merits more study due to its duplicity. It disarms because of its emancipation façade over the oppressive subtext and thus is subtle but serious. *Insidious oppression* is less visible, more resilient and infiltrating, and hence more deleterious. To use an analogy, *insidious oppression*, when compared with visibly blatant oppression, works more like chemical and biological weaponry rather than conventional weaponry.

Insidious oppression via the medium of imagistic rhetoric is doubly dangerous. Images, compared with verbal rhetoric, possess more cognitive immediacy because of their easier mental decoding and cognitive reception (Lu, 2001). Research by Jameson (1988) and Olson (1983) corroborates that images possess greater persuasive potency in the sense-making process of the audience. Therefore, if conveyed via the medium of images, *insidious oppression* becomes more unconsciously osmotic and infiltrating in that the emancipation façade more easily conceals the oppressive nature.

However, as Evans (1999) contends, poster images as an important form of rhetoric have not received adequate scholarly attention. This essay intends to help make up for this deficit, and to direct scholarly attention toward the "double dangers" of *insidious oppression* contained in images, and toward the manifestation of *insidious oppression* in various human contexts and arenas.

The analysis in this essay benefits from the authors' unique frame of reference because of their heritage and experience. Xin-An grew up in China and lived in many different areas of the country for 29 years. He acquired an insider's understanding of the language, history, and culture of China, as well as the symbolic signification of the Chinese images. In contrast, Linda, who was born in England, spent most of her life learning how to perform her gender not only from her British parents but also from the socialization she received from being a part of various institutions in the United States. She also has a background in feminist studies and understands the subtleties of women's oppression.

As an overview, this essay will first explain that the status of women, as described in Western feminist literature, is largely one of oppression. Second, the essay will show, with documented evidence, how women's status in pre-liberation Chinese history also was largely one of oppression. Actual poster images from the pre-liberation period will be used to illustrate the oppressed position of women. Third, the essay will explicate the post-liberation rhetoric of "women's emancipation" and illustrate how this rhetoric is visually reflected in propaganda posters of this period in Chinese history. Finally, the essay will explain why women's emancipation, as depicted in post-liberation poster images, was indeed emancipation of an oppressive core or *insidious oppression*.

THE OPPRESSED POSITION OF WOMEN IN PRE-LIBERATION CHINESE HISTORY

Women's position in pre-liberation Chinese history consisted largely of obedience, obeisance, passivity, seclusion, and instrumentality, a condition worse than women's overall status globally. Men were considered the superior sex, and women existed for men's needs and enjoyment; women's purpose was to reproduce sons, so that the father's family name did not perish.

A virtuous and properly bred woman was expected to adhere to an elaborate set of Confucian precepts and disciplines. Among these precepts and disciplines were "The Three Obediences" and "The Four Virtues," as catalogued in *Nu er Jing* (cited in Headland, 1914, pp. 69–80), or the *Bible for the Daughter*. "The Three Obediences" were (1) the obedience to the authorities of father and elder brothers when the woman was young (2) the obedience to the authority of husband when the woman was married, and (3) the obedience to the authority of sons when the woman was widowed. "The Four Virtues" were (1) that a woman should know her place in the universe and behave in total compliance with the time-honored ethical codes (2) that she should be reticent in words, taking care not to chatter too much and bore others (3) that she must be clean of person and habits and adorn herself for the purpose of pleasing the opposite sex, and (4) that she should not shirk her household duties.

According to *Nu Jie* (Precepts for Woman), the qualitative difference between male and female lies in the very different but complementary virtues of firmness and flexibility. *Nu Jie* stipulates that a woman should be subservient, yielding, timid, reticent, respectful, and selflessly caring to others. Her husband is the "Heaven," and thus she should revere him and endure his reproach: "Heaven is unalterable; it cannot be set aside," and "if the wife does not serve her husband, the rule of propriety will be destroyed" (*Nu Jie*, p. 8). *Lie Nu Zhuan* (or *Biographies of Filial Women*. Cited in Asycough, 1937) enumerates the stories of virtuous and exemplary women whom every woman should emulate. Enumerated in *Lie Nu Zhuan* were women who were "far-sighted" and "benevolent" in service, who would sooner meet death than dishonor their husbands, and whose devotion to "womanly duty" was above reproach and worthy of emulation. The preface of *Lie Nu Zhuan* reads, "The wife leans on the man. Gentle, yielding, she eagerly listens to the words of others. She has the nature and emotions of those who serve others and controls her person in the way of chastity" (Asycough, 1937, p. 267).

A practice that lasted for thousands of years in Chinese history and epitomized the secondary and oppressed position of women was footbinding. The purpose was the "gradual confinement and silencing of the female body" (Croll, 1995, p. 20). From a very early age (7–8 years old), a girl's feet were tightly bound with long bandages for over a year. The feet had no space in which to grow. Consequently, the arch was broken, and the toes were bent permanently. Because of the great difficulty of walking on tiny feet, the practice of binding feet effectively crippled women's physical mobility and their mental aspirations for the external world and "manly affairs." This practice confined

women to the single choice of household duties, such as serving the daily needs
of their husbands and bearing and rearing children, especially sons (Pruitt,
1967).

From birth, the inequality between men and women or between boys and
girls was vividly reflected in the unequal perceptions of sons and daughters.
Such perceptions were recorded in *Shi Jing* or *Book of Poetry,* a text depicting social life in ancient China:

> When a son is born
> Let him sleep on the bed,
> Clothe him with fine clothes.
> And give him jade to play with.
> How lordly his cry is!
> May he grow up to wear crimson
> And be the lord of the clan and the tribe.
> When a daughter is born,
> Let her sleep on the ground,
> Wrap her in common wrappings,
> And give her broken tiles for playthings.
> May she have no faults, no merits of her own,
> May she well attend to food and wine,
> And bring no discredit to her parents.

Inculcated with Confucian precepts that were endorsed and reinforced in
social practice, women before the Chinese liberation in 1949 were largely objectified as instruments for practical purposes designed by men. Women were
instruments for bearing children, or rather, sons. Women were instruments to
maintain domestic hygiene and order. Women were instruments to serve all
the men in the household, the father, the husband, and the son. And, no less
important, women were instruments for men's visual and physical pleasure.
Later on, when the influence of Western commerce infiltrated and increased
in China, women became instruments to promote the sale of commercial
products, many of which were purely for men's consumption.

The secondary position of women—a position characterized by submission, passivity, obedience, obeisance, and instrumentality—was reflected in
the portrayal of women in pre-liberation poster images. Figure 12.1 is a poster
advertisement for cigarettes in the 1930s. The "lady" in the image is juxtaposed with a houseplant, implying that women served a similar function as
did the houseplants. The function was to give fragrance and be decorative, as
indicated by the advertising message: "wafting fragrance of the orchid and
the cigarettes and, probably, of the beautiful lady." Although cigarettes were
almost exclusively for men's consumption in traditional Chinese culture, the

promotional image on the cigarette packages was that of women. The brand name for the cigarette was "Beauty" (as signified by the large Chinese words in the poster image), beauty as represented by the beautiful woman, who, like the cigarette, was for men's consumption.

Figure 12.2 also dates from the 1930s. The woman in the advertisement is portrayed as seductive bait. The brand name of the soap, as indicated in the large Chinese words, was "Medicinal Soap for Virility," targeting men as potential consumers. The function of the medicinal soap is reified through the image of the woman.

In summary, similar to women's status elsewhere, as documented in much feminist literature, women in pre-liberation Chinese history were oppressed and forced into obedience, obeisance, passivity, seclusion, and instrumentality. Women existed for the purpose of men, who were considered the superior sex.

WOMEN'S EMANCIPATION AS DEPICTED IN POST-LIBERATION CHINESE POSTERS

The Liberation of China in 1949 greatly changed women's situation. Maoist culture advocated egalitarianism between men and women. Mao himself claimed, "Women hold up half of the sky. . . . Times have changed. Women can do the same as men" (pp. 29–30). According to Harriet Evans (1999), since the Party's early years, the Chinese Communist Party defined the goals of the women's movement in classical Marxist-Leninist terms. That is, the liberation of women lay in their participation in the revolution against feudalism and imperialism and in their contribution to the liberation of the people as a whole. Later an editorial in the *New China* publication in Yan'an defined women's liberation in even more comprehensive terms, to include participation in all movements that benefited the state and the nation.[1] Thus, immediately after the Liberation in 1949, when the Chinese Communist Party consolidated its state power, the official approach to "women's liberation" had shifted to emphasize women's equal entry into the public sphere of production and labor (Evans, 1999). Deng Yingchao, chair of the All China Women's Federation, commented in 1953, "Ten years of practice has proven that mobilizing the masses of women to participate in production is the basic key to improving equality between men and women and to achieving the thorough liberation of women" (p. 381).

Because of prevalent efforts in ideological propaganda, the prominence of women in various aspects of national life was greatly promoted. More pertinent to this study, as indicated by Clunas (1999), the Maoist rhetoric of

"Women can hold up half of the sky" is definitely reified in post-liberation propaganda posters, especially those created during the Cultural Revolution (1966–1976). This section of the chapter illustrates that women's emancipation is depicted in four different ways in the post-liberation Chinese posters. First, many posters portray women as engaged in work that traditional Chinese mentality would associate only with men. Second, post-liberation Chinese posters frequently delineate women as equal participants in national life. Third, women are given a new prominence that often dominates the holistic composition of the poster images. Finally, women are occasionally pictured as equal to men in authority.

First, many posters show women engaged in "men's" work, which is a departure from traditional Chinese mentality. Figure 12.3 is an illustration of the "Iron Girl Brigade" cultivated by Chen Yonggui, the leader of the village of Dazhai, which was then promulgated as the national paragon for agricultural production. With Chen standing in the center, the "Iron Girls" are shown happily engaged in the masculine work of harnessing and terracing the mountains through detonation, so that the infertile mountainous land could be transformed into arable, productive, terraced soil. The gender of the subjects in the poster is discernible not only from hairstyles and brightly colored clothing, but also from the observation of one girl covering her ears, an indication of the stereotypical "feminine" fear of loud explosive sounds. Under the heroic inspiration of the "Iron Girl Brigade," millions of "imitation boys" (*jia xiaozi*) and "iron women" (*tie nuren*) emerged during that time to promote agricultural production (Wen & Liang, 1977).

In Figures 12.3, 12.6, 12.12, 12.16, and 12.18 women are shown either engaging in "masculine" work or operating machinery that conventionally only men would maneuver. For instance, in Figure 12.18, a woman is depicted pushing the wheelbarrow, which is generally perceived as heavy manual work expected to be done exclusively by men.

In Chinese mentality before the liberation, women were rarely associated with the military. The only exception was perhaps *Mulan* in ancient Chinese history (the same Mulan as in the Disney production). She joined the army out of a filial duty so that her old father would not have to be enlisted. She could do this only by disguising herself as a man, knowing that she risked being beheaded because of this dishonesty to the king. Yet in Figure 12.4, women are portrayed as militia soldiers and no longer need to disguise themselves as men. Furthermore, no men are seen in this image; women are the only players on the "stage." The portrayal of these women standing on huge protruding rocks is symbolic and significant. The protruding rock enhances the three women in the holistic composition of the poster image. Common associations attached to the image of rock (such as firmness, will power, and strength) are almost antithetical to those traditionally delegated to femininity (such as gentleness, softness, and weakness). The portrayal of women in this poster not only gives prominence and a new image to women, but also romanticizes the idea of women as tough soldiers. The Chinese title of the picture literally means "aurora over the sea," metaphorically indicating that women may have conquered a strong force, and therefore providing them with a sense of enlightenment and empowerment. Several scenes contribute to this romanticized picture: the waves crashing on the shore, the lone sailboat cruising on the horizon, the sea birds hovering against the background of the vast sea, and the sunset aurora shining in the background. In its visual composition this poster presents women in a new, enlarged, centralized, and romantic image.

Second, post-liberation Chinese posters frequently portray women as equal participants in national life. This equal participation is fully signified in the title of Figure 12.5, "Share the Labor and Share the Fruit." All of the women as portrayed in this poster are entitled to "Labor," the labor to build the new national life in the socialist New China. Logically, they are also entitled to sharing the "Fruit" from the "Labor." They become entitled to new rights. Interestingly, women in this poster, as seen by their different ethnic clothes, are from all Chinese minority nationalities. This seems to intend a broader representation of women of more backgrounds. Their jubilant dancing around the tree conspicuously delineates the new status of women and a new unity among them. The image in this poster, like that in Figure 12.4, is also highly romanticized. These women's imagination for a new life will fly on the wings of birds, over the vast expanse of the fields, into the infinite future beyond the horizon. Ready to share the fruits from their labor, the women wear euphoric smiles on their faces and exude a sense of empowerment, entitlement, and contribution.

In Figure 12.6, the "New Chinese Woman" is seen as a constructor, building the edifice of the socialist New China. Traditionally, women were almost never perceived as builders nor given the opportunity to do this type of work. The term and image of construction are fraught with symbolic implication. The women are depicted as contributors, builders, and thus as important participants in the national life. Both the title of the poster ("New Chinese Women") and the name of the publisher ("New Chinese Women Association") connote a revolutionary redefinition of women.

Third, women not only enjoy equal participation in national life and socialist construction, but they are also given a new prominence that often dominates the holistic composition of the poster images. For instance, women's unprecedented achievements in world sports competition helped dramatically to promote women's prominence in the national mosaic. Figure 12.7 portrays the former Chinese women's volleyball team who won the world championship consecutively for many years. Their victories almost became iconic of the athletic clout of China in the world, as visually represented in the word "China" printed on their clothes. Lang Ping, the captain of the women's volleyball team, is depicted in a much larger size and thus given special attention.

Women in Figure 12.8 are seen engaged in the glamorous profession of mass broadcasting, which confers popularity, fame, and even charisma. Chinese women employed in this kind of profession would have been inconceivable in the conventional mentality. The young woman in Figure 12.9 is again portrayed as larger-than-life, dwarfing the background of the rural China. Her exaggerated size, once again, signals the new prominence for women as important participants in the national life.

Finally, besides their new roles, new participation, and new prominence, women are frequently, though not always, portrayed as equal to men in authority. In Figure 12.10, the woman is the larger-than-life heroic leader of the crowd, whom she is motivating, inspiring, and directing. In Figure 12.11, women are shown as national models, standing on the Tiananmen Rostrum where Mao declared the founding of the People's Republic of China in 1949.

After the liberation in 1949, March 3rd was designated as "the Women's Day." The women in Figure 12.12 are building the "Women's Day Channel," a channel of their own.[2] In this sense, women are becoming new molders of the face of the New Socialist China in their own right. Women were not only given equality in terms of participation in the national life, they were also given equality as participants in the "ruling class" of the "proletariat." Armed with the ideological weapon of Mao Zedong thought (as indicated by the *Selected Works of Mao Zedong* held in her hand) and the physical weapon of the bayonet, women in Figure 12.13 constitute half of the members of the ruling class of the proletariat dictatorship.

In short, depiction of women in post-liberation Chinese posters helps promote the prominence and emancipation of women.[3] The posters attempt to achieve this through the pervasiveness of visual images of women and through illustrating women as engaged in work traditionally associated only with men.[4]

THE OPPRESSION IN WOMEN'S EMANCIPATION
AS DEPICTED IN POST-LIBERATION CHINESE POSTERS

Post-liberation posters display women engaging in work previously done by men, creating a perception of total equality for women. Although the poster images show women in these roles, the underlying messages are both am-

biguous and contradictory. In a number of posters we see an illusion of emancipation under a black cloud of oppression. In this section we deconstruct and
analyze the posters from a feminist perspective, noting any incongruous messages concerning women's status contained in these texts.

We tack back and forth from feminist and gender theory to the ways in
which these notions apply to the posters. As a framework for our analysis and
interpretation, we rely on four of the five faces of oppression articulated by
Young (1990a). These include *exploitation, marginalization, powerlessness*,
and *cultural imperialism*. We did not include the fifth face, *violence*, because
we did not discover examples of it in our analysis.

The first face of oppression, *exploitation*, takes place when members of
one social group—typically women and people of color—work exclusively to
benefit others. Women work in jobs where they must depend on their em-
ployers, take orders, and receive minimal, if any, recognition or autonomy in
return for their services. In most cases, women who are exploited often work
in menial jobs and are compensated with low wages for the expenditure of effort, time, and energy. Second, the exclusion of an entire category of individuals from participation in various forms of social life results in *marginalization*, or "the deprivation of cultural, practical, and institutionalized conditions
for exercising capacities in a context of recognition and interaction" (Young,
1990a, p. 53). Third, some individuals feel a sense of *powerlessness* when social divisions bisect a culture into "middle class" (i.e., professionals) and the
"working class" (i.e., nonprofessionals). Professionals garner authority, autonomy, recognition, and respect, whereas nonprofessionals lack the status,
authority, knowledge, and capacity to make decisions that affect their lives.
Cultural imperialism is the fourth, and last, face that we use to characterize
oppression. Young points out, "To experience cultural imperialism means to
experience how the dominant meanings of a society render the particular perspective of one's own group invisible at the same time as they mark it out as
Other" (pp. 58–59). Furthermore, she argues that the wide dissemination of
the cultural expressions of the dominant group ensues because of the array of
accessible media and institutions that promote the dominant values, ideals,
and behavioral norms. These norms and expectations are prescribed, adopted,
and ultimately considered the standard of behavior for the entire population
within a culture and permeate all aspects of the culture.

The posters serve as a barometer to assess the position of women in China
as one inferior to that of men. We refer to the phenomenon of oppression that
is hidden behind an illusion of freedom as *insidious oppression* because it is
not obtrusive or blatant. Admittedly, Chinese women may have increased their
status because they were given the opportunity to work in agriculture or the
military. However, in spite of the vocational changes, some posters illustrate

the maintenance of the status quo because women did not achieve their full human and individual rights. Masked behind the emancipatory façade in the images in the posters is a reality that is more oppressive than liberating.

Private Sphere—Family and Domestic Life

Exploitation of women takes place in the private sphere because the responsibilities demanded of them in this domain often benefit others. Thus, women's ambitions, needs, goals, and interests become secondary, and must be sidelined. Taking on the responsibilities of the home and child rearing might offer mothers and wives feelings of satisfaction; nonetheless, the underlying assumption is that a woman's obligations in the private sphere come first. In the posters, women appear to be independent as they are situated in work environments formerly reserved for males; meanwhile, the family and the domestic environment are exclusively associated with women. Figure 12.14 provides evidence for this claim. We observe a woman at work while, at the same time, she tends to the needs of the child. Moreover, the props in the room, for example, the needlework and quilt, are customarily identified with women's interests. Cultural practices assume that women will take care of the children, despite the fact that they also participate in the labor market.

A sense of powerlessness might be part of a woman's experience of oppression when she remains in the home. Women do not receive financial remuneration for any work done in the private sphere and rarely receive recognition or rewards for their efforts. In addition, women lack independence because they often must depend on men for economic resources and take orders from their husbands, or even their children. Typically, men's work is more valued and honored than work done by women, whether inside or outside the domestic sphere.

Women may feel powerless when they work in the home because they would be deemed nonprofessionals rather than professional. Moreover, they do not play an integral role in the business or legal community and cannot be a part of making decisions that would significantly affect their lives. They might even feel that they are under "house arrest" because they have few other options available and must stay close to home. Taking orders from a patriarchal husband or demanding children undermines women's positions of authority and autonomy. Communicating exclusively with young children all day and not developing interpersonal relationships with adults might cause women to feel powerless and isolated physically, emotionally, mentally, and socially. As an example, in Figure 12.14, we do not see any other adults with this woman. This alienation, isolation, and lack of recognition or worth can negatively affect a woman's self-esteem.

Public Sphere—The Business World

As explained previously, confinement of women in the private sphere of family and housework represents oppression of women. Yet women's participation in the public sphere (e.g., the workforce, leadership and authority), as depicted in the posters, does not reflect genuine liberation either. Rarely are women portrayed as leaders or in positions of authority. Women seem to obtain leadership and authority only through defeminization.

In Figure 12.3, Chen Yonggui, the only male character in the poster, is placed in the center. His height and stature are larger than the other figures in the poster, giving the impression that he is the leader and holds the position of authority. Conversely, the women are marginalized, standing at the outskirts of the picture and surrounding Chen.

The woman in Figure 12.10 is presented as a leader, visible in her exaggerated size and extended arm, a typical Maoist gesture. Although she has gained some authority as a leader, the image of this woman is still masculinized. For instance, the clothes she wears are drab and lusterless. Her physical features are rather masculine: she has a flat chest, broad large musculature, and big, strong hands. What gives the woman the leadership position is not her femininity but her transformation through masculinization. The display of any characteristics associated with females or being feminine deprives a woman of her authority. The woman in the foreground of Figure 12.15 is relatively feminized, as can be seen in her hairstyle and bright red clothes (visible in the original color image). The leaders in this poster image are apparently the young man and the old man behind him. The leadership position of the young man is symbolized by his visual prominence, large stature, and left arm extended forcefully upward. Likewise, he holds tightly in his right hand a book that appears to be Mao's *Selected Works*—a symbol of leadership. The leadership of the old man is symbolized in his old age (a traditional indicator of authority in the case of men) and his towel hat (iconic of Chen Younggui), as well as by his visual prominence.

The presentation of women participating in the public sphere mirrors several faces of oppression as explained by Young (1990a). First is the face of marginalization. Women are allowed to participate only at the periphery of the public sphere, not occupying significant positions of leadership and authority. Powerlessness is the second face of oppression. Because of women's inability to acquire positions of senior managers and executives, women suffer from a sense of powerlessness. Marginalization is the third face of oppression, which contributes to the abuse of women. As an example, in numerous cases in both Chinese and Western history, leaders reap disproportionately greater rewards not from their actual contribution, but from supervising and controlling others, namely women. This is exploitation.

Education and Creative Expression

During the Cultural Revolution, the campaign to "go up to the mountains and down to the villages" forced women away from schools, colleges, and universities and repositioned them into physical labor in the fields. This practice deprived women of access to educational resources that promote women's liberation (e.g., books containing Western feminist ideas, intellectual discussion, and publication).

Figure 12.9 romanticizes and glorifies the image of the "educated youth going up to the mountain and down to the villages." The Chinese title of the poster says, "After graduation, return to the countryside to make revolution and vow to become a generation of new peasants." The viewer sees a scene of idyllic serenity and empowering pride in the face of the character; nevertheless, several of Young's faces of oppression are hidden under the surface.

One face of oppression hidden in the poster is powerlessness. Young explains that the social distinctions between professionals and nonprofessionals usually give a sense of powerlessness to nonprofessionals. Despite large-scale propaganda, peasants have not been professionals in any period of Chinese history. Some may even claim that peasants occupy one of the lowest rungs on the Chinese social ladder. The pledge or theme of "going up to the mountains and down to the villages" largely confines the participants to the manual work of agriculture and the low status of the working class. This lower socioeconomic class position not only diminishes the chance of recognition for their labors, but also limits their access to institutions for intellectual development or to privileges afforded to members of a higher class.

The second hidden face of oppression is cultural imperialism. When the educated youth leave educational institutions, important support for women's emancipation may be gone. Consequently, this facilitates the voice and ideology of the ruling class to dominate the culture. Reality is no longer defined by a diversity of voices but by a single dominant voice. This is cultural imperialism.

There is another facet to the face of cultural imperialism. The campaign of "going up to the mountains and down to the villages" foregrounds one understanding of national prosperity and obscures others. That is, the emphasis on agricultural and industrial development creates a situation in which the intellectual and moral sinew of the nation atrophies. One explanation for this situation may be that agrarian and industrial development is perhaps more conspicuous than intellectual or moral development and thus more easily grants credit to the leader. Another explanation may be that a nation of individuals who are not intellectually or morally developed is more vulnerable to dictatorial control. Whatever the underlying reasons or intentions, the accentuation of one form of national prosperity over other forms also represents cultural imperialism.

Figure 12.1

Figure 12.2

Figure 12.3

Figure 12.4

Figure 12.5

Figure 12.6

Figure 12.7

Figure 12.8

Figure 12.9

Figure 12.10

Figure 12.11

Figure 12.12

Figure 12.13

Figure 12.14

Figure 12.15

Figure 12.16

Figure 12.17

到工农兵群众中去 到火热的斗争中去
Go Among the Workers, Peasants and Soldiers and into the Thick of Struggle!
Allons parmi les ouvriers, paysans et soldats! Jetons-nous dans la lutte ardente!   coll. SRt
Unter die Massen der Arbeiter, Bauern und Soldaten gehen, in flammenden Kampf gehen!

Figure 12.18

CONCLUSION

The portrayal of women in post-liberation Chinese propaganda posters presents an interesting and unique paradox. This display of images forms a contrast between women's generally oppressed status, as explained in feminist literature, and with women's status in pre-liberation China. These posters seem to promote women's prominence in national life, to portray them as "women of the New China" disburdened from their traditional "womanly" duties, and even occasionally to elevate them as figures of authority and leadership. Regardless, the portrayal of women in these posters is oppressive. The depicted liberation of women occurs largely within a masculine framework, and the women characters continue to be disadvantaged by several of the faces of oppression explicated by Young (1990a). As a result of *insidious oppression*, women have to "walk the tightrope" of balancing myriad factors of femininity and masculinity, whether conventional or imposed. They may gain new importance and access to "manly" occupations, yet they have to undergo a metamorphosis of masculinization. Moreover, while they may engage in new types of work, they still need to maintain a feminine image incompatible with physical exertion.

We contend that the kind of oppression that lies behind a façade of emancipation represents a more deleterious and covert form of oppression. We also advocate that *insidious oppression* via the rhetoric of images is "doubly dangerous" due to the power of audient immediacy of the images. We invite further scholarly research not only to *insidious oppression* in visual depiction, but also to the *insidious oppression* latent in different contexts of human activity and communication.

NOTES

1. Research Department of the All China Women's Federation on the history of the women's movement. (1986). *Materials on the history of the Chinese women's movement*. Beijing: People's Press.

2. Women's Association of Shaanbei Province. (1982). Commemorate international women's day and widely develop the women's movement. In Selected materials on the women's movement in the Shaan-Gan-Ning border region. Xi'an: Women's Association of Shaanbei Province.

3. Most of the poster images used in this essay were originally in color. Because of practical constraints in publication, they can only appear as black and white images in this book.

4. All of the poster images in this essay are used with permission from their sources. In the case of Minick & Ping, the authors have made repeated and continued efforts to search for their contact information. The efforts were not very fruitful because of unavailability of their contact information from their book publisher. We remain indebted to all the sources of the poster images.

REFERENCES

Asycough, F. (1937). *Chinese women yesterday and today*. Boston: Houghton Mifflin.

Bureau of Labor Statistics. (1992). S*tatistical Abstract of the United States, 1992*. Washington, DC: U.S. Department of Commerce.

Clunas, C. (1999). Souvenirs of Beijing: Authority and subjectivity in art historical memory. In H. Evans & S. Donald (Eds.), *Picturing power in the People's Republic of China: Posters of the Cultural Revolution* (pp. 47–62). New York: Rowman & Littlefield.

Croll, E. (1995). *Changing identities of Chinese women: Rhetoric, experience and self-perception in twentieth-century China*. Hong Kong: Hong Kong University Press.

Deng, Y. C. (1953). Work report at the Second National Congress of Chinese Women, 10 April 1953. In *Forty years of the All China Women's Federation*. Beijing: Chinese Women's Press.

Evans, H (1999). "Comrade sisters": Gendered bodies and spaces. In H. Evans & S. Donald (Eds.), *Picturing power in the People's Republic of China: Posters of the Cultural Revolution* (pp. 63–78). New York: Rowman & Littlefield.

Jameson, F. (1988). *Eloquence in an electronic age*. New York: Oxford University Press.

Lee, W. S. (1998). In the names of Chinese women. *Quarterly Journal of Speech, 84*, 283–302.

Lu, X. A. (2001). Dazhai: Imagistic rhetoric as a cultural instrument. *American Communication Journal 5.1*. [Available online at http://www.acjournal.org].

Nu er Jing, Sections IV and V, see Headland, I. T. (1914). *Home life in China today*. London.

Nu Jie, Chapter 3, see Headland, I.T. (1914). *Home life in China today*. London.

Olson, L. C. (1983). Portraits in praise of a people: A rhetorical analysis of Norman Rockwell's icons in Franklin D. Roosevelt's "Four Freedoms" campaign. *Quarterly Journal of Speech, 69,* 15–24.

Pharr, S. (1993). Homophobia: A weapon of sexism.

Pruitt, I. (1967). *Daughter of Han: The autobiography of a Chinese working woman* (as told to her by Ning Lao Tai-tai). Stanford, CA: Stanford University Press.

Shi Jing, quoted in *North China Herald*, Shanghai, 10 February 1931.

Wen, Y. & Liang, H. (1977). *Dazhai: The red banner*. Peking, China: Foreign Languages Press.

Young, I. (1990a). *Justice and the politics of difference*. Princeton, NJ: Princeton Univ. Press.

SOURCES OF POSTER IMAGES

Figures 1, 2, 4, 5, and 6: Minick, S. & Ping, J. (1990). *Chinese graphic design in the 20th century*. New York: Van Nostrand Reinhold. Copyright held by writers.

Figures 3, 7, 10, 11, and 14-18: IISH Stefan R. Landsberger Collection (http://www.iisg.nl/~landsberger/).

Figure 8, 9, 12, and 13: the Chinese Poster Collection, Centre for the Study of Democracy, University of Westminster.

Part Three

PORTRAYALS OF POLITICAL ACTIVISM

Chapter Thirteen

Butterflies and Boobs: (Or, How to Manufacture an Environmental Pin-Up Girl)

Tina Richardson & Audrey Vanderford

Julia "Butterfly" Hill and Erin Brockovich are the most widely known female environmental activists in contemporary American popular culture, propelled into fame in no small part by the mass marketing of their respective stories: the autobiography *The Legacy of Luna* and the movie *Erin Brockovich*. Both women have received a flurry of media coverage, elevating them from "grassroots activist" to "celebrity" status. As a result, their stories and images have become the exclusive popular culture representations of women in the environmental movement. While their stories appear to present a critique of contemporary practices of environmental devastation, they are in fact far less radical than they appear. Indeed, we argue that Hill and Brockovich serve as "environmental pin-up girls," images of sexual titillation, not social transformation, manufactured and promoted by dominant ideological forces, more regressive than radical.

Within the context of a 246-page book, a 212-minute movie, the tree is saved, the case is closed, and in both instances, the check delivered. Through this structure the narratives of Julia "Butterfly" Hill and Erin Brockovich present the successful resolution of environmental problems through appeals to established power structures. The environmental problems they dramatize are isolated occurrences with no connection to more systemic cultural practices and values. As a result, the corporate interests that profit from environmental degradation remain intact and uninterrogated.

Effectively neutralizing other types of environmental narratives, these stories betray the ongoing suffering of those affected by toxic environmental contamination and the continued widespread practice of "resource" extraction. Presented as potential feminist narratives emerging from the environmental movement, these narratives are yet another means of trivializing the important work of women: in this case the work of women in environmental and environmental justice groups. In the course of this essay we will consider why these women and their narratives have gained access to dominant cultural image making apparatuses and examine what is at stake in the creation of Julia "Butterfly" Hill and Erin Brockovich as environmental pin-up girls.

Environmentalists and environmental sympathizers may well question a critique of any story that brings environmental issues to the forefront of dominant discourse; yet our purpose in examining the role of these women and their narratives developed from the observation that the gains they make in popular environmental awareness are far outweighed by the manner in which they reify established power relations among gender, the environment, and capitalist interests. The manner in which these stories are presented—the methods by which these narratives are constructed, the appearance and actions of the heroines placed at their center, and the location of the environmental issue at each story's fringe—all combine to eradicate any critical discussion of "cause" from the environmental discourse they evoke.

ERIN BROCKOVICH

The major Hollywood film production *Erin Brockovich* swept into mainstream culture the real life story of an uneducated, working class, foulmouthed, sleazily dressed, twice divorced, single mother of three who, through intuition and individual effort, investigates the curious presence of medical records in the file of a client involved in a *pro bono* real estate case. This case, taken on by the law firm at which Brockovich has pushed her way into employment, becomes an investigation into the connection between environmental contamination and human health problems in the community of Hinkley, California. Ironically, the film *Erin Brockovich*—named for the central female character around which the narrative revolves—is the horrific true story of mega-corporation Pacific, Gas, and Electric's (PG&E) willful poisoning of an entire community. In the film's rendering of this story the suffering of the citizens of Hinkley, California, becomes the emotional backdrop for the center stage focus on the title character. Marginally sympathetic as a social underdog, Brockovich appeals to the all-powerful myths of American individualism by successfully making her way in a world that has thus far excluded her. Embodying the ideals of hard work and commitment, Brockovich assembles the largest toxic tort case ever settled in the United States. However, the film's focus on Brockovich and her process of finding, investigating, and pursuing this case to its economic "windfall" conclusion—a windfall that most greatly benefits Brockovich and the law firm for which she works—

serves to marginalize the experience of the residents of Hinkley. The toxic contamination of the Hinkley watershed and the resulting pain, suffering, and deaths of its citizenry are incidental to the plot of the film. Instead, this real life tragedy functions within the narrative as a device to move the triumphant story of the film's heroine, Erin Brockovich, forward.

JULIA "BUTTERFLY" HILL

The narrative of Julia "Butterfly" Hill has a similarly self-serving relationship to the community out of which it emerges. For nearly two decades, radical environmental groups such as Earth First! have utilized treesits to both protest and prevent the clearcutting of old growth forests. Perched in platforms a hundred feet or more above the ground, treesitters risk their own physical safety to protect that of the trees. Julia "Butterfly" Hill, undoubtedly the world's best known treesitter, spent two years atop Luna, a thousand-year-old redwood in Humboldt County, California, in imminent danger of being logged. Her brave and tenacious act drew immense media attention; however, at least as much coverage was granted to Hill and her hygiene habits as to the unsustainable logging practices that spurred treesitters to this form of direct action in the first place. After 783 days in the tree, Hill and her lawyers made a deal with Pacific Lumber, agreeing to pay the company a $50,000 "fine" in exchange for the preservation of Luna and a surrounding twenty-foot buffer zone of trees. Many within the radical environmental movement felt as though she had betrayed them, not only by compromising with a logging company infamous for its rapacious practices, but by agreeing to a price tag on an invaluable ancient redwood. Luna was saved, but whole forests of other trees continue to be felled. However, dissent and criticism from within the movement have not hampered Hill's success. Her autobiography *The Legacy of Luna* is as much a personal tale of spiritual enlightenment as it is a story of political activism. On store shelves a mere four months after her descent, *The Legacy of Luna* documents Hill's action and eventual triumph; yet the community of activists that supported her during her two years in Luna is hardly mentioned. Furthermore, the inhabitants of Stafford, the community economically dependent upon logging the forest in which Luna was located, appears only in the prologue: absent from the body of Hill's narrative, the community is reduced from characters to setting. Since her descent, Hill has traveled extensively, speaking about her time in Luna. Adopting a public persona more akin to a motivational speaker than a radical activist, Hill exalts love, "connectedness," and personal growth over political critique and direct action.

CELEBRITY

On the surface, the stories of Erin Brockovich and Julia "Butterfly" Hill can be lauded for generating media attention for their respective causes—the toxic contamination of watersheds and the destruction of the ancient forests. However, in both of these stories, that media attention is narrowly focused on the women themselves, elevating them to celebrity status at the expense of the larger radical environmental and environmental justice movements from which the stories emerge. Indeed, the celebrity of Julia "Butterfly" Hill and Erin Brockovich far exceeds the press coverage that environmentalism usually receives—for either the causes or for the individuals working in them. Hill and Brockovich have appeared in publications beyond the typical liberal fare known to report on "green" politics; in fact, one would be hard-pressed to name a mainstream news or news-entertainment source that has not covered one or both stories. From *Time* to *Rolling Stone*, from *The Today Show* to *Oprah*, these women have become the faces of environmental activism. Despite the potentially radical claims Hill and Brockovich appear to espouse—an end to clearcutting and toxic pollution—these women have been applauded by mainstream organizations. Hill was named *Good Housekeeping* magazine's Woman of the Year; Brockovich was presented with the Association of Trial Lawyers of America's "Champion of Justice" award; and at the 2000 Academy Awards ceremony, Julia Roberts won the Best Actress Oscar for her title role in the movie *Erin Brockovich*. The prominence of these stories in popular American culture is striking. Typically, mainstream media organizations condemn radical environmentalists as "ecoterrorists" and belittle women working in the environmental justice movement as "angry housewives" or "hysterical mothers"; Julia "Butterfly" Hill and Erin Brockovich have sidestepped these charges and have instead been embraced and promoted.

What we know of these women is based almost exclusively on what is filtered through mass media, through writers, directors, and publicists. It becomes difficult then to draw a clear distinction between the individual and the representation, between the book, the movie, and the actual woman. As the movie promotions declare, Julia Roberts "is" Erin Brockovich. The final credits of the film reveal that the "real" Erin Brockovich appears in a cameo role as a waitress; yet even the actress Erin Brockovich is not Erin Brockovich—according to the credits she is Erin Brockovich-Ellis. Erin Brockovich no longer exists as a real person, but only as a media construction. We should not be surprised. Post-structuralism challenges the notion of an "authentic" story; we cannot know the "real" Erin Brockovich or Julia "Butterfly" Hill. Whether through a screenplay or an autobiography, both women and both women's stories are to some extent fabrications, constructed, narrated, filmed, edited, and promoted in such a way that blurs fact and fiction, Humboldt, Hinkley, New York, and Hollywood. The political implications of this transposition were apparent at the Academy Awards when Julia Roberts neglected to mention the environmental justice movement, the residents of Hinkley, or even Erin Brockovich in her acceptance speech. Brockovich's own struggle for financial survival as well as the struggles of numerous others to end toxic contamination and hold corporations accountable for their reckless, polluting practices were out-performed, so to speak, by the glitz, the glamour, the gown, the grin.

It is perhaps no coincidence that both of these stories emerge from California, hub of American cultural influence. Unlike environmental struggles that occur in other locations, proximity to established celebrities aided both women in gaining media attention and eventually their own star status. As Hill notes in her autobiography, musicians Bonnie Raitt, Joan Baez, and Mickey Hart of the Grateful Dead, as well as actor Woody Harrelson, all visited her in Luna, lending their own fame to her cause. Similarly, Brockovich was approached about the movie deal after her chiropractor told her story to another client, the wife of movie producer Michael Shomberg. Presented to the public by Harper Collins and by Universal Pictures, these stories are products of a particular image-manufacturing apparatus, better known for promoting dominant values than social transformation.

ENVIRONMENTAL RACISM

Certain characteristics of these women and their stories make them particularly attractive to this apparatus; without doubt these are the characteristics that propelled Hill and Brockovich to the status of environmental pin-up girls in American culture. Most obviously, Hill and Brockovich are both white women. While the environmental movement is largely made up of middle class white folks (creating some level of justification for Hill as a representative image) the environmental justice movement is not. The environmental justice movement can be defined as the intersection where issues of race, class, and environment meet. It is the convergence of the social justice movement with environmental concerns. Environmental justice draws a connection between the health of humanity and the health of the planet by examining the policies and practices that are being applied to each. These policies and practices are often the result of what Benjamin J. Chavis, Jr. (1993) describes as environmental racism in his introduction to Robert Bullard's environmental justice anthology, *Confronting Environmental Racism: Voices from the Grassroots*.

Environmental racism is racial discrimination in environmental policymaking. It is racial discrimination in the enforcement of regulations and laws. It is racial discrimination in the deliberate targeting of communities of color for toxic waste disposal and the siting of polluting industries. It is racial discrimination in the official sanctioning of the life-threatening presence of poisons and pollutants in communities of color. And, it is racial discrimination in the history of excluding people of color from the mainstream environmental groups, decision making boards, commissions and regulatory bodies (p. 3).

It is therefore noteworthy that the story that has generated such widespread attention in popular culture to issues of environmental justice portrays a white woman as its central character. Additionally, the story takes place in a white community: the race issue is effectively erased from any environmental justice discussion the film might raise. The dominant status of white America is reinscribed through an environmental narrative that "casts" neither victim nor heroine as a person of color.

One reason communities of color are discriminated against is that they are perceived by governing bodies and polluting industries to lack political agency. This perception extends to low income communities as well, and while white, the communities of Hinkley and Stafford are both working class. In addition, both communities are economically dependent upon the companies engaged in practices of environmental destruction that put the lives of their citizens in danger: Hinkley is dependent upon PG&E, whereas Stafford is dependent upon Pacific Lumber. As a result, neither community is predisposed to "challenge the hand that [feeds] them" (Hill, 2000). In this context the presence of Brockovich and Hill could be read as that of an outside agent pushing a political critique into public dialogue, yet this does not appear to be the motivation underlying the actions of either of the main characters within these narratives.

In spite of their narrative construction as members of marginalized groups, neither of these women's positions emerges organically from community membership, nor do they "adopt" membership by taking direction determined by the community through group process. Instead, each of these women enters her narrative as an isolated individual, and through her efforts—supposedly on behalf of the environment and underrepresented individuals—becomes a powerful member of the dominant group. In this way both Hill and Brockovich function as outsiders; in addition, their use of their positions as outsiders neutralizes the power and empowerment emerging from the work of other women in grassroots activism. Celene Krauss (1993) asserts that "central to feminist theory and practice is the notion of conscious-raising, the reinterpretation of the individual, private experience of oppression as a public, political issue." She goes on to say that "until women have made the connections between . . .their own lives and the larger world of public policies and power that cause them, they cannot act politically" (p. 109). This critical awareness is notably missing from the characters central to both these narratives; as outsiders involved in activism disconnected from their personal experiences, neither Hill nor Brockovich engages in a critique that examines her own subject position or any resulting maginalization. Although *Erin Brockovich* reveals some of the struggles of working class single motherhood, and *The Legacy of Luna* documents some of the issues of those involved in direct action campaigns, such issues are not the subject of either the book or the film. Furthermore, in neither instance do the everyday experiences of those living within the communities affected by environmental degradation gain access to the narrative. The personal is not political in these narratives; instead, the cause becomes a career—a catalyst to membership within the dominant group. The ability of Hill and Brockovich to make this change in their own status is a direct result of their willingness to appeal to heterosexual desires.

SEX APPEAL

This sex appeal is a critical quality to an environmental pin-up girl; no doubt, Hill and Brockovich are attractive women. Before becoming an environmental activist, Hill was a model; Brockovich was a beauty queen. Despite Hill's two years living in a tree, photojournalists always captured her looking clean: no matted hair, no dirty feet. While Hill's fresh, clean, "natural" beauty was captured in many photographic images—one of her first interviews after descending from Luna involved a photo-shoot in Central Park for *Elle Magazine*—the media does not often remark on her appearance in print. However, they invariably do so in regard to Brockovich. Seemingly a useful marketing strategy, the video cover quotes movie reviews that describe Brockovich as "provocative," "revealing," and "miniskirted." In one scene in the movie, Brockovich dons her tiara, explaining to her new (male) lover that she was once Miss Wichita. "A real live fuckin' beauty queen." To Brockovich, the crown signified that she would do something important with her life. Reliving her acceptance speech, she pronounces, "I will devote my entire reign as Miss Wichita to ending world hunger and to the creation of a peaceful earth for every man, woman, and child." This big screen reiteration of Brockovich's self-perception betrays an underlying cultural assumption that external beauty—recognized, acknowledged, and awarded beauty—is what provides the platform from which women can become useful and active participants in the greater global community.

Although both women claim to have found "inner beauty" through their activism, their actions demonstrate that external beauty remains a crucial element of their political persuasiveness[1]. As Nancy Armstrong (1987) argues in *Desire and Domestic Fiction*, this sexual objectification does not render women powerless. On the contrary, these women are able to manipulate those around them to attain political ends by exerting power that is revealed in specifically female ways. Both Hill and Brockovich deploy their beauty in ways that pander to heterosexual desire. For example, while contemplating how to convince loggers of the merits of her position, Hill asks herself,

> . . . how can I get them to let go of their stereotypes of me? Because in their mind, I was a tree-hugging, granola-eating, dirty, dreadlocked hippie environmentalist. They always managed to say this word with such disgust and disdain! As I thought about this one afternoon, I remembered that I still had copies of one of the nicest snapshots ever taken of me, from my dear friend's birthday just three months before I'd come up into the tree. . . . Maybe seeing me made up and dressed in a silk suit and heels would shake up their stereotypes of me! (pp. 69–70)

She proceeds to lower her photograph (with a baggie of granola) to a logger on the ground, encouraging the logger to "consume" the image—and the cereal—and rethink his opinion of her.

"Damn!" the logger exclaims. "You really look like this?"

"Yeah."

"Then what the hell you doing up in a tree?" . . . The loggers joked that I had climbed into a tree simply because I hadn't found the right guy. (p. 71)

Hill insists this exchange made the logger receptive to her on a human level; however, it seems more accurate to say she reached him on a heterosexual level.

The persuasive force of beauty and heterosexuality occurs throughout *Erin Brockovich.* Early in the film Brockovich spends several days visiting town residents, a government agency, and a college campus compiling a preliminary report on PG&E's poisoning of the Hinkley watershed. Upon her return to the law office, she finds that her boss, Ed Masry, has fired her. He later admits he misconstrued her absence from work because she "looks like someone who has a lot of fun." When he recants and rehires her, Masry demands to know how she managed to access files from the Lahonton Regional Water Board. "They're called boobs, Ed," Brockovich replies. Determination and hard work are rendered irrelevant as sex appeal prevails. In a later scene, Brockovich is quizzed about her successful field methods: "How did you do this?" the lawyer stutters. "Well, um, seeing how as I have no brains or legal expertise. . .I just went out there and performed sexual favors. 694 blowjobs in five days. I'm really quite tired," she retorts. Although a tongue-in-cheek response, Brockovich's self-deprecating acknowledgement of her sexual caché somehow becomes an acceptable account of her ability to obtain claimants' agreement to binding arbitration. Furthermore, while the movie shows Brockovich interacting primarily with women and with families, her flippant remark about fellatio implies sexual encounters with men. In this way the film shows the heroine using heterosexuality, even "faking" heterosexuality, as a means to justify her legitimacy within the system.

Undeniably, both these women are very intelligent. Although neither has formal training in the professional field in which her narrative is embedded— either law or sustainable forestry—each manages to present herself as a legitimate expert when necessary. Hill discusses the complex intersection of science and economics as they relate to the devastation of clearcutting; Brockovich demonstrates knowledge of legal processes, as well as health issues. But in scene after scene, both defer to their looks, playing down their intelligence to appeal to men, to heterosexual desire, and to the established structure of gender relations.

Their status as objects of heterosexual consumption is further enhanced by their position as single women. In this way Hill and Brockovich are "available" to both the characters in their stories and to an outside audience. Yet in spite of the cultural acceptance of their manipulation of heterosexual desire to achieve their political ends, some element of punishment exists for this overtly sexual behavior. The threat of violence and particularly sexualized violence appears in both stories. Hill (2000) expresses concern about what Pacific Lumber security forces or loggers might do to her: "[Guards] trained floodlights on the tree, the generators going *grrrr*. They screamed at me, calling me dirty names that I don't even like to think back on. They threatened me" (p. 92). Interestingly for a woman living alone in the woods, Hill does not specifically mention fears of rape until she describes her relationship with a particular security guard: "Kalani's presence kept me from going insane during that period. I was so afraid of what those other men were going to do to me, but every other twelve-hour shift, Kalani would be on duty. If something went down while he was there, I knew I wouldn't be beaten or raped or whatever else the others wanted to do to me" (p. 93).

In *Erin Brockovich*, the overtures of Charles Embry are quite ominous. He approaches Brockovich several times in a manner that she (and the audience) interprets as sexualized. These meetings culminate when, after a long day of getting residents to sign legal documents, Brockovich stops at a bar. Embry is there, and as he sidles close to her at the bar, the super-confident Brockovich is visibly uncomfortable. His remarks begin in a way that can only be interpreted as threatening: "I'm watching you. I have my eye on you. Saw you talking to everybody, writing down a lot of stuff. When I saw you, I said to myself, 'I really like that girl.' . . . I feel like I can talk to you. Like you're the type of person I can say anything to." As Brockovich starts to leave the bar to escape this unwanted sexual attention, Embry grabs her arm. "Would it be important if I told you that when I worked at the Hinkley plant I destroyed documents?" In a single utterance the stalker—the potential attacker—transforms into hero. Yet Brockovich does "escape" Embry and the bar to call Masry, seek his advice, and strategize. Just like Hill, Brockovich is portrayed as a female in need of a male protector. Encouraged by Masry's guidance, Brockovich forgets Embry's threatening mannerisms—or at least, her own personal safety becomes secondary to her potential achievement. Although this character turns out to be the one who can provide the all-important "smoking gun" linking corporate PG&E to the Hinkley contamination, his appearance as a predator implies the dangers associated with a strategy dependent upon the arousal of heterosexual desire.

Recounting the simultaneous presence of danger and protection, these narratives contain a cautionary note: the rules of heterosexual engagement are clear: male protection is required. This is not a strategy that can be used to subvert patriarchal control. Yet this reliance upon male protectors is consistent with how Hill and Brockovich seek political resolution; their willing deferral to white men fails to hold those in power accountable. In saying she *loves* Charles Hurowitz (the head of Maxxam Corporation and parent company to Pacific Lumber), Hill absolves Pacific Lumber and the corporate structure of their crimes. Translated into the larger cultural arena, this reliance upon a male protector is readily adapted to reliance upon established power structures that perpetually fail to address acts of social and environmental injustice. Furthermore, Hill and Brockovich's seemingly natural adoption of this strategy indicates a lack of critical awareness of the relationship between gender, environmental, and political oppression prevalent in patriarchal societies.

ECOFEMINISM

In contrast, ecofeminism argues that there are important connections between the domination of women and the degradation of the environment. In an article entitled "Ecofeminism and Grass-roots Environmentalism in the United States" Barbara Epstein (1993) states that "[P]erhaps the greatest strength of ecofeminism is that it has developed a theory that addresses both gender relations and the relationship between human society and the natural environment, showing how the structures of domination in these realms shape and reinforce one another" (p. 146). Within this context, any appeal to heterosexual desire aligns itself with patriarchal values and the structures of domination that oppress both women and the environment. This is an obvious compromise of the cultural work ostensibly being accomplished through the environmental narratives of Julia "Butterfly" Hill and Erin Brockovich. Epstein goes on to say, "[E]cofeminists also believe that capitalism is linked to domination" (p. 145). In this light an examination of capitalism itself must become part of any inquiry into environmental degradation.

As a result of their working class origins, both Julia "Butterfly" Hill and Erin Brockovich could engage in an economic critique of environmental degradation; but they do not. Neither argues for a re-examination of the values that have caused the environmental degradation their "activism" addresses, but argues instead for a re-distribution of the profits generated by those practices. As a result their critiques leave the dominant power structures intact. Hill does not question whether it is appropriate to place a value on a tree: her efforts merely culminate in negotiating a price, transferring ownership, and, given the fact that forests activists do not possess the same economic resources as do the timber/lumber industry, establishing a monetarily unachievable precedent for saving forests. By the same token, Brockovich does not question whether or not a dollar figure can be placed on a breast, uterus, or life; she merely barters about what that figure should be. In this way both Hill and Brockovich side with the powerful legal and economic systems to arbitrate "justice." Both opt for money as resolution, seemingly unaware of how their collaboration with systems of power might impinge on the lives of others. The residents of Hinkley get less money, for example, as Masry and Brockovich take their full 40% cut of the settlement; Hill gets national celebrity, while Earth First! remains a national threat.

Of course, the image making apparatus out of which both these narratives emerge is first and foremost profit driven industry. Industries gain their power and financial affluence through their participation within the capitalist structure; as such it is unlikely that they would engage in a capitalist critique. Thus, for those voices that gain access to large audiences through dominant modes of production it is difficult, if not almost impossible, to raise "questions about what values govern our society and what values we want it to be governed by" (Epstein, 1993, p. 150). In this light the narratives of Hill and Brockovich clearly reveal their inability to provide any critique of for-profit practices that compromise the integrity of the environment. Rather, both women have been commodified. They have "sold their stories" to Harper Collins and Universal Pictures in what has become a profitable move for all involved. For example, *Erin Brockovich* earned well over $100 million in box office sales within the first few months of its release. Hill has parlayed her stint in Luna into a book deal, as well as an almost perpetual speaking tour schedule. However, it is not just the commodification of the women and their stories that is objectionable, but the commodification of the causes. In selling their stories, these women lose control over them. For the dominant cultural structures that now own them, profit becomes more important than the stories or the social movements behind them.

INDIVIDUALISM

Because environmental narratives developed by the publishing and movie producing industries equate to environmental narratives with economic sponsorship, Robert J. Brulle's (2000) discussion (in *Agency, Democracy, and Nature: The U.S. Environmental Movement from a Critical Theory Perspective*) of how foundation funding influences environmental organizations sheds relevant light on the political limitations imposed on Hill and Brockovich and their narratives. Arguing that "foundation funding influences an organization to move away from confrontation and protest and toward noncontroversial positions and nonconfrontational practices" (p. 261), Brulle goes on to quote Craig J. Jenkins: "Foundation patronage . . . could be interpreted as creating a neocorporatist system of political representation in which elites exert increasing control over the representation of social interests" (p. 262). Unfortunately, this type of influence negates any expression of the fundamental conflicts of interest that exist between corporate (in both its for-profit and philanthropic manifestations) and environmental organizations. Subordinated to the decision making of those elites at the helm of the publishing and movie industries and thereby enmeshed in the reproduction of ideological dominance, these narratives "block or mask the social origins of ecological degradation" (Brulle, 2000, p. 273). It then becomes obvious that no real social transformation will be achieved through the sponsorship of "established institutions of economic power" (Brulle, 2000, p. 264). Thus the narratives of Julia "Butterfly" Hill and Erin Brockovich become instruments of propaganda rather than cultural critiques.

In part this is accomplished through each narrative's use of the rhetoric of individualism that defines American ideology; without the tenacity and passion of these particular women, there would have been no victory. These stories therefore reinforce the notion that social change occurs through the heroic acts of committed individuals—not through groups, not through movements. The supremacy of the individual over the social movement is apparent not only in the media's focus on Hill or Brockovich, but within the narratives themselves. For example, in *The Legacy of Luna,* Hill overtly states her rejection of Earth First! despite the fact that the Luna sit was initially an Earth First! treesit. Early in her story, local activists make the decision to move the treesit to another threatened location; Hill becomes furious and denounces the group process. "The thought of all these people sitting down there in a circle talking about me and determining that I didn't have a right to be in Luna, as if they owned the tree, made me crazy" (Hill, 2000, p.87). Hill claims that saving Luna was something she achieved alone (or, at least with the help of a few lawyers); this was "her" sit, not the group's, despite the fact that every treesitter—including Hill—always relies on a whole team of ground support to trek food and water in and transport waste out.

Erin Brockovich presents a similar distortion by presenting the story out of the context of any larger movement, as if Erin Brockovich were the first or only person to seek redress for the consequences of toxic waste contamination. According to Barbara Epstein (1993) "[a]ntitoxics activity provides the focus for about five thousand groups around the United States" (p. 149–9). However, the only reference to other environmental justice struggles in *Erin Brockovich* comes as a critique: at a meeting in the Hinkley Community Center, attorney Ed Masry tries to convince residents of Hinkley to forego a jury trial in exchange for binding arbitration. As people begin to leave with their hopes for justice dashed, Masry shouts out, "1978. That's the year of the Love Canal controversy and those people are still waiting for their money. Think about where you'll be in fifteen years." The Hinkley residents are convinced to agree to binding arbitration. The implication is obvious; the actions of the Love Canal litigants, or more precisely, their failure to take a certain type of legal action, and not the justice system, are at fault for their inability to achieve a just and timely settlement. Hooker Chemical, the company responsible for the toxic waste poisoning the residents of the Love Canal neighborhood, is not even mentioned.

The titles of both stories emphasize the women as individuals. *Erin Brockovich* masks Hinkley, toxic pollution, and cancer. Hill's autobiography, *The Legacy of Luna*, is subtitled *the Story of a Tree, a Woman, and the Struggle to Save the Redwoods*—apparently one tree at a time. The title obscures the destruction of old growth forests and the people who act to defend them. In the very titles, then, the movement is concealed, the larger struggle made invisible, and the role of the individual given dominance. With the flurry of attention and hype on Julia "Butterfly" Hill and on Erin Brockovich, other stories—the stories of Earth First! and other treesitters, the stories of other communities or activists fighting for environmental justice—fail to be told. One would never guess that "[a]cross the country, similarly situated citizens are fighting civic battles that require the same levels of tenacity, creativity and intelligence" (Nader, 1998, xiii). Instead, in the narratives of Hill and Brockovich, two beautiful white women are victorious through a combination of serendipity and sex appeal—consumable, obviously and for obvious reasons, but hardly representatives of environmental activism.

As these stories become the mainstream representation of women in the environmental movement, their cultural prominence gives rise to the establishment of a canon of environmental narratives. In writing about the process of literary canonization, Derek Attridge (1992) states that "canonization inevitably involves, as a condition of the audibility of the canon, a continuous act of silencing (p. 228). Thus, the real cost of manufacturing these types of images as representative of women in the environmental movement is the stories they force to the margins, exclude, and silence: the women who remain unheard (of) and unseen.

ENVIRONMENTAL PIN-UP GIRLS

Whether an intended effect or not, the narratives of Julia "Butterfly" Hill and Erin Brockovich function as a kind of social control. Environmental pin-up girls offer images of male pleasure and political pacification. By portraying what women in the environmental movement look like—white, heterosexual, beautiful, and ultimately able to succeed in the world as it is currently constructed—they exclude images of women who provide real critiques of the value system responsible for environmental degradation. According to Lois Gibbs, a white, heterosexual, beautiful environmental activist whose narrative has not been adopted into popular culture, "we can't protect our health and the environment without finding the courage to change the way government works. To begin this process of change, we have to create a national debate, community by community, on the nature of our government and our society. We have to explore how people become powerless as the corporations become powerful. We have to discuss why our government protects the right to pollute more than it protects our health. We have to figure out how to speak honestly and act collectively to rebuild our democracy" (1998, p. xv). This critical interrogation of domination and exploitation fails to occur in the narratives of Hill and Brockovich. For this reason and this reason alone these narratives serve as substitutes in popular culture for the more radical project of feminist environmentalism.

Without due process Julia "Butterfly" Hill and Erin Brockovich have become the representation of women in the environmental movement. That they have gained that position neither through merit nor election, but through the efforts of a self-serving capitalist apparatus functioning to maintain cultural hegemony, has been of little consequence in the mainstream reception of these women and their narratives.

The project of critically examining these narratives "is a small component of a much greater struggle . . .to fashion cultural and political structures and procedures that will allow us not just to hear each other's stories . . .but to hear—and this will entail a different mode of hearing—each other's silences" (Attridge, 1992, p. 231). It is our sincere hope that our reading of the narratives of Julia "Butterfly" Hill and Erin Brockovich have given readers cause to listen for the stories of women in the environmental movement that these stories exclude.

NOTES

1. *Oprah*. (2001) <http://www.oprah.com/tows/pastshows/tows_past_20010131_k.jhtml> (2001, January 31).

REFERENCES

Armstrong, N. (1987). *Desire and domestic fiction: a political history of the novel.* Oxford: Oxford University Press.

Attridge, D. (1992). Oppressive Silence: J.M. Coetzee's *Foe* and the Politics of the Canon. In K. R. Lawrence (Ed.), *Decolonizing tradition: new views of twentieth-century "British" literary canons* (pp. 212–238). Chicago: University of Illinois Press.

Brulle, R. J. (2000) *Agency Democracy, and nature: the U.S. environmental movement from a critical theory perspective.* Cambridge: MIT Press.

Chavis, B. (1993). Foreward. In R.D. Bullard (Ed), *Confronting Environmental Racism: Voices from the Grassroots* (pp.3–6). Boston: South End Press.

Epstein, B. (1993). Ecofeminism and grass-roots environmentalism in the United States. In R. Hofrichter (Ed), *Toxic Struggles: The Theory and Practice of Environmental Justice.* (pp.144–152). Philadelphia: New Society Publishers.

Erin Brockovich (1999).

Hill, J. B. (2000). *The legacy of Luna: the story of a tree, a woman, and the struggle to save the redwoods.* New York: Harper Collins.

Krauss, C. (1993). Blue-collar and toxic-waste protests: the process of politicization. In R. Hofrichter (Ed), *Toxic Struggles: The Theory and Practice of Environmental Justice.* (pp.107–117). Philadelphia: New Society Publishers.

Nader, R. (1998). Foreword. In L. M. Gibbs, *Love Canal: the story continues.* (pp.xii–xv). Gabriola Island, BC: New Society Publishers.

Chapter Fourteen

Performing Politics: Media Aesthetics for Women in Political Campaigns

Lori Montalbano-Phelps

INTRODUCTION

Defining communities is an essential part of the political process. For national candidates, it is imperative to create a persona that millions of voters can connect with. For a woman in national politics, special consideration must be given to carving out the role of a powerful candidate, who balances idealized standards of what constitutes womanhood within a given nation. This process leads candidates with an unending process of re-defining themselves, and a female candidate with a constant re-negotiation of political roles and individual identities.

Over the past two decades, America has experienced an increasing amount of women entering national political campaigns, and in national office. Currently, the number of women in Congress has reached its highest point in our nation's history, although it still falls significantly short of any balanced percentage. Accompanying this participation is media attention regarding the performance aesthetics which *should* be embodied by those who seek or serve in national politics. By "performance aesthetics," I mean, questions of behavioral expectations, such as opposite-sex interaction, appropriateness in language use, and the performance of various roles. These performance aesthetics represent a few issues that have captured media attention.

Women candidates often confront unique challenges in formulating their public personae. For example, Benze and Declercq (1985) explain that in television ads, research showed that female candidates "suffer from stereotyping in several areas, most notably that they are viewed as not tough enough or lacking competence or experience for an office" (pp. 279–280). Consequently, concerns include positioning the candidate "to have her appear strong but certainly not too aggressive and to have her look professional and not too attractive . . . negative advertising had to be used even more carefully than is usually the case for fear of voter backlash" (Benze and Declercq, 1985, p. 283 and p. 288).

These challenges are present in all political coverage, including that which appears in print media. To answer these questions, I examined over one hundred examples of print media coverage of three female political players who have campaigned in national politics within the past two decades. Specifically, I examined the media coverage of Geraldine Ferraro's 1984 Vice Presidential campaign, Pat Schroeder's 1988 bid for the Democratic Presidential nomination, and Hillary Rodham Clinton's role in the 1992 and 1996 Presidential campaigns, as well as her performance as "First Lady," and subsequent role as candidate for New York Senate. This analysis seeks to add to an understanding of the socially-constructed performance of the public personae which leads to formed "communities" of constituencies. Three categories of performance aesthetics have emerged from the research; behavioral expectations and the "Presidential Character," the physical appearance of the candidate, and issues of credibility.

BEHAVIORAL EXPECTATIONS AND THE *PRESIDENTIAL CHARACTER*

Biological sex of the political candidate brings to bear certain expectations of gender performance, according to prescribed notions of what constitutes *acceptable* behavior for a man or a woman in a given culture. The way in which we "do gender" influences campaigning behavior significantly. West and Zimmerman (1987) explain that "doing gender means creating differences between girls and boys, women and men, differences that are not natural, essential, or biological. Once the differences have been constructed, they are used to reinforce the 'essentialness' of gender" (p. 137). Consequently, these differences are not only reinforced by the candidates' behavior, but by the media coverage which promotes dominant ideology regarding judgments on appropriateness of the candidates' actions. Further, these actions perpetuate specific gender roles within a given society. Carrigan, Connel, and Lee (1987) suggest that "the very idea of role implies a recognizable and accepted standard . . . society is organized around a pervasive differentiation between men's and women's roles" (p. 77). The political players examined in this essay, particularly Rodham Clinton, confronted issues of gender with varying degrees of success. Each of their candidacies have contributed to the current positioning of women in national politics. The "Presidential character" is influenced by political stereotypes, rules of opposite sex interaction, and a "woman's role" in national campaigns.

POLITICAL STEREOTYPES

Traditionally, male candidates seeking national office are positioned as possessing strong leadership qualities that mirror stereotypical gender roles. Daughton (1993) found:

> the president is the national patriarch: the paradigmatic American Man . . . a strong leader: decisive, fit, visionary, and competent . . . the president's duties involve being the guardian of moral values (hence scandals when candidates are accused of infidelity), [and] the protector of hearth and home (including defense against international foes, fighting domestic crime, and more recently, protecting the environment) (p. 37).

This view is typified by print coverage which described Bill Clinton the candidate as "tough", "strong under pressure," a "political powerhouse" during his 1992 campaign, as well as the coverage which noted Clinton's deviation from the more traditional behavioral expectations, for example, touching other men during the campaign:

> Bill Clinton hugs other men, usually—more like a full shoulder squeeze. Women get it too, but the gesture is more striking in its generational freshness when applied to the same sex. He softens the old fashioned backslap into something more sensitive. These guys are touching each other! It's unselfconscious, gender neutral, very 90's ('President's Best," 1992, p. 49).

Despite the claim of gender neutrality proposed in the above quote, such nurturing behavior is often more traditionally attributed to female behavior. Negative sex-role stereotyping perpetuates notions of the female as nurturer, the "weaker sex," more emotional, less logical, and dependent upon males. Women seeking national political office often combat such stereotypical expectations. In reflections on her candidacy for Vice President, Ferraro (1985) explains that, "throughout the campaign I knew that if I had displayed any vulnerability, allowed for any sign of weakness, it would have been construed as a typically negative female trait" (p. 314).

Perhaps the most notorious occurrence during the Schroeder campaign was when she announced that she was ending her candidacy. Reminiscent of Edmund Muskie's tearful scene in the 1968 campaign, Schroeder began to cry. "To the embarrassment of her supporters, Schroeder burst into tears and had to be comforted by her husband James for a full minute before she could continue with her announcement" (Church, 1987, p. 24). Other accounts added that "she finished her speech and threw herself into his arms" (Ferraro, 1990, p. 30). Schroeder's behavior caused considerable controversy, and many feminists cringed at the thought of her showing weakness, that is emotion, in public. This event was intensified by the burdensome expectations that plagued the Schroeder campaign early on, a candidacy which some claimed, "could do more for the power of sisterhood than any single campaign since suffrage" (Kopkind, 1987, p. 77).

Hillary Rodham Clinton and her husband, Bill Clinton, experienced similar constraints during Clinton's campaign and during the White House years. Perhaps one of the most striking reactions to their lack of conformity to gender role expectations is reflected in the following excerpt:

> The Democrats have become the party whose cultural trend is to blur gender differences. . . . The Clintons are born leaders of this party. Sharing his office, they shift gender roles. He insinuates. She orders. He seduces. She demands. He wants people to love him. She wants to be feared. Her hunger for power is open and palpable; his, buried in layers of charm. She does not bake cookies. He does not draw blood. . . . The Clinton's political traits seem in marked public contrast. She is brash, single minded, tone deaf to nuance. He is malleable, pliant, eager to please. His features are soft, hers much harder. Her smile is avid, his sly (Emery, 1993, p.49).

The above quote is one of the most blatant accounts of gender stereotyping that appeared in print regarding the '92 campaign. Yet, a significant amount of coverage of that and subsequent campaigns, although more subtle, creates similar mental images and continues to raise sedimented issues of what constitutes appropriate behavior for men and women. The issues manifest themselves in concerns over female-male interaction in campaigns and a person's role within the political arena based on sex.

FEMALE-MALE INTERACTION IN POLITICAL CAMPAIGNS

One of the most challenging tasks for a female candidate to negotiate is determining how to interact with her male counterpart or runningmate in the campaign. Schroeder's inclusion of her husband's support as campaign manager in 1988 raised questions of appropriateness, as did Rodham Clinton's role in Bill Clinton's bid for the Presidency and subsequent terms in office (which manifested itself in significant questions regarding women's participation in national politics). The issue of determining appropriate behavior/interaction strategies for opposite-sex runningmates on a national ticket emerged in the 1984 campaign, for the first and only time in America's history. During their campaign, Ferraro and her runningmate, Walter Mondale, were careful not to embrace, or engage in any other behavior that might be misconstrued as sexual contact. Ferraro (1985) explains that:

> The whole issue of my being the first female candidate made other people feel more awkward than it did me. There had been such a fuss in the campaign and media about Fritz and me not touching at all, not even raising our joined hands. (p. 201).

This constraint was realized even more completely when Ferraro's campaign was in trouble. When charges of wrongdoing were made against Ferraro, Mondale kept a low profile, so not to be perceived as a "protective male" rescuing the "helpless woman": a "damsel in a medieval romance, praying for a man to come to her rescue" ("Show and Tell," 1984, p. 27). This choice had consequences on the campaign as well; it:

> contributed to a picture of the presidential candidate as essentially a passive bystander while his runningmate was fighting her way out of a burning building. That picture may not have been an accurate one, but in politics, perception is often more important than reality (Germond and Whitcover, 1985, p. 446).

Similar constraints surfaced when Ferraro was scheduled to debate then Vice President George Bush:

> The president's strategists preferred that Bush not debate Ferraro at all. Their view rather was that it was a no win situation for Bush and the ticket—Ferraro would come out ahead merely by walking on stage and holding her own (Goldman and Fuller, 1985, p. 327).

Because this was an unprecedented occurrence, Bush was placed in a difficult position as well. "He could not, under the new sexual etiquette, attack Ferraro too vigorously, for fear he would look like a bully" (Goldman and Fuller, 1985, p. 327).

Similar issues arose in the campaigning and debate strategies used by Lazio in the 2000 New York Senate campaign. Attempting to slander his opponent, Lazio was criticized frequently for personal attacks against Rodham Clinton's character, and it didn't play well with the voters or in the polls.

Female-male interaction can play a significant role in campaign strategizing and the formation of a sense of community with constituents. This constraint is complicated by larger considerations of women's role(s) in national politics.

Despite Schroeder's bid for the Presidency, little consideration was given to women's participation as major political players in the 1988 campaign. The sense was that considering a woman for a national position was analogous to succumbing to special interests:

Democrats and Republicans agree that Walter Mondale badly miscalculated in 1984 when he bowed to feminist pressure to *take a woman* (emphasis added) as his runningmate. And as a result, political consultant Carter Eskew says, "male candidates are particularly wary this time not to be perceived as pandering to special interests, whether they be women or any other" (Jacoby, 1987, p. 20).

Such coverage seems to emphasize a strategy to marginalize women's participation in national political campaigns, hence reducing the credibility of potential candidates.

Questions of appropriate roles and behavior surfaced early for Rodham Clinton. Her claim, "if you elect Bill, you get me" (Cooper, 1992, p. 34), and the media focus on the so-called, "Hillary Factor," raised considerable controversy. Articles with titles such as, "Will Hillary Clinton Stand By Her Man on Child Care?" (Fields, 1992), "Nepotism for the Nineties," ("Nepotism, 1993), "Mr. And Mrs. President," (Deacon, 1993), accompanied claims that "Republican spinmeisters whisper that Hillary is a woman scorned who clung to marriage because she wants to be first lady" (Clift, 1992, p. 24).

More controversy developed when Rodham Clinton was criticized by opponents for continuing to practice law while her husband was Governor of Arkansas. To these critics, Rodham Clinton scoffed, "I suppose I could have stayed at home, baked cookies, and had teas" (Carlson, 1992, p. 30). This expression was not well received, because of its seemingly sarcastic overtones, yet it was quite revealing of attitudes regarding a political wife's "duties," which pervade our society:

According to Ruth Mandel of the Center of the American Woman and Politics at Rutgers University, the unspoken rule of political life is that a wife will tend to home and family and be by her husband's side when he runs. Working violates that rule. Being successful in a primarily male profession shatters it, as Hillary Clinton is learning (Carlson, 1992, p. 3).

An example of these constraining notions was vocalized by former President Richard Nixon who said of Rodham Clinton: "If the wife comes through as too strong and too intelligent, it makes the husband look like a wimp" (MacDonald, 1992, p. 22). Throughout the 1996 campaign and Clinton's second term in office, Rodham Clinton's behavior was continually debated and contested. Gardetto (1997) explains:

> In the hands of conservative political cartoonists, talk show hosts and even respected columnists, Hillary Clinton seems to be a dangerously non-conformist first lady. To her admirers, on the contrary, Hillary Clinton represents a trailblazer who has, in the tradition of Eleanor Roosevelt, reinvigorated the first lady role to include social activism (p. 225).

Similarly, Winfield (1997) contends that "the first lady has been a difficult news topic for journalists who are used to traditional first lady stories. For them, she is a surprise; they see a contradiction between expected female roles and her policy making and political power, areas calling for more critical analysis" (p. 243).

Stereotypical gender roles pervade the media coverage and political rhetoric of national campaigns. These stereotypes limit the perceived ability of the candidates, implying inappropriate behavior by anyone who deviates from the status quo. These behavioral constraints further manifest themselves in questions of the political player's credibility, an issue which is often overshadowed by media coverage of the player's appearance.

APPEARANCE OF THE POLITICAL PLAYER

Appearance of the political player, particularly a female player, is highlighted by media coverage of the player's physical attractiveness and media image.

Media coverage of the physical appearance of political players often includes an analysis of physical stature and physical shape (i.e., weight control issues). "Everything is political—what you wear, what you eat, even how you make love. Politics has become inseparable from style, fashion, entertainment, etiquette and general self presentation" (Sobran, 1993, p.40). For female candidates, clothing and hair style can become major media events. Ferraro (1985) explains:

> Male candidates have it easy. All they have to worry about is which striped tie to wear with which dark suit. Before the first presidential debate. . . . Walter Mondale evidently ran through some forty ties before one was declared the most presidential looking. My problem as a woman was how to look vice-presidential . . . short sleeve dresses are a no no. . . . "You should wear only suits" was another campaign dress theme I ignored, except for the vice-presidential debate. Why dress like an imitation man? I never wore slacks in public, of course. It could have been considered offensive in the more conservative areas of the country. (p.8).

Clothing has become a media favorite for women in politics. Schroeder's appearance was once described this way: "At a recent hearing of Schroeder's sub-committee on Military Installations and Faculties, she wore a tomato-red dress and a wide-shouldered royal blue sweater; her bright insouciant style seemed to dominate a room full of military uniforms and dark business suits" ("The Prime of Pat Schroeder," 1990, p. 15). What was it that happened at the meeting? Enough said. Rodham Clinton's attire experienced a certain overhaul in the '92 campaign. Commenting upon the "overhauled model," media journalists note:

> no longer did Hillary sport her trademark headbands—too corporate? Too professional?. . . . Television Producer Linda Bloodworth-Thomason, a Hollywood buddy of the Clintons, dispatched advisers on wardrobe, hair, and makeup, so that Hillary would look more "natural." By natural, let us assume Bloodworth-Thomason meant "acceptable" (Bruning, 1992, p. 9).

Of course, as is traditional in American politics, scrutiny over the appearance of the First Lady has always captured media attention. The Clinton years in the White House were a continuation of this tradition, despite Rodham Clinton's aversion to such coverage. "Acceptable physical appearance" of a major political player can contribute significantly to that player's overall media image. Recently, an article entitled, "Another Clinton Wears the Pants," appeared in *People* magazine. They reported that Senator-elect Hillary Rodham Clinton, "gave a nod to her 'six black pantsuits' in her victory speech . . . tailored to her pear shape, the suits (including two from Oscar de la Renta that are similar to ones that sell for $3500) transformed her into a powerful figure" (p. 133). Of course, it was her pantsuits, not her character, that were credited with her "powerful" transformation.

For Rodham Clinton, juggling media images, which were placed on a continuum ranging from "Lady MacBeth of Little Rock," or a "feminazi" to "Co-President" or "Superwoman," wasn't easy. During the '92 campaign, for example, her image underwent several modifications. "With her direct manner and aggressive style, she was not coming across as Little Woman or Supermom" (Bruning, 1992, p. 9). Consequently, her image evolved "no fewer than three times during the course of the campaign" (Clift, 1992, p. 38). When her non-traditional-wife-of-the-candidate image began overshadowing the media coverage of her husband, Rodham Clinton was re-marketed as wife and mother, photographed with her daughter Chelsea, with children on the campaign trail, and eventually as if she were American royalty, sporting an ivory suit, traditional pearl necklace and earrings (Kelly, 1992). This image transformation seemed to indicate a desire upon the part of the Democratic team to create a closer match between Rodham Clinton's role in the campaign and traditional expectations of a potential First Lady. Once she became First Lady, her media image would be scrutinized, commented upon, and watched in wonder as the various scandals regarding her husband's infidelity, their seemingly unscrupulous business activities, and so on were thwarted over the course of their eight years in the White House. "Stand by her man" was often the theme projected by her public stance; however, speculations regarding what her "true" motives might be, what her own political aspirations were, and so on, fueled the fire and required several re-writings of the public personae Rodham Clinton would portray over the course of the administration. Somehow, as time would show, she was able to establish a wide-based (I'm avoiding the use of the term broad-based) community of support across the nation.

Tests of media image were not new to politics with Rodham Clinton's emergence into politics, of course. For Ferraro, similarities existed in image constraints. She was often viewed as too aggressive, and media sound bites made Ferraro appear "smart-aleky;" one journalist concluded, "her own negative ratings had been rising as a consequence" (Goldman, 1984, p. 330). And Peter Teely, Bush's press secretary, "called the congresswoman screechy, scratchy, and bitchy" (Blume, 1985, p. 303).

Consequently, Ferraro attempted to display a more Presidential style of delivery in her subsequent debate with Bush and throughout the campaign. She attempted to be more "subdued" and more "lawyer-like" in her delivery in an attempt to combat the negative media image, which arose in the early part of her campaign (Ferraro and Franke, 1985, p. 251).

CREDIBILITY OF THE POLITICAL PLAYER

Issues of credibility are confronted by all candidates or political players in national campaigns. Due to historically limited participation of women in national politics, questions of credentials, and consequently legitimacy for participation in national politics, become major campaign obstacles.

One method that is often used to carve out credible public personae for women in politics is to emphasize their "non-traditional" accomplishments and, at the same time, balance these images with more sedimented ideals of women's perceived "functions" in society and family. During her campaign, Schroeder was quoted as asking whether America was "man enough to back a woman" (Kempton, 1989, p. 20). More than a clever play on words, this expression borrowed from outmoded ideas that man equals strength, man equals power. Such phraseology does little more than perpetuate negative stereotypes. Schroeder found establishing credibility to be difficult at times:

I'd talk about my issues, and often the first question would be: "Does your husband know you're doing this?" And you had to deal with the fact that people were playing with the novelty of your sex and not listening to what you're saying (Kempton, 1989, p. 22).

At the same time, media coverage included an attempt to mark her non-traditional accomplishments:

despite two grown children and my campaign manager who happens to be her husband, Schroeder is not a traditional woman. A licensed pilot, she has spent nearly 15 years on the House Armed Forces Committee, and she can argue nuclear technicalities more knowledgeably than most congressmen (MacDonald, 1987, p. 30).

Throughout Ferraro's campaign, she attempted to reinforce her image as a serious, and consequently, a credible candidate (Goldman, 1984, p. 330). Her attempts were most successfully realized during her press conference over her individual taxes and the Vice-Presidential debate. By "taking the heat" during the press conference in particular, and "standing on her own," without the direct support of her runningmate, she gained the credibility she needed. "Her credible performance quieted critics who had doubted whether Ferraro—or any other woman—had the experience, depth, and temperament to hold high office" (Doerner, 1984, p. 30). Because of the potential impact of her candidacy on future participation of women in national politics, Ferraro was careful to maintain a credible public persona.

Although Rodham Clinton was not the candidate in 1992 or in 1996, her behavior and credentials were questioned throughout the campaigns. In the '92 campaign, she was labeled, "Superwoman, the role model for the 90's," (Quinn, 1993, p. 25). "Hillary's role" became one of the most debated issues of the campaign. She continually redefined what constitutes First Lady in the U.S., and according to Fineman and Miller, realized "unprecedented clout" in that role (Fineman and Miller, 1993, p. 18). While the role of First Lady itself carries clout, clout which women such as Eleanor Roosevelt exercised to what were then "unprecedented" levels, this clout raised controversy which has been scrutinized by media analysts. These journalists claim, "Hillary's unique role will raise the issue of who's really in charge in the oval office" (Fineman and Miller, 1993, p. 18). While one could argue that this is more an issue of nepotism than feminism, media polls have asked questions over the past decade that focus, to a great degree, on Rodham Clinton's credibility, including issues of her intelligence, being a potential role model for girls, admiration for her, and her behavior (Carlson, 1993, p. 35), in addition to polls on her role as First Lady. Achieving a balance of power, especially power which is housed in "unofficial" or unpaid capacities, was a significant challenge to Rodham Clinton. Never before, as media analysts put it, has there been a First Lady "who could qualify to be White House counsel, if only her husband were not President" (Carlson, 1992, p. 40). Similarly, "the fact that Hillary brings independent credentials to the White House should be celebrated, but like most Firsts, this makes people nervous" ("Hillary: Behind," 1992, p. 23).

Consequently, when credibility is no longer questioned, legitimacy of participation is placed under scrutiny regarding Rodham Clinton's participation within the campaign and presidency of Bill Clinton. The aforementioned quotes demonstrate the qualifications from which a female political player is scrutinized, implying that her accomplishments are valued only when they mirror male standards of success.

However, opinion of Hillary Rodham Clinton runs high. Cohen (2000) reports that since 1993, when the Clinton Administration began—through November 1999, "there have been thirty-one polls that ask the public to rate the jobs Mrs. Clinton has been doing as First Lady" (p. 376). In a summary of the polls and poll findings, Cohen (2000) writes:

> In 1993 and 1994, her "job approval" ratings were quite high, ranging from the mid-50's to the mid-60's. However, once she appeared in the public spot-light because of her role in leading the health care reform effort and strategy and assorted scandals, her polls began to decline. In 1995, her polls began dropping and seemed to bottom out in early 1996 in the low 40's With the 1996 presidential election campaign, we see an upsurge in her polls ratings to the mid-50's by late 1996, and surpassing the 60 percent mark by early 1997, after the re-election. Throughout 1997, they stayed in the 60 percent region and even crept passed the 70 percent mark by early 1998 (p. 376).

These numbers are quite high and indicate popularity among the American public; this, of course, may or may not be directly related to issues of credibility in the media coverage. It is often the media that raise speculation about improprieties of political figures.

SUMMARY

The accomplishments of women in national politics within the past two decades represent important steps in facilitating the future participation of women in the political arena. Yet, the performance aesthetics that are imposed upon female candidates, which include sedimented images of "appropriate" behavior, appearance, and credibility, define narrow boundaries a woman must conform to when engaging in national politics. The female candidate must be careful not to conform to stereotypical traits which may make her appear unqualified for holding high office (for example, those which contrast to male standards of positive political traits). She cannot be too non-traditional, for fear she will appear part of some lunatic fringe. She must dress appropriately —like her male counterpart, however, never forgetting that she is a woman— no pants allowed? She must be a credible candidate—that is, her accomplishments must mirror her male counterpart's, but never be earned at the expense of her duties as wife and mother.

Media performance aesthetics tend to focus on three categories of female candidates' coverage. The first category perpetuates the ideal of woman as traditional wife and mother, dutifully committed to her family and home. The second category presents the woman "as man," in other words, as *no* different from her male counterpart, except, of course, for her style of appearance. Finally, there is the woman as a member of a marginalized group, a "special interest" that must be "handled," *regretfully*, in national politics. The three preceding categories are isolating. Karlyn Kohrs Campbell (1983) contends:

> Each female is socialized into the woman's subculture; thus eliminating gender-based differences is difficult and painful. Women are asked to invent new identities and to develop new patterns of behavior while discarding the roles and support systems that have sustained them. Just as early feminists were unable to maintain an unswerving commitment to personhood, so contemporary feminists have yet to synthesize the values characteristic of feminine subculture with the goal of a society in which gender-based distinctions are irrelevant (p. 104).

By minimizing differences, the current state of American politics fails to acknowledge the contributions individuals can offer through public service. By emphasizing differences, the current system perpetuates a very narrow definition of what constitutes an effective national leader. Either approach makes defining communities which connect with female candidates in national politics a significant challenge.

REFERENCES

"A credible candidacy and then some." *Time*, 19 November 1984, 84–85.

"A feisty Ferraro takes the offensive." *Maclean's*, 3 September 1984, 28–29.

Adams, J. R. "The lost honor of Geraldine Ferraro." *Commentary*, 81 (Fall 1986): 34–38.

Anrig, G. Jr. & MacDonald, E.M. "How Hillary manages the Clinton's Money." *Money*, 21 July 1992, 112–120.

Barone, M. "Entering the combat zone." *U.S. News and World Report*, 30 March 1992, 39.

Benze, J.G. & Declercq, E.R. "Content of television political spot ads for female Candidates." *Journalism Quarterly,* 62, 278–282 (1985).

Blankenship, J., Mendez, S.M., Kang, J.G., & Giordano, J. "Initial construction of Ferraro in newspaper editorials." *Journalism Quarterly*, 63 (Summer, 1986): 378–382.

Brubach, H. "Right and fitting." *The New Yorker*, 68, February 1993, 33.

Bruning, F. "Tough, smart, and a presidential bedmate." *Maclean's*, 12 December 1992, 9.

Campbell, K.K. "Femininity and feminism: To be or not to be a woman." *Communication Quarterly*, 31:2, Spring 1983, 101–108.

Carlson, M. "A different kind of First Lady." *Time*, 16 November 1992, 40–41.

———. " A room at the top." *Time*, 10 May 1993, 28–36.

———. "At the center of power." *Time*, 4 January 1993, 38–41.

———. "Hillary Clinton: Partner as much as wife." *Time*, 27 January 1992, 19.

———. "We've had some good times." *Time*, 10 May 1993, 37.

Carrigan, T., Connel, B., & Lee, J. (1992). "Toward a new sociology of masculinity." In Brod, H. (Ed.) *The making of masculinities: The new men's studies. . .* New York: Routeledge.

Carroll, G. "Will Hillary hurt or help?" *Newsweek* , 30 March 1992, 30–31.

Clark, J. "Getting there: Women in political office." *The Annals of the American Academy of Political and Social Science*, 515, 63–76.

Church, G.J. "The dwarfs in disarray." *Time*, 12 October 1987, 22–23.

Clift, E. "First Lady culture clash." *Newsweek*, 8 June 1992, 24.

———. "Hillary: Then and now." *Newsweek*, 20 July 1992, 38–39.

———. "Hillary's ultimate juggling act: As First Lady, she's free to be herself." *Newsweek*, 16 November 1992, 42.

———. "I'll try to be who I am." *Newsweek*, 28 December 1992, 24–25.

———. "The re-selling of the First Lady." *Newsweek*, 26 April 1993, 34.

Cohen, J.E. (2000). "The Poll's: Public attitudes toward the First Lady." *Presidential Studies Quarterly*, 30:2, 374–381.

Cooper, M. "A mother, a wife, a woman." *U.S. News and World Report*, 11 October 1993, 10–11.

———. "Co-President Clinton?" *U.S. News and World Report*, 8 February 1993, 30–32.

———. "The Hillary Factor." *U.S. News and World Report*, 27 April 1992, 30–35.

Daughton, S. "Women's issues, women's place: Gender-related problems in Presidential campaigns." Paper presented at the Speech Communication Association, Miami, November 1993.

Deacon, J. "Mr. And Mrs. President." *Maclean's*, 1 February 1993, 38–41.

Doerner, W.R. "Co-Stars on center stage: A close battle for best performance in a Supporting role." *Time*, 22 October 1984, 30.

Duffy, M. "Operation Hillary." *Time*, 22 March 1993, 36–39.

Emery, N. "The androgyny party." *Commentary*, June 1993, 49.

————. "Hillary R." *National Review*, 52, 17 July 2000, 33.

Farley, C.J. "Commander Hillary." *Time*, 26 April 1993, 7.

————. "Making a name for herself." *Time*, 17 May 1993, 13.

"Ferraro: A tough lady draws the crowds." *U.S. News and World Report*, 24 September 1984, 25.

"Ferraro denies any wrongdoing." *New York Times*, 22 August 1984, A1.

"Ferraro faces the past." *Maclean's*, 27 August 1984, 33.

"Ferraro's first week." *Newsweek*, 30 July 1984, 20.

Ferraro, G. and Franke, L.B. (1985). *Ferraro: My story.* New York: Bantam Books.

Ferraro, S. "The prime of Pat Schroeder." *Newsweek*, 27 June 1987, 32.

"Ferraro weathers the storm." *The Economist*, 3 September 1984, 25.

Field, S. "Will Hillary Clinton stand by her man on child care?" *U.S. News and World Report*, 22 June 1992, 18–19.

"Fighting on thrift, wit, and feminism." *Insight*, 27 June 1987, 32.

Fineman, H. & Miller, M. "Hillary's role," *The Economist*, 15 February 1993, 18–23.

Gardetto, D.C. (1997). "Hillary Rodham Clinton, symbolic gender politics, and the New York Times: January-November, 1992." *Newsweek*, 14, 225–240.

Germond, J. & Witcover, J. (1985). *Wake us when it's over: Presidential politics of 1984.* New York: MacMillan.

Goldman, P. & Fuller, T. (1985). *The quest for the presidency 1984.* New York: Bantam Books.

Harbrecht, D.A. & Fly, R. "Can Pat Schroeder be more than 'the woman's candidate'?" *Business Week*, 5 October 1987, 35–36.

Hehir, B. "Leading roles: The stature of Schroeder and Nunn." *Commonwealth*, 20 November 1987, 645–646.

Kaus, M. "Tribal hatred." *The Republic*, 21 June 1993, 4.

Kelly, M. "Saint Hillary." *The New York Times Magazine*, 23 May 1993, 22.

Kempton, B. "Bowing out: A tough choice." *New Choices for the Best Years*, October 1989, 20–22.

King, F. "The great girl." *National Review*, 11 May 1992, 64.

Klein, J. "We're all in this together." *Newsweek*, 15 February 1993, 22.

Kopkind, A. "Now redux." *The Nation*, 1 August 1987, 76–78.

Lindberg, T. "Healthcare from A to Zzzz . . ." *Insight*, 19 April 1993, 40.

Lippert, B. "Execu-Bob Angst." *Working Woman*, November 1993, 111.

"Making the price too high." *Time*, 3 September 1984, 18.

Masliek, J. "The view onstage at the debate." *U.S. News and World Report*, 22 October 1984, 23.

McDonald, M. "His best defense." *Maclean's*, 24 February 1992, 22–24.

————. "The fall of a contender." *Maclean's*, 5 October 1987, 30.

"Mondale: This is an exciting choice." *Time*, 22 July 1984, 12.

Morganthau, T, Shannon, E. & Agrest, S. "The veepstakes: Bush prepares to Debate Ferraro—gently." *Newsweek*, 15 October 1984, 41.

Miller, M. "Lessons of a lightning rod." *Newsweek*, Nov–Dec 1992, 11.

"Nepotism for the nineties." *The Economist*, 30 January 1993, A26.

"Now for the real fight." *Time*, 30 July 1984, 18.

O'Brien, P. "The First Lady with a career?" *Working Woman*, August 1992, 44–48.

Olson, W. "The hand that rocks the cradle." *National Review*, 11 May 1992, 34.

O'Reilly, J. "Our candidates/ourselves: Ferraro touches women's lives in a way No politician ever has." *Time*, 29 October 1984, 33.

O'Reilly, J. & Jacobs, G. "Watch Pat run." *Ms. Magazine*, February 1988, 44.

Pollitt, K. "The male media's problem: First Lady bashing." *The Nation*, 17 May 1993, 657–660.

Raines, H. "GOP seizes 'genderless issue' of tax return to attack Ferraro." *New York Times*, 14 August 1984, A1.

"The rising star of Queens." *Time*, 4 June 1984, 24–25.

Scott, S. & McIntyre, S. "Another Clinton Wears the Pants." *People*, 27 November 2000, 133.

Shapiro, W., Fineman, H, & Shannon, E. "Shoot-out at the gender gap: Bush won at the Polls but Ferraro held her ground." *Newsweek*, 22 October 1984, 29–30.

"Show and tell." *Time*, 3 September 1984, 17.

Sobran, J. "The rise of style." *National Review*, 21 June 1993, 40–41.

Stanley, A. "Run, Pat, run: Colorado's Pat Schroeder is expected to join presidential Pack." *Time*, 3 August 1987, 20.

Walsh, K. T. "America's First (working) couple." *U.S. News and World Report*, 10 May 1993, 32–34.

Walsh, K.T. & Cooper, M. "There's a lot more coming." *U.S. News and World Report*, 3 May 1993, 42–44.

West, C. & Zimmerman, D.H. (1987). "Doing gender." *Gender and Society*, 1:2, 125–151.

Will, G.F. "Her sound bites draw blood." *Newsweek*, 27 August 1987, 76.

Willis, G. "A doll's house?" *The New York Times Review of Books*, 22 October 1992, 6–10.

———. "Hillary Rodham Clinton's Case." *The New York Times Review of Books*, 5 March 1992, 3–5.

Winfield, B.H. (1997). "The making of an image: Hillary Rodham Clinton and American journalists." *Political Communication*, 241–253.

———. (1997). "Introductory note." *Political Communication*, , 221–224.

"Women politicians: A growing breed." *U.S. News and World Report*, 23 July 1984, 9.

"The year of Hillary." *People Weekly*, 25 October 1993, 158–161.

Chapter Fifteen

A Million Moms, MADD Mothers, and Feminists: Media Coverage of Women Activists

Angela High-Pippert

When the relationship between women, politics, and the media is explored, researchers typically concentrate on political elites. Political scientists have been interested in how a candidate's gender affects media coverage both during a political campaign (Kahn and Goldenberg, 1991; Kahn, 1994) and once the candidate is elected to office (Carroll and Schreiber, 1997). Media coverage of women activists is an important area that has been overlooked in this body of research. Understanding the role of the media in framing women's political participation at the mass level seems imperative to understanding the media's role at the elite level. Messages that citizens receive concerning women holding signs on street corners and women holding meetings with constituents reinforce one another. Both messages create an impression about women's roles in the political world, and both are significant. This article begins to fill this gap in the research by examining media coverage of women activists.

In an effort to determine what types of messages citizens receive about women activists, I examined national newspaper coverage of three political organizations: the National Organization for Women (NOW), Mothers Against Drunk Driving (MADD), and the Million Mom March (MMM). A brief description of each organization follows.

Feminists: The National Organization for Women (NOW) is the largest feminist organization in the United States, with more than 500,000 contributing members and 550 chapters nationwide. The mission of NOW is to make legal, political, social, and economic change in society in order to eliminate sexism and oppression. Established in 1966, "NOW has dominated news coverage of the women's movement during the last thirty years and has been most strongly identified in the media with feminism" (Huddy, 1997, p. 198).

MADD Mothers: According to its website, Mothers Against Drunk Driving is the most popular non-profit cause in the United States and has helped pass more than 2,300 anti-drunk driving and underage drinking laws. Founded in 1980, MADD has approximately 2 million members and supporters, with more than 600 chapters across the country. Its mission is to stop drunk driving, support the victims of drunk driving, and prevent underage drinking.

A Million Moms: Founded in 1999, the Million Mom March is a national grassroots organization working to prevent gun death and injury by seeking responsible limits on gun access and use. In May of 2000, more than 750,000 supporters marched in Washington, D.C. while thousands more people marched in cities across the United States. There are 230 MMM chapters nationwide.

I chose to analyze media coverage of NOW, MADD, and MMM because of the potential to compare coverage of women as feminists to coverage of women as mothers. Specifically, I wanted to focus on the framing of "mom discourse" and "policy discourse" among women activists.

"THE MYSTICAL POWER OF MOM"[1]

Framing is about presentation and interpretation. Activists may frame their own political participation in certain ways, or journalists may frame their political involvement for them. In either case, the purpose of the frame is to provide meaning. News frames provide journalists with a "hook" or "peg" for their article, helping them to decide what elements of an event to focus on or ignore (Carroll, 1997). Framing is comfortable for both journalists and readers, as it allows new information to be compartmentalized into familiar categories. According to Gitlin (1980, p. 7), "Media frames are persistent patterns of cognition, interpretation, and presentation, of selection, emphasis, and exclusion, by which symbol handlers routinely organize discourse, whether verbal or visual." Framing affects public perceptions by the way stories are constructed or events are portrayed.

The process of framing is related to the interdependence of social movements and the media. Social movements need the media in order to get their message out to the public, since they need to mobilize other potential activists and establish credibility (Gamson and Wolfsfeld, 1993). For example, the plan for the Million Mom March was first announced on CBS's *The Early Show* and quickly picked up by the Oprah Winfrey and Rosie O'Donnell shows. It helped the MMM cause that founder Donna Dees-Thomases worked as a publicist for CBS and knew what journalists need from social movements—good copy. Stories that are dramatic, personalized, and effective in providing photo opportunities are what the media needs from social movements. Although the relationship between activists and the media may be symbiotic, it is not equal. Activists need the media more than journalists need them. Therefore, activists may choose to frame their own political behavior in a manner that will attract journalists' attention. Framing simplifies the process by making it easier for activists to get attention and for journalists to do their job.

In this paper, I examine two possible frames for women activists: mom discourse (Eliasoph, 1998) and policy discourse. Eliasoph writes of mom discourse among women activists in her fascinating study of citizen involvement and apathy. Among the citizens Eliasoph studied, "momism" was the women activists' "standard fare for their frontstage discourse, despite their wide variety of discourses in more backstage settings" (1998, p. 183). This mom discourse emphasized the women's concern for their own children. As Eliasoph (1998, p. 4) explains,

> One activist said to every reporter she met, "She's a new mom and I'm an old mom. That's why we're in it. We're worried." She had been an activist since the civil rights movement, but she always presented herself as a 'Mom' in more formal settings.

Whether the discourse was a conscious choice or an unintentional habit for the women in Eliasoph's study is significant because it has to do with responsibility for framing. The implications are different if women activists frame their political participation as mom discourse than if journalists frame women activists as moms. Eliasoph (1998, p. 185) gives one example of an activist, Ginny, who "tried to get attention any way she could, and calculated that Momism would get her a foot in the door." According to Ginny, "All the media people want is a Mom and an Expert" (Eliasoph, 1998, p. 196).

While the women in Eliasoph's study tended to incorporate mom discourse, the men tried to implement expert discourse, or what I will refer to as policy discourse. Policy discourse is more rational and technical than mom discourse and more closely resembles the speech of officeholders than constituents. It is not personalized, and it may not be particularly good copy for a journalist. In this study, I define mom discourse and policy discourse in the following way. Mom discourse frames political participation in terms of women's status as mothers, rather than their expertise on policy issues. Policy discourse frames the issue in terms of political rather than personal aspects.

My first set of hypotheses concern the type of discourse presented in media coverage of NOW, MADD, and MMM.

Hypothesis 1: National newspaper coverage of the National Organization for Women will focus on policy discourse rather than mom discourse.

Hypothesis 2: National newspaper coverage of Mothers Against Drunk Driving will focus on policy discourse rather than mom discourse.

Hypothesis 3: National newspaper coverage of the Million Mom March will focus on mom discourse rather than policy discourse.

My fourth hypothesis concerns whether the media or the organization is responsible for this focus on mom discourse. Since the Million Mom March is the only organization with significant amounts of mom discourse to analyze, I focus on MMM for this part of the analysis.

Hypothesis 4: Women involved with the Million Mom March are framing their political participation in terms of mom discourse.

My final hypothesis concerns the differing amounts of media coverage that these organizations received during the time frame of this study.

Hypothesis 5: The Million Mom March will attract more newspaper coverage than the National Organization for Women or Mothers Against Drunk Driving.

This research is based on both systematic content analysis and a contextual reading of 509 articles published in three major U.S. newspapers between August 1, 1999 and June 30, 2001. The three newspapers included in the data set are *The New York Times, The Washington Post*, and *USA TODAY*. According to the Lexis-Nexis Academic Universe, *The New York Times* "bears the reputation of being the United States' unofficial newspaper of record," *The Washington Post* is "standard breakfast-time reading" for members of Congress and journalists, and *USA Today*'s 6.3 million readers make it the most widely read daily newspaper in the United States. The time frame of this study is almost two years, from the inception of the Million Mom March in August of 1999 through June of 2001. In order to locate newspaper articles about each organization, I searched the online Lexis-Nexis database using the keywords "National Organization for Women," "Mothers Against Drunk Driving," and "Million Mom March." I conducted all searches, coding, and analyses for this research. In addition to analyzing national newspaper coverage, I also conducted a content analysis of each organization's website in order to determine the type of discourse that emerges when the organization has complete control of its message.

MEDIA COVERAGE OF WOMEN ACTIVISTS

Table 15.1 presents the number of times that the National Organization for Women, Mothers Against Drunk Driving, and the Million Mom March had mom discourse linked to their organization in national newspaper coverage during the time frame of this study. The National Organization for Women had only one such example, in a *Washington Post* article about an abortion rights rally in Washington, D.C. The article notes, "The thousands of participants in the capital's largest abortion rights rally in recent years included college students, mothers, and daughters from across the country" (Leonnig, 2001). This is noteworthy because it is the only example of a journalist using the term "mothers" in conjunction with NOW. The article also includes a quote from a participant in the rally, an inclusion that somewhat qualifies as mom discourse.

Chapter 15.   Use of Mom Discourse

NOW	MADD	MMM
1	1	95

Source: Lexis-Nexis search.

Although the woman is not identified as a member of NOW, she is described as a "New Hampshire grandmother who joined the abortion rights rally." After describing a friend's experience with an illegal abortion in 1967, she adds, "She came back to my apartment and almost bled to death. And I don't want that ever happening to my granddaughter" (Leonnig, 2001). The woman presents herself as participating in the rally on behalf of her granddaughter, just as the women activists in Eliasoph's (1998) study present themselves as participating on behalf of their children.

Another example is significant in its distancing from mom discourse. The article is about NOW's opposition to presidential candidate Al Gore's anti-poverty plan, due to its possible funding of right-wing, "father's rights" groups. The article mentions that NOW sent an e-mail alert to its members, warning that Gore's plan is "'bad for women and children' largely because it funnels money away from custodial parents to the absent parent" (Connolly, 1999). While acknowledging that the plan was bad for women, NOW's language did not acknowledge that the plan was bad for women precisely because of their status as mothers, since they are more often the custodial parents. Although the subject of the article created the potential for mom discourse to surface, it appears as though NOW deliberately avoided even the use of the term "mother" in its message.

Of course, the mission of NOW is equality for women, not just equality for mothers, so we would not expect to find as many examples of mom discourse in the organization without "mothers" or "mom" in its title. As I argue in the conclusion, it is probably better for women activists if their political participation is not framed this way, as it may reinforce the role of women as private (mothers) rather than public (citizens). However, the perception that a woman is either a feminist or a mother, but never both, is a separate issue, and is not discouraged by media coverage of the nation's largest and most recognizable feminist organization.[2] This adds fuel to the fire of prominent anti-feminists, such as Phyllis Schlafly, who often pit the rights of women against the rights of children. It may also contribute to the perception that women who participate in politics in order to advance feminist policy goals do so only out of self-interest.[3] The idea that a feminist mother might protest or write a letter to a public official concerning an issue such as violence against women, which would be important to her as well as her children (regardless of their gender), is not considered.

Given the name of the organization, it may be surprising that Mothers Against Drunk Driving also had only one example of mom discourse linked to its organization during the time frame of this study. The article is about the 20th anniversary of MADD's founding, and the national president is quoted as saying, "Today, we return to the U.S. Capitol, where 20 years ago, grief-stricken mothers met and launched the nationwide MADD movement and a war on drunk driving" (Santana, 2000). The combination of past tense with mom discourse is significant. Although a content analysis of media coverage of MADD since its inception in 1980 is beyond the scope of this study, the use of past tense to describe the role of mothers is indicative of the possible evolution of MADD from a mother's organization into a public policy organization. An examination of MADD's website lends support to this idea, as the first words that appear use the term "mom" but would not qualify as mom discourse ("You don't have to be a mom to be a member of MADD. MADD is made up of moms, dads, young people and other individuals working to make a difference on our roadways and in our communities"). There are no examples of mom discourse on MADD's website, not even in the description of Millie Webb, the national president. This is significant because Millie Webb is frequently identified in newspaper coverage as having "lost a daughter and nephew in a crash with a driver with a 0.08 blood-alcohol level" (Bowles, 2000). Most of the information provided on MADD's website concerns public policy, such as a guide to Congress, detailed and comprehensive position statements, and a link to MADD's public policy department. It appears as though MADD emphasizes policy discourse in its own materials, and that media coverage of MADD follows this trend. As with NOW, media coverage of MADD is dominated by policy discourse rather than mom discourse. Hypotheses one and two are supported.

In stark contrast to NOW and MADD, the Million Mom March had 95 examples of mom discourse linked to its organization. Women involved with the Million Mom March are referred to (and refer to themselves) as "the moms," "stroller moms," "soccer moms," "marching moms," "star moms," "everyday moms," "quintessential suburban mothers," "professional moms," "just moms," "ticked-off moms," and "a few good moms." Examples of mom discourse are not only plentiful, but also diverse. Hypothesis 3 is strongly supported.

The first set of hypotheses begs the question as to who is responsible for framing women's political participation in terms of policy discourse or mom discourse. Specifically, who is responsible for framing women's participation in the Million Mom March as mom discourse? Hypothesis 4 identified the MMM itself as the culprit. As Table 15.2 shows, there is support for this hypothesis as well. Although journalists used many of the descriptions in the previous paragraph and wrote phrases such as "the hand that rocks the cradle rules the world," "mind your mothers," and "mom power," the media is not solely or even primarily responsible for this framing. The media was the source of the mom discourse within newspaper coverage of MMM less than one-fourth of the time. Another possibility was that this framing occurred from outside the MMM organization and therefore was beyond its control. This does not appear to be the case, however. The mom discourse came from outside the organization less than one-fifth of the time. Examples of this category range from opponents to supporters, with National Rifle Association (NRA) spokespersons referring to MMM activists as "misled moms" and "a million misinformed moms" and President Clinton predicting that the gun lobby would be no match for "America's moms"[4] (Stolberg, 2000).

As Table 15.2 shows, the leaders of the Million Mom March provided the mom discourse for about one-fourth of the media coverage, while members emphasized this framing in more than one-third of the media coverage. Taken together, this accounts for more than half of the examples of mom discourse reported by the media.

It is entirely possible that there is a relationship between these two categories, with MMM leaders using mom discourse and setting the tone for members to follow. Based on a contextual reading of the 95 MMM articles in which mom discourse appears, as well as an examination of the MMM website, there is evidence that mom discourse has been encouraged and promoted within the Million Mom March since its founding in August of 1999. Beyond

Table 15.2. Source of Mom Discourse Within MMM (n = 95)

Media	*23%*	*(22)*
Outside the Organization	19%	(18)
Leadership	24%	(23)
Members	34%	(32)

Source: Lexis-Nexis search.

the obvious aspects such as the title and date of the march, founder Donna Dees-Thomases implemented mom discourse from the start. She has been quoted as saying that her "maternal instincts kicked in" after a shooting at a Jewish Community Center day care center in California (Toner, 2000). Once she thought of the idea for a million mom march, she applied for a march permit for the following Mother's Day, "hoping to harness what she calls the 'mystical power of mom'" (Koch, 2000a). At an early press conference for the event, Dees-Thomases explained, "If we mothers can make babies in nine months, surely that's enough time for Congress to make tougher gun laws to protect them" (James, 1999). According to Dees-Thomases, "Word about the march spread from 'stroller mom to stroller mom'" (Koch, 2000a). The slogan for the march was "We're looking for a few good moms." Dees-Thomases repeatedly emphasized that she was a political novice until her involvement with the Million Mom March, commenting, "I didn't know the Brady Bill from the Brady Bunch" (James, 1999). Mom discourse has continually won out over policy discourse. Even when Dees-Thomases was passing the MMM torch to new leadership, she relied on mom discourse, using the term "chair-mom" to describe Mary Leigh Blek's new position in the organization. Dees-Thomases chose that term even though Blek was a founding member of the Bell Campaign, a national movement to prevent gun violence (METRO in Brief, 2000). Her qualifications as a mother seemed to outweigh her policy expertise.

This emphasis on mom discourse has been picked up by MMM members and activists. Of course, this emphasis is not necessarily top-down and may have been present in activist circles even without the apparent endorsement of such language by Million Mom March leaders. Either way, mom discourse certainly prevails in newspaper coverage of MMM activists. The most blatant example is from an MMM member seeking permission to distribute materials about the march to spectators at a sports center. "I'm nobody. I'm just a mom," she told the director of the center (Levine, 2000). "The mothers of the world are angry, and you never, never tick off a mother. The hands that rock the cradle rule the world" (Koch, 2000b) is another such example. Another MMM activist told a reporter, "We are going to the Hill, and any politician who doesn't recognize that the moms mean business is going to timeout in November" (Witt, 2000). One activist began with mom discourse and then shifted toward policy discourse by mentioning lobbying her congressional member. "Motherhood is sacred in this country. I've already e-mailed my congressman . . . this rally has to bring some attention to the issue" (Gerber, 2000a).

There are signs that this shift toward more of a policy discourse among the MMM could be reflected in a larger sense as well. A current examination of the Million Mom March website reveals more of a policy message than was

Table 15.3.   Number of Articles in which Organization Mentioned

NOW	MADD	MMM
32%	24%	44%
(161)	(123)	(225)

Source: Lexis-Nexis search (n = 509 articles).

previously highlighted. The website contains a summary of national policy priorities and now more closely resembles the MADD website. However, MMM is not abandoning all of its mom discourse in favor of policy discourse, as its website still contains a "timeout chair" for opponents of gun control and an "apple pie award" for supporters. Recent newspaper coverage indicates that the "chair-mom" of the Million Mom March, Mary Leigh Blek, does not engage in mom discourse to the degree of Dees-Thomases. However, Blek did refer to "the moms" as "becoming a force, alongside the gun lobby" (Gerber, 2000b).

Now that I have examined aspects of the content of newspaper coverage of NOW, MADD, and MMM, I turn my attention to the amount of newspaper coverage received by each organization. Hypothesis 5 states that the Million Mom March will receive more newspaper coverage than the National Organization for Women and Mothers Against Drunk Driving. Tables 15.3 and 15.4 address this hypothesis from different perspectives. Table 15. 3 shows that MMM was mentioned in 44 percent (225 articles) of the 509 newspaper articles analyzed for this study, as compared to 32 percent (161 articles) for NOW and 24 percent (123 articles) for MADD. This supports Hypothesis 5.

In Table 15.4, we go beyond whether the organization was mentioned in a newspaper article to whether the organization is the subject of the article. The most striking aspect of Table 15.4 is the distinction that develops between the Million Mom March rally and the Million Mom March organization. Although a quick glance might indicate that MMM was the subject of many more articles than NOW and MADD, we must consider that the bulk of these articles were about the march itself (19 percent), rather than the organization (3 percent). Since there were two Mother's Day marches during the time frame of this study, it seems logical that coverage of the marches would tip

Table 15.4.   Number of Articles in which Organization is Subject of Article

NOW	MADD	MMM (Orgn)	MMM (Rally)
4%	7%	3%	19%
(6/161)	(8/123)	(6/225)	(42/225)

Source: Lexis-Nexis search (n=509 articles).

the scales in favor of MMM. When only media coverage of the organizations are concerned, the numbers and percentages are much closer, and Hypothesis 5 is somewhat contradicted.

Media coverage of NOW, MADD, and MMM differs in other significant ways as well. One interesting aspect of the newspaper coverage of each organization concerns how it is portrayed in the article. Is the organization portrayed as its members, its leadership, or merely as a nameless, faceless organization? Tables 15.5, 15.6, and 15.7 present the differing portrayals of the National Organization for Women, Mothers Against Drunk Driving, and the Million Mom March. As Table 15.5 shows, NOW is most often presented as an organization without members (43 percent). The next most common portrayal is equating Patricia Ireland, the national president during the time frame of this study, with NOW (29 percent).[5] The most striking aspect of Table 15.5 is that members, activists, or protestors account for only 4 percent of how NOW is portrayed in national newspapers. The National Organization for Women most commonly appears as an organization without members, which may affect perceptions that citizens have about NOW, and therefore about feminists. It's difficult to imagine a feminist activist if you never hear about one. It may not be as difficult to conjure up an image of a "stroller mom," since MMM members and supporters account for 56 percent of its newspaper coverage.[6] Mothers Against Drunk Driving is most often portrayed as an organization (58 percent) rather than its members (7 percent). As

Table 15.5. Portrayal of NOW Within Article

Organization Name	43%	(69)
Patricia Ireland (President)	29%	(46)
Kim Gandy (Ex VP)	6%	(10)
Other Natl Leadership Positions	6%	(10)
President of Local Chapter	12%	(20)
Members/Activists/Protestors	4%	(6)

Source: Lexis-Nexis search (n = 161 articles).

Table 15.6. Portrayal of MADD Within Article

Organization Name	58%	(71)
Millie Webb (President)	8%	(10)
Public Policy Liaison/Lobbyist	9%	(11)
Other Natl Leadership Positions	11%	(13)
President of Local Chapter	8%	(10)
Members/Activists/Volunteers	6%	(7)
Mothers	<1%	(1)

Source: Lexis-Nexis search (n = 123 articles).

Table 15.7.   Portrayal of MMM Within Article

Organization Name	7%	(15)
Rally	30%	(67)
Founder/President	4%	(10)
Chapter President/Director	3%	(7)
Members/Marchers/Activists/ Supporters/Protestors/Organizers	14%	(32)
Names of Individual Members	36%	(80)
Mothers/Moms	6%	(14)

Source: Lexis-Nexis search (n = 225 articles).

with NOW, this presentation fits with an emphasis on policy discourse over mom discourse. The Million Mom March is a relatively new organization, and therefore lighter on the organization portrayal (7 percent) than NOW and MADD.

CONCLUSION: MOTHERS AND CITIZENS

This paper is a first step toward adding to what we know about women, politics, and the media. By examining media coverage of women activists, we may better understand media coverage of women candidates and officeholders. This study focused on the framing of women's political participation by both activists and the media, specifically in terms of mom discourse. I found that members, leaders, the media, and individuals outside the organization created the connection between the Million Mom March and mom discourse. The Million Mom March also attracted more national newspaper coverage than the National Organization for Women and Mothers Against Drunk Driving during the time frame of the study. It is too soon to tell whether this pattern will continue once the focus of MMM becomes less about actual marches and more about sustaining the organization.[7]

Eliasoph (1998) suspects that women activists often receive more media attention than men activists due to their easier access to mom discourse, which is a more legitimate-sounding language for citizen involvement than the expert discourse typically incorporated by men. While this may appear to be a benefit for women activists, it is not only the quantity but also the content of the coverage that matters. With mom discourse, women are often portrayed as emotional (rather than rational) and unreasonable. The perception that women are too emotional is linked to the perception that they are less suited for politics than (rational) men. This is linked to another potential problem concerning maternalist politics, which is that the only suitable motivation for women's political participation is "for the sake of the children." Taken to the extreme, the message is that women are emotional and more concerned with people (particularly children) while men are rational and more concerned with politics. However, women are the experts where children are concerned, and so it is appropriate for them to be politically involved on their behalf. Whether is it appropriate for women to participate on their own behalf is another matter. As Pollitt (2000, p. 10) writes, "Under the rubric of maternalism, women can fight for kids but not for themselves." While mom discourse may gain media attention for women activists, it also may cost them in the long run. Since most citizens are more apt to learn about women's political participation from reading a newspaper than reading a college textbook on American political behavior or feminist theory, the way women activists are portrayed in the media matters.

NOTES

1. Quoted by Donna Dees-Thomases, founder of the Million Mom March (Koch, 2000a).

2. However, an examination of NOW's website indicates that the organization may not always avoid any connection with motherhood. In 2001, NOW announced a Mother's Day Picket for Women's Rights on its website. The announcement had elements of both mom discourse and policy discourse. NOW Action Vice President was quoted as saying, "While the country celebrates and honors mothers, the Bush administration works to pass a budget and tax cuts that will hurt women and our families." The remainder of the information on the website focused on public policy.

3. The fact that many members of society participate in politics because they want something for themselves, and are able to do so without being labeled as selfish or self-interested, is yet another (important) issue. However, it is beyond the scope of this paper.

4. The risk of mom discourse becoming a weapon for opponents to use in order to patronize and discount women activists resonates with these examples.

5. Ireland is frequently presented as "the feminist position" on a variety of issues, from which movies are potentially offensive to women to whether Barbie for President is a positive or negative agent of political socialization for young girls.

6. The percentages in the last three rows of Table 7 total 56 percent.

7. The Million Mom March merged with the Brady Campaign and Brady Center to Prevent Gun Violence on October 1, 2001.

REFERENCES

Bowles, S. (2000). National Drunken-driving Standard Passes. *USA TODAY,* October 4, 3A.

Carroll, S. & Schreiber, R. (1997). Media Coverage of Women in the 103rd Congress. In Norris, P. (Ed). *Women, Media, and Politics.* New York: Oxford University Press.

Carroll, S. J. (1999). The Disempowerment of the Gender Gap: Soccer Moms and the 1996 Elections. *PS: Political Science and Politics* 22, 7–11.

Connolly, C. (1999). Gore's Anti-Poverty Plan Alarms NOW. *The Washington Post,* October 23, A8.

Eliasoph, N. (1998). *Avoiding Politics.* Cambridge: Cambridge University Press.

Gamson, W. A. & Wolfsfeld, G. (1993). Movements and Media as Interacting Systems. *Annals of the American Academy of Political and Social Science* 528, 114–125.

Gerber, A. (2000). Bus Brings Moms Together for Rally. *USA TODAY,* May 15, 3A.

———. (2000). Million Moms Say their Group is Becoming a Force. *USA TODAY,* September 5, 6A.

Gitlin, T. (1980). *The Whole World is Watching.* Berkeley: University of California Press.

Huddy, L. (1997). Feminists and Feminism in the News. In Norris, P. (Ed). *Women, Media, and Politics.* New York: Oxford University Press.

James, G. (1999). Mothers Hope They're One in a Million. *The New York Times,* October 31, 14NJ.

Kahn, K. F. and Goldenberg, E. N. (1991). Women Candidates in the News: An Examination of Gender Differences in U.S. Senate Campaigns. *Public Opinion Quarterly* 55, 180–199.

Kahn, K. F. (1994). Does Gender Make a Difference? An Experimental Examination of Sex Stereotypes and Press Patterns in Statewide Campaigns. *American Journal of Political Science* 38, 162–195.

Koch, W. (2000a). Leaders of Mom March Call it a Starting Step. *USA TODAY,* April 24, 9A.

Koch, W. (2000b). Marchers Tell Congress: Mind your Mothers. *USA TODAY,* May 15, 3A.

Leonnig, C. D. (2001). Abortion Rights are Rally's Cry. *The Washington Post,* April 23, B1.

Levine, S. (2000). Fight Against Guns Gives Moms a Cause. *The Washington Post,* April 19, B1.

METRO in Brief, 2000. Moms March Effort Plans Strategy. *The Washington Post,* May 17, B3.

Pollitt, K. (2000). Moms to NRA: Grow Up! *The Nation,* June 12, 10.

Ruddick, S. (1989). *Maternal Thinking.* London: The Women's Press.

Santana, A. (2000). On 20th Anniversary, MADD Urges National 0.08% Standard; Rally Targets Drunk Drivers. *The Washington Post,* September 7, A6.

Stolberg, S. G. (2000). On Eve of Million Mom March, Clinton Calls Mothers the Stronger Voice in Gun Debate. *The New York Times,* May 14, 1–16.

Toner, R. (2000). Mothers Rally to Assail Gun Violence. *The New York Times,* May 15, A1.

Witt, A. (2000). Maryland Mom Does her Part for a 'Safer Society.' *The Washington Post,* May 15, A15.

Chapter Sixteen

A Life's Work: Preserving and Transcending Immigrant Culture and Gender Roles

Linda Brigance

Catch-22. Between a rock and a hard place. No-win situation. Caught in a double bind. These are familiar expressions used to describe those moments when circumstances trap someone between two equally undesirable options. Few people make it through their personal and professional lives without experiencing such dilemmas. Tell a white lie or offend a friend. Put in the extra hours to finish a project or attend a special family celebration. The practical and moral consequences of such problematic choices are as varied as the scenarios from which they arise. On an individual basis such situations occur rarely and are situationally driven. There are entire groups of people, however, whose double binds are not the result of circumstances, but identity. These people exist inside the fault line between the principles and practices of the dominant culture and those of their sub-culture. They are under pressure to conform to two sets of standards even if these standards are polar opposites, and even if success in terms of one set of standards assures failure in terms of the other.

W. E. B. DuBois (1903/1999), described African Americans' double bind as a sense of "double consciousness . . . [where one is] . . . always looking at one's self through the eyes of others, of measuring one's soul by the tape of a world that looks on in amused contempt and pity . . . two warring ideals in one dark body" (p.164). Frye (2001) explains it this way: "the experience of oppressed people is that the living of one's life is confined and shaped by forces and barriers which are not accidental or occasional and hence avoidable, but are systematically which related to each other in such a way as to catch one between and among them and which restricts or penalizes motion in any direction" (p. 50). Jamieson (1995) defines it as a "rhetorical construct that posits two and only two alternatives, one or both penalizing the person being offered them" (p. 13). This paper focuses on two groups that histori-

212

cally have faced identity-based double binds in America: immigrants and women. Specifically, it examines the life of Maria Kowalska, a second generation Polish American woman, who faced a complex double bind (in essence, a double-double bind) of gender and ethnic identities. However, her role as publisher of an immigrant newspaper, *Slowo Polskie* (*The Polish Word*), provided her with an opportunity to utilize her double bind status to transcend limitations imposed by her gender and ethnicity. In turn, her unique standpoint as a woman immigrant contributed to the success of *Slowo Polskie* as a vehicle for community building within the immigrant community and as a bridge between the immigrant and non-immigrant populations. Kowalska's story, therefore, offers an opportunity to better understand the multifaceted intersection of media history, immigrant culture and gender. This essay first examines the double bind status of immigrant women. Second, it establishes the need to focus on the role of immigrant women's history in order to enrich a variety of areas of scholarship. Third, it provides an overview of the role of the immigrant press in America. Finally, it presents the story of Maria Kowalska and *Slowo Polskie* as a case study for learning about women, immigrants and the media.

As a member of a close-knit immigrant community in Utica, New York, in the early twentieth century, Kowalska faced a double bind. While nomenclature like "German American," "Italian American," and "Polish American" has been offered as proof of assimilation into the great American melting pot, such twofold designations are also evidence of the double bind faced by newcomers. With ethnic pride and comfort in the Old World language and traditions on one side and the pressure to be a "real" American on the other, immigrants often face a no-win situation. According to Schneider and Schneider (1993), during the peak of European immigration to the United States in the early twentieth century, "the nativism aroused by this sizable immigrant population operated almost as unjustly and cruelly as the racism directed against America's black population" (p. 6). Clearly marked by their clothing, language, and customs, immigrants were expected to live with their own kind and fill jobs at the lowest rung of the economic level. Poor wages forbade immigrants from purchasing the American appearance of ready-made clothes and cosmetics (Ewen and Ewen, 1982) or escaping their ghettoized communities. Only through a strong sense of ethnic identity could immigrants find a refuge from the prejudices of the dominant society. Yet, the glue that bound members of an ethnic community was made of those very values and practices that distinguished them from the non-immigrant community and devalued them as "un-American." Because the choice between what it meant to be a "good" ethnic community member and a "good" American was a mutually exclusive one, immigrants lived within the confines of a double bind.

Women are another group whose identity places them in what Jamieson (1995) has characterized as "a bundle of binds" (p. 8). Women are regularly trapped between standards for behavior that are deemed appropriately feminine and the devaluation of those same behaviors by a patriarchal culture. For example, for centuries laws and custom limited women's activities to the private sphere; yet, women were devalued *because* those activities were interpreted to be of little value to the public sphere. The result is a conundrum in terms of sexual activity (Fry, p. 50), management style (Bem, 1993), communication practices (Kramarae, 1991; Tannen, 2001), and political participation (Jamieson, 1995). While Jamieson (1995) contends that women are continually breaking out of the double bind, Faludi (1991) argues that women's perpetual double bind status consistently undermines aspirations for social, political, and economic equality. The enthusiasm with which Faludi's book, *Backlash: The Undeclared War Against American Women* (1991), was received suggests that many women continue to identify with and experience gender-based Catch-22 situations.

The immigrant woman faced a double dose of conflicting restrictions and expectations. For example, because the majority of immigrants came from rural backgrounds but settled in urban areas, women's traditional ways of contributing to the family's livelihood were no longer available to them, placing them in a double bind. As part of a family trying to establish themselves in a new homeland, women were needed to contribute to a household's economic stability; yet, "immigrant families were adverse to living off the wages of wives and mothers. . . [despite the fact that] . . income earned by immigrant fathers was rarely enough to support a family" (Woloch, 1984, p. 231). Women were trapped between the immigrants' economic reality and gender role expectations. In Polish immigrant communities, for instance, economic survival often depended on the income women could earn from jobs outside of the home as millworkers or domestics. Yet, it was "a rule almost without exception" that married women were to stay at home regardless of whether they had large families or were childless (Knothe, 1997b, p.316.) Thus, their roles as economic contributor and family nurturer were compromised, and success in one area meant failure in the other.

Another example of the double bind facing immigrant women had to do with their domestic practices. On one hand, the immigrant community expected mothers to follow traditional ethnic child rearing practices that were transmitted from one generation to another. According to Knothe (1997b), in the Polish communities, "baby care did not change much in America" (p. 317). On the other hand, however, traditional practices were viewed with ridicule by the mainstream community whose "scientific methods of homemaking and childcare . . . were disdainful of time-honored old world traditions" (Seller, 1994, p. 179). Thus, immigrant women consistently were caught between the rules, roles and expectations of the Old World and the New World and trapped in no-win situations.

Scholarship focusing on media history, women and the media, and immigrant culture has left out or marginalized the perspectives provided by the other two topics. As Hardt (1999) points out about media history, "the immigrant or foreign languages press in the United States has received scant attention. . .and [this situation] reflect[s] negatively upon press historians and their understanding of American culture" (p. 155). Women, too, have been left out of the traditional studies of newspaper culture. Thanks to efforts of a few pioneering scholars, women's contributions to print media history are being discovered and acknowledged. Beasley and Silver (1977), Belford (1986), and Marzolf (1997) identify and celebrate the accomplishments of women who worked professionally as journalists from colonial times to the present. Streitmatter (1994) acknowledges the leadership and contribution of African American women journalists. Yet, out of the hundreds of women mentioned in these combined works, there are no representatives of the immigrant press. Also, by focusing exclusively on women journalists, women's contributions and to editing and publishing are not represented.

In addition to the omissions addressed above, there is also a gender gap in the scholarship of immigrant culture. According to Weinberg (1992) "the study of immigrant history has been distorted and impoverished" because it has been based primarily on the experiences of immigrant men (p. 25). There has been a move to focus on how and why immigrant women fit their traditional roles into the economic and social milieu of America (Harzig, 1997; Seller, 1994). However, exploration of the professional careers and other non-traditional activities of immigrant women have rarely been explored. The goal of this study is to begin to fill in the gaps in media history, immigrant culture, and women's history by recovering the story of one woman who used her role as a newspaper publisher to challenge the bundle of double binds she faced as an immigrant woman.

Between 1900 and 1920, immigrants fleeing the chaos of World War I Europe arrived in America in unprecedented numbers. In 1907 alone, a record 1,285,000 newcomers entered the United States ("Growth of a Nation," 1985, p. 35). When Maria Kowalska became the publisher of *Slowo Polskie* in 1918, it was one of more than 1,300 foreign-language newspapers published in the U.S., including sixty-eight Polish language dailies, weeklies and monthlies that served an audience of approximately 500,000 (Pliska, 1965, p. 52). In the period 1900 to 1920 alone, "over 170 new journals were launched" (Kuzniewski, 1987, p. 278). These papers were published either by individuals motivated by political ideology, churches attempting to exert social and moral control over their parishioners, or secular organizations devoted to a variety of concerns (Olszyk, 1940, p.13–17). Regardless of the ownership structure or differences in editorial intentions of specific papers, the immigrant press as an institution served unique and invaluable functions for Polonia[1] as well as the larger communities in which the immigrants settled.

A primary function of immigrant newspapers was community building through the preservation of ethnic consciousness. This was accomplished both by facilitating connections with the homeland and helping to create and maintain networks with immigrant communities in the United States. News reports of conditions and activities in the old country were a focus of most immigrant newspapers. In the early decades of the twentieth-century, this was particularly true of the Polish-language newspapers, whose audiences were caught up in a nationalist fervor[2]. In the days before and during World War I, *Slowo Polskie* was filled with reports about growing hostilities in Europe as well as the local community's efforts in support of the war, such as fund-raising events and activities of the Blue Army.[3] After the war, it closely followed the conditions in the fledgling Polish state, even publishing appeals for donations from the local Polish community (*Slowo Polskie*, May 5, 1922). For the immigrant populace, the immigrant press was the most consistent source of news from abroad.

An equally important community building function of the press was the maintenance of a cohesive local community. By reporting on local events ranging from club meetings and sports competitions to entertainment opportunities and the opening of new businesses, *Slowo Polskie* served as a clearinghouse for the social and civic life of Polonia. It utilized correspondents from nearby cities such as New York Mills, Whitesboro, and Rome to keep Poles throughout New York state's Mohawk Valley connected with each other. In addition to news coverage, the paper served as a public forum for the voices of immigrants by printing letters to the editor as well as creative works such as poems and short stories.

Immigrant newspapers fulfilled an important function by providing the community with information vital to their survival in America from sources outside of their ethnic group. Because so many immigrants were unable to read newspapers written for English-reading audiences, they relied on the immigrant press to bring them information from the world beyond their ethnic enclaves in their own tongue. Coverage of local, state and national news provided readers with a window to the world outside of their immigrant community that they might otherwise lack. Thus, papers like *Slowo Polskie* gave immigrants a glimpse of the latest fashions, public debates, and civic controversies that characterized the larger culture within which they resided. Much of the information they received from these papers was of immediate and practical value, such as *Slowo Polskie*'s serialization of a tutorial for the U.S. citizenship examinations (*Slowo Polskie*, September, 9, 1922).

In addition to serving these important functions for the immigrant community, the immigrant press was essential to the dominant (non-immigrant) community. In Utica, this consisted primarily of the descendants of English, Welsh and Scottish settlers who first came to the Mohawk Valley in 1634 (Pitcher, 1914, p. 4). The dominant culture needed a way to communicate with the large influx of newcomers whose language, customs and values made direct communication a problem. Because most immigrants raised their children, worshiped, organized, and spent their leisure time primarily within ethnically homogeneous enclaves, members of the dominant community had limited access to individual immigrants or their organizations. Mayoral candidates, banks, furniture stores, and community charities all counted on these newspapers to take their message to the immigrants in a language the readers could understand. The relationship between the immigrant press and the non-ethnic community was a symbiotic one. The immigrant newspaper provided the larger community with a voice to the immigrants. The paper delivered voters, community volunteers and consumers to the dominant community. And, the dominant community provided the newspapers with advertising revenue that was essential to their economic stability.

Slowo Polskie was founded in 1911 by Jan Gomolski, a Polish community activist. The paper, like others during this time period, echoed the nationalistic leanings of most people in Utica's Polonia (Baretski, 1969, p. 72). For example, Gomolski rallied the community against the German, Austrian, and Russian regimes that had occupied a partitioned Poland since 1772 (Halecki, 1992, p. 276) and advocated a free, independent Polish state (*Slowo Polskie*, September 25, 1911, p. 1). In addition, the paper called for political activism against oppressors in the immigrants' new home. In the first months of the paper's publication, for example, it not only reported on a worker's strike at a nearby textile mill where the majority of workers were Polish immigrants (Pula and Dziedzic, 1990), but admonished anyone in the community who did not support the action (*Slowo Polskie*, October 12, 1911, p. 7).

At this time it was the custom for single men to board with established families (Nobel, 1999, p. 65). Gomolski lived with the family of Thomas and Louise Kowalski, a founding family of the Utica Polish community.[4] By this time the Kowalskis were members of Utica's small Polish American middle class. While the majority of Poles in the area worked as unskilled laborers in the mills, Thomas Kowalski was self-employed. In addition to running a tailor shop from the family home, he was in the insurance business and owned several properties in Utica. In keeping with tradition and economic necessity, Thomas trained his three sons and three daughters to work in the family businesses. Louisa fulfilled the traditional domestic roles of wife, mother and housekeeper. In addition she cooked and kept house for boarders, which was one of the few socially acceptable ways for married women to contribute to the family's income. (Knothe, p. 318). While daughter Marie complained that her father was a strict taskmaster, she learned the family trades well enough to become an entrepreneur in her own right and opened her own dressmaking business. Like many unmarried Polish women, Kowalska earned her own living and contributed to the family's income until she married. In 1914, Kowalska married Jan Gomolski and turned her business acumen to *Slowo Polskie*.

The marriage lasted only a few years during which Gomolski continued as a political activist. He served as a leader in a Utica-based regiment of the Blue Army (*Zlota Ksiegas*, 1920, p. 23). The Gomolskis lived separately after Gomolski's return from the war in Europe, although they continued to publish the newspaper together for another year. The urge to return to Europe to help restore an independent Polish state was strong among Polish nationalists, and Gomolski may have returned to his native land after the war. After 1920 his name no longer appeared in city directories and *Slowo Polskie* listed only Maria K. Gomolska as the paper's publisher. The fact that most publishers of the Polish American press were men (Olszyk, 1940, p. 31) did not deter Kowalska from continuing to publish *Slowo Polskie* on her own. As a once-again single woman from an entrepreneurial family, the opportunity to continue as an independent business owner would have been an appealing challenge.

In 1928, Kowalska married Louis K. Bienkowski, who hosted one of the nation's longest running Polish language radio shows, *Echoes of Poland* for over fifty-four years (John, 1984), until shortly before his death in 1984 ("Former," 1984). Although Bienkowski's name intermittently appeared in the paper alongside his wife's as co-publisher, family members report he had little to do with the daily operations of the paper, instead directing his energy toward the radio program and a variety of community charities efforts (M. Kran, personal communication, July 15, 1999; B. Stanulevich, personal communication, August 8, 2001).

Kowalska's primary role with *Slowo Polskie* was as a publisher, not a journalist. In the early days of the immigrant press, journalistic experience was not a prerequisite for establishing and operating a newspaper. Barszczewski (1902), commenting on Polish American publications in the early part of the twentieth-century said, "establishment of a periodical in the United States requires no more difficulty than setting up a store or repair shop or tailoring establishment" (15). In other words, the newspaper business was first and foremost a business. Tailors provided the community with clothing; newspapers publishers provided the community with information. For the first three years following Gomolski's departure from Utica, Kowalska held the combined position of editor and publisher. This meant that she handled editorial functions such as obtaining, choosing, revising and preparing what was to be printed as well as publishing functions such as advertising sales, distribution, and the technical aspects of the printing process. By 1925, however, Kowalska was able to focus her attention on the business side of the paper by hiring an editor, Jan Labuz, who held this position off and on until the paper ceased publication after Kowalska's death. Even with an editor on the staff, however, all editorial policies would have been "subject to approval of the publisher" (Olszyk, 1940, p. 29).

The most visible evidence of Kowalska's impact on the newspaper and the community is the longevity of *Slowo Polskie*. According to Olszyk (1940), "one of the characteristics of the Polish American press is its instability and activity. During the 30-year period from 1870 to 1900 some 120 publications were launched and by 1950 only 49 remained" (p. 43). In 1922, Park characterized the future of the immigrant press in the U.S. as "the survival of the fittest" (p. 328). Publishers of immigrant newspapers faced the same financial struggles as the rest of the newspaper industry such as the Great Depression of the 1930s and competition for advertising revenue. They also faced an obstacle unique to the immigrant press. As first generation immigrants died out and their children and grandchildren became increasingly "Americanized," the immigrant press experienced the decline of "a captive [native] speaking readership" (Obidinski, 1997, p. 46). Obidinski (1997) reported that "in order to survive, the press must attract enough readers and sufficient resources to justify publication . . . through various adaptations . . . [such as] finding or preserving financial support to supplement advertising and subscription revenues . . . appearing in a language and style attractive to readers . . . addressing diverse interests of readers" (p. 49).

In order to maintain the financial stability that would allow *Slowo Polskie* to succeed in the community building work previously identified, Kowalska had to make sure the paper served both its advertisers and its readers. This is the focus of the upcoming section. However, because advertising and subscription revenues alone rarely assure the financial success of a publication, she also had to look beyond meeting the needs of these two constituencies. For example, a primary strategy she initiated was to expand the business into a full-service printer, operating first as Slowo Polskie Publishing (1928–1939) and later as Fort Schuyler Press (1940–1964). A steady flow of revenue was assured by obtaining outside printing contracts with Hamilton College, the New York State Art Teachers Association, Utica Catholic Academy, DeSales High School, the *Civil Defense News*, and others (*Slowo Polskie*, December 11, 1964). By consistently upgrading the technological capabilities of the printing business as well as expanding the scope of the paper's readership and advertising base, Kowalska built the paper into a business that succeeded for decades when failure was the norm for immigrant newspapers.

Kowalska's upbringing prepared her well for the role of newspaper publisher. As a member of one of the founding families of Utica's Polonia, she was raised in an environment of civic responsibility and witnessed first-hand the work necessary to build a thriving community. For instance, her family was instrumental in founding Holy Trinity Catholic Church, an institution which has been at the center of the Polish community in Utica for more than a century. Such early experiences provided her with a sense of community and a sense of self as an integral part of that community which was key to running a successful newspaper. This consciousness would have been vital in terms of knowing what information people wanted and needed as well as knowing where to go to acquire such information. Because of her family's position in the community, Kowalska would have had access to information and resources that otherwise may have been unavailable to a woman taking on such a public role.

She would have been comfortable in the role of community builder, also, because this was a traditional function of women in Polish communities. In Poland, for example, women were at the center of rituals and religious activities vital to the social and cultural life of the community (Knothe, 1997a, p. 151). According to Radzilowski (1996), immigrant women adopted this tradition role in America. "Polish immigrant women carried on the work of [social reproduction of communal networks] as operators of boarding houses; as teaching and nursing nuns; as founders of a myriad of local, parochial, regional, and national social, religious, educational, and insurance organizations; and most important, as wives, mothers, and relatives" (p. 70). Kowalska's use of role as publisher to help build community did not violate gender expectations. But she did expand the method of fulfilling this function beyond those methods more traditionally and directly related to the domestic sphere.

Because of the nature of the immigrant press and its functions within the immigrant society, Kowalska's position as a daughter of one of Utica's first Polish families, her entrepreneurial experience, and her business acumen, she was able to transcend traditional gendered restrictions and limitations. Rather than be confined by the roles and expectations of a gendered double bind, she inverted them to establish her legitimacy as a newspaper publisher and to fulfill the paper's community-building function. She built on her traditionally sanctioned roles as helpmate-wife and industrious immigrant daughter to establish a place for herself in the male-dominated, public sphere enterprise of publishing. She fashioned the role of newspaper publisher as an extension of acceptable roles for women in traditional Polish immigrant families. Rather than allowing those roles and expectations to restrict her opportunities, she legitimized her role as publisher through them.

Just as she inverted her gendered double bind status to her advantage, Kowalska capitalized on the double bind she faced as an immigrant. She used her immigrant status to make the paper a success and, in turn, used her position as publisher as a vehicle for transcending her immigrant status. While most immigrant-owned businesses relied on their own ethnic group for a customer base, the nature of the newspaper business necessitated that publishers secure advertising revenue from outside the immigrant community. In the case of *Slowo Polskie*, the majority of ads placed by immigrant businesses were one-inch column ads—the smallest and least expensive type of display ad. In contrast, ads for local banks, furniture stores and department stores usually were one-fourth, and occasionally even, one-half page ads. These larger ads meant greater income for the paper. Assuring a steady income from advertising sales required an astute understanding of both the immigrant and non-immigrant communities in order to facilitate exchanges between consumers and providers of good and services. Therefore, Kowalska had to become knowledgeable about the non-immigrant community in a way that most immigrants, regardless of gender, did not. The paper could not have survived for more than fifty years without this understanding.

In order to be a successful newspaper publisher, Kowalska constructed an insider/outsider standpoint for herself.[5] By virtue of being born into the heart of Utica's Polish community, she was an accepted member of that community, had an ethnic consciousness, and possessed an accumulation of knowledge specific to that community. In addition, as the owner of a business that served an important function for the non-immigrant community and depended on the non-immigrant community for economic stability, she became an adjunct member of the larger, non-immigrant community. This dual identity is illustrated by the diverse types of organizations with which she was involved, such as the White Cross (a Polish relief organization), the Polish Women's Business Club (a Polish social organization), the Oneida County Tuberculous Society, and the Munson-Williams-Proctor Institute (one of Utica's most prestigious performing arts venues). Success of the paper demanded that she understand and serve an "insider" audience (immigrant readership) and "outsider" audience (civic and business leaders of the non-immigrant community.) It was her status as a member of the immigrant community that made her (and *Slowo Polskie*) a valuable resource for the non-immigrant community and her relationship with the non-immigrant community that made her valuable to the immigrant community. Once again, the double bind that might have limited her was inverted to expand her influence.

As publisher of an immigrant newspaper, Kowalska successfully lived and worked within the intersection of gender and ethnic boundaries. She was a woman working in a man's world, and she was a member of an immigrant group operating with and within the dominant community. Because of the role of the immigrant press in the community, *Slowo Polskie* was a enterprise that benefited from Kowalska's double bind status. She understood the informational needs of Utica's Polonia and for more than five decades supplied that information from both inside of and outside of the community. In turn, the newspaper business became a vehicle that enabled her to transcend the role expectations proscribed by her status as a woman and a member of an immigrant group. She stretched the limits of the ethnic and gender boundaries that created her double bind. She did this skillfully enough that she was accepted as a woman, a newspaper publisher, a representative of the immigrant community, and the voice for the dominant community.

Millions of men and woman have immigrated to the United States. Thousands of different immigrant newspapers have been published. Was Marie Kowalska an exception or a representative of a larger group of women whose involvement with the immigrant press is unknown? Gaps in scholarship make it difficult to answer this question. This essay is an attempt to bring such questions to the forefront by recovering one woman's story for immigrant, women's and media history.

NOTES

1. "Polonia" is the term used to refer to "American urban communities of Polish immigrants" (Noble, 1990, p.63).

2. 1772 marked the first of three partitions (the others occurred in 1793 and 1795) that "erased . . . (Poland) from the map of Europe" (Halecki, 1993, p. 202) by dividing it among Austria, Russia, and Prussia. Many of the men who immigrated from Poland to the United States, did so to avoid serving in the armies of their oppressors (Preston, 1994, p. 6; Knothe, 1997a, p. 58). During the period leading up to, including, and following World War I, the Polish communities in America exhibited a profound nationalist spirit that motivated them to support the Allied war effort in return for the promise of a free Poland at the end of the war (Wytrwal, 1969, p. 299–347). Through a series of treaties, Poland became a free and independent state with the adoption of a constitution in 1921.

3. Through the cooperation of the governments of Canada, France and the United States, more than 138,000 men joined the Polish-American Army (or Blue Army, so called for the color of their uniforms) to fight as part of the Allied Forces in Europe (Pliska, 1965, p. 50).

4. Thomas Kowalski came to Utica from Galicia (the Austrian occupied section of Poland) in 1880 just before the period of mass immigration from Poland which began in the late1880s and peaked in 1913 (Noble, 1999, p. 63.)

5. "Inside/outside" status is a term frequently used by feminist anthropologists. It signifies ethical concerns about power relationships that are inherent in the ethnographic

methods used by researchers who study groups with which they ethnically or culturally self-identify (Zavella, 1993, p. 53). This term is a useful one to characterize any situation in which a person simultaneously identifies as belonging to a group, yet plays important roles outside of that group. It is in this way that I use the term. In the case of Maria Kowalska, as a voice of the dominant, non-immigrant (more powerful) community to her immigrant (less powerful) culture, she occupied an insider/outsider standpoint.

REFERENCES

Barszczewski, S. (1902). *Poles in America*. Warsaw: Arct Publishing.

Baretski, C. A. (1969). *A content analysis of the Polish American journal newspaper in reflecting the political attitudes, issues and perspectives of the Polish-American group during the period, 1950–1966*. Unpublished doctoral dissertation, New York University.

Beasley, M. and Silver, S. (1977). *Women in media: A documentary source book*. Washington, D.C.: Women's Institute for Freedom of the Press.

Belford, B. (1987). *Brilliant bylines: A biographical anthology of notable newspaperwomen in America*. New York: Columbia University Press.

Bem. S. (1993). *The lenses of gender*. New Haven: Yale University Press.

DuBois, W. E. B. (1903). Double-consciousness and the veil. In C. Lemert (Ed.) *Social theory: The multicultural and classic reading*. (1999), pp. 163–168.

Ewen, S. and Ewen, E. (1982). *Channels of desire: Mass images and the shaping of American consciousness*. New York: McGraw Hill.

Former radio show host dead at 87. (16 December, 1984). *Utica Observer Dispatch*.

Faludi, S. (1991). *Backlash: The undeclared war against American women*. New York: Crown.

Frye, M. (1983/2001). Oppression. In M. Anderson and P. H. Collins (Eds.) *Race, class, and gender: An anthology*. Belmont, CA: Wadsworth, pp. 48–52.

Growth of a nation: The numbers tell the story. (8 July, 1985). *Time*, pp. 34–35.

Halecki, O. (1992). *A history of Poland*. New York: Barnes and Nobles Books.

Hardt, H. (1998). Alien culture, immigrant voices: The foreign-language press in journalism history. *Interactions: Critical studies in communication, media, and journalism*. Lanham, MD: Rowan and Littlefield, pp. 155–237.

Harzig, C. (Ed.). (1997). *Peasant maids, city women: From the European countryside to urban America*. Ithaca, NY: Cornell University Press.

Jamieson, K. (1995). *Beyond the double bind: Women and leadership*. New York: Oxford University Press.

John, S. (1984, June 29). `Echoes of Poland' signs off after 54 years." *The Utica Observer Dispatch*, p. F1.

Knothe, M. A. (1997a). Land and loyalties: Contours of Polish women's lives. In C. Harzig (Ed.) *Peasant maids, city women: From the European countryside to urban America*. Ithaca: Cornell University Press, pp. 143–181.

Knothe, M.A. (1997b). Recent arrivals: Polish immigrant women's response to the city. In C. Harzig (Ed.) *Peasant maids, city women: From the European countryside to urban America*. Ithaca: Cornell University Press, pp. 299–338.

Kramarae, C. (1989). *Women and men speaking: Frameworks for analysis.* Rowley, MA: Newbury.

Kuzniewski, A. J. (1987). The Polish-American Press. In S. Miller (Ed.) *The ethnic press in the United States.* Westport, CT: Greenwood Press, pp. 275–290.

Marzolf, M. (1997). *Up from the footnote: A history of women journalists.* New York: Hastings House.

Nobel, A. G. (1999). *An ethnic geography of early Utica, New York: Time, space and community.* Lewiston, NY: Edwin Mellen Press.

Obidinski, E. (1977). The Polish American press: Survival through adaptation. *Polish American Studies, 34,* p 38–55.

Olszyk, E. G. (1940). *The Polish press in America.* Milwaukee: Marquette University Press.

Park, R. (1922/1970). *The immigrant press and its control.* Westport, CN: Greenwood.

Pliska, S. (1965). The Polish-American Army 1917–1921. *The Polish Review, 10,3,* pp. 46–59.

Pitcher, C. A. (1914). *Official program and book of words of the pageant of Utica.* Utica Public Library.

Preston, Douglas. (1994). A city of immigrants. In J. S. Pula (Ed.) *Ethnic Utica.* Utica, NY: Ethnic Heritage Studies Center, pp. 3–18.

Pula, J. S. and Dziedzic, E.E. (1990). *United we stand: The role of Polish workers in the New York Mills textile strikes, 1912 and 1916.* New York: Columbia University Press.

Radzilowski, T. C. (1996). Family, women, and gender: The Polish experience. In J. J. Bukowczyk (Ed.) *Polish Americans and their history: Community, culture, and politics.* Pittsburgh: University of Pittsburgh Press.

Schneider, D. and Schneider, C. (1993). *American women in the progressive era, 1900–1920.* New York: Doubleday.

Seller, M.S. (Ed.). (1994). *Immigrant Women.* Albany: State University of New York Press.

Slowo Polskie. (1964, December 11). Historja 'Slowa Polskeigo.'

Slowo Polskie. (1922, September 9). Jak mozna zostag obywate lem stanow zjedn.

Slowo Polskie. (1922, May 5). Powracajacym do Polski pod rozwage.

Slowo Polskie. (1911, October 12), p. 7.

Slowo Polskie. (1911, September, 25), p. 1.

Streitmatter, R. (1994). *Raising her voice: African-American women journalists who changed history.* Lexington: University of Kentucy Press.

Tannen, D. (2001). *Talking from 9 to 5: Women and men in the workplace: Language, sex and power.* New York: Quill.

Weinberg. S. S. (1992, Summer). The treatment of women in immigration history: A call for change. *Journal of American Ethnic History,* pp. 25–46.

Woloch, N. (1984). *Women and the American experience.* NY: Alfred A. Knopf.

Zavella, P. (1993). Feminist insider dilemmas: Constructing ethnic identity with 'Chicana' informants. *Frontiers, 3,* pp. 53–76.

Zlota Ksiega. (1920). Utica, NY.

Part Four

MEDIA PIONEERS

Chapter Seventeen

Joan Ganz Cooney: Children's Crusader and Founder of the Children's Television Workshop and Sesame Street

Margaret O. Finucane

Children's educational television, a term considered an oxymoron by many, became a reality for Joan Ganz Cooney in 1968. Drawing on her experience as an education major with an interest in the positive values of mass media, Ganz Cooney persuaded major foundations to provide eight million dollars to start The Children's Television Workshop (CTW) (Kanfer, 1970). What began as a dinner party comment about the poor quality of children's television programming developed into a successful educational corporation that has stood the test of time. Joan Ganz Cooney's contributions to the development of a strong, well-funded production of quality programming enabled children's educational television to become a reality in America.

Lloyd Morrissett, vice-president of the Carnegie Corporation, met Ganz Cooney's dinner table comment about the poor quality of children's television with a challenge to produce something better (Kanfer, 1970). Ganz Cooney's background as a television producer for Channel 13, the Public Broadcasting System (PBS) station in New York, enabled her to begin laying the groundwork for the proposal. The goal of the programs would be to provide children, especially low-income children, with opportunities to learn from television (Ganz Cooney, 2001).

Working with educational psychologist Gerald Lesser of Harvard, Ganz Cooney studied children, television, and the impact of viewing. She noticed that the jingles and advertisements on television were attention-getting for the children "face it—kids love commercials" ("Public TV," 1969). Ganz Cooney explained, "parents kept telling me how compelled their children were by commercials . . . the fun and the challenge were to use television in a new and highly specific and purposeful way" (Gilbert & Moore, 1981, p. 294). Thus was born the idea of having letters and numbers "sponsor" each show. Ganz

Cooney (2001), reflecting on the beginnings of Sesame Street, wrote, "We believed that if we created an educational show that capitalized on some of commercial television's most engaging traits . . . we could attract a sizeable audience" (p. xi). *Sesame Street* was different from all other programs because the producers worked with researchers on an ongoing basis to determine what techniques, stories, and characters most successfully reached and educated their young audience. Ganz Cooney, reflecting on over 30 years of success with the program, wrote that the initial creators met with resistance and ridicule. She noted that almost everyone in television scoffed at the idea that researchers could help produce a hit show. "Producers believed exclusively in intuition and experience as the means to a successful show" (Ganz Cooney, 2001, p. xi).

THE EARLY YEARS

Joan Ganz was born November 30, 1929 in Phoenix, Arizona. Her parents, Pauline and Sylvan Ganz, were strong Catholics who raised their three children in their faith. Through her parents Joan Ganz became involved with the Christophers, a Catholic group which emphasizes the importance of using communication for humanitarian reasons (Williams-Rautiolla, n. d.). Father Keller, founder of the Christophers, encouraged Catholics to utilize the media for positive goals. Ganz Cooney told Gilbert and Moore (1981) she was very idealistic as a child. Father Keller believed mass media were very powerful and that idealistic people needed to work within the system to shape it for positive outcomes. According to Ganz Cooney, he said that if idealistic people were not instrumental in shaping the media, the other kind of people would (Gilbert & Moore, 1981). With this Catholic influence shaping her beliefs, Joan Ganz began her college career.

Although she graduated from the University of Arizona with a bachelor's degree in education, Ganz Cooney worked for the government for one year in Washington, D. C. "I majored in education in college, but I wasn't really interested in teaching. It was something that girls of my generation did because teaching was very acceptable" (Gilbert & Moore, 1981, p. 295). She returned to Arizona and took a job as a reporter for the *Arizona Republic.* After one year she quit her job to move to New York City, a move that alarmed her parents (Golden & Findlen, 1998). Ganz Cooney's first position in New York was with NBC as a publicist.

After eight years in publicity, Ganz Cooney moved to public television, joining the newly opened Channel 13, WNDT-TV (now WNET-TV) in New York (Willliams-Rautiolla, n. d.). While at WNDT, Joan Ganz married Tim

Cooney, a civil rights advocate. She was 34 years old. Although societal pressures pushed most young women to marry early and give up any career aspirations, Ganz Cooney believed that she needed to establish herself in a career, giving herself something to return to after marriage and children. She stated, "In fact, it was when I started doing work that I adored, producing shows at Channel 13, that my work made me happy enough and competent enough to finally get married" (Gilbert & Moore, 1981, p. 296).

Ganz Cooney produced documentaries for WNDT, including the Emmy award-winning *Poverty, Anti-Poverty, and the Poor.* One documentary, *A Chance at the Beginning,* examined an educational project in Harlem that was a forerunner to *Project Head Start.* The research and production of that documentary alerted Ganz Cooney to the tremendous need among low-income families for high quality, affordable preschool education (Gilbert & Moore, 1981).

Morrissett's challenge to Ganz Cooney in 1966 started her study of children and television. After more than one year of speaking with experts, talking with parents, and studying children's use of television, Ganz Cooney produced her report, *The Potential Uses of Television in Preschool Education.* From her earlier documentary work and current social policy initiatives, Ganz Cooney argued that television could be used as a tool for preparing children for school, especially those from lower socioeconomic backgrounds who needed additional help. Wright, Huston, Scantlin, and Kotler (2001) wrote

> The War on Poverty rested on the premise that the disadvantages of poverty could be overcome by providing the poor with the skills and capabilities needed for success. Interventions for young children, including Head Start and other early education initiatives, were a major part of this effort (p. 97).

Ganz Cooney's strong belief that she could change the world propelled her to create the Children's Television Workshop, parent company of *Sesame Street.* "So thoroughly has her creation embedded itself into our lives that anyone asked to rattle off some famous street names would probably include hers. There would be Pennsylvania Avenue, Broadway, Rodeo Drive, State Street, Route 66—and Sesame Street" (Moreau, 1989, p. 88).

At the time Ganz Cooney began investigating children's television, there was very little creative, stimulating programming. Most programming was unappealing, overly commercialized, or violent. Palmer and Fisch (2001) noted that most children's programming was merely an imitation of other forms of media. They identified "storybook television," programming that used "shots of book covers and static, illustrated pages" (p. 6) as representative of the types of programming for children. Quoting sociologist Wilbur Schramm, Kanfer (1970) wrote, "'[t]he media dare small changes, but not fundamental ones; their whole impact is to retain status quo.' Until now, that status has been nothing to quo about" (p. 68).

Ganz Cooney's *Sesame Street* changed the status quo for children's television permanently. She believed the Children's Television Workshop should move into new areas and set the standard for children's television (Gilbert & Moore, 1981). Realizing that educational programming in the past failed because it was developed by educators and implemented by production people, Ganz Cooney created a team that included educators, child development specialists, research specialists, television production specialists and Morrissett (Williams-Rautiolla, n. d.). Ganz Cooney led the team by giving voice to the vision of a program that would simultaneously entertain and educate American children. Ganz Cooney said, "the leadership was not just myself . . . [t]he idea was an idea around which everyone could coalesce. I was the keeper of the flame " (Gilbert & Moore, 1981, p. 293).

The result of Ganz Cooney's extensive research was a proposal to establish a foundation based on educational research that would produce quality, educational children's programming. Ganz Cooney was more successful than even she expected to be. She said, "When we started out it was considered a phenomenon that $8 million was raised for a children's program. Nobody was spending that on children . . . but we did it" (Gilbert & Moore, 1981, p. 297). The funding period specified that within two years, CTW must produce 130 hour-long programs directed toward children 3 to 5 years of age (Palmer & Fisch, 2001). Ganz Cooney's success in financing her vision moved the project ahead.

According to Polsky (1974), "commercial programmers were unwilling to take the financial and creative risks necessary to create quality children's programming on a regular basis" (p. viii). When the Carnegie Corporation presented an offer of funding, the alliance with National Educational Television was a stipulation. This allowed CTW access to administrative and legal services (Polsky, 1974). Polsky noted that some of the funding organizations were hesitant to provide the eight million dollars of funding to a fledgling group. The alliance placed the control of funds for the project with an established agency. The independence of the Workshop was maintained by keeping the development and production areas separate. This move also placed the programming of CTW firmly in the realm of public television. CTW retained the broadcast rights to the programs the organization created. The loose alliance that was formed with NET lasted until 1970 when Ganz Cooney was named president of the Children's Television Workshop (William-Rautiolla, n. d.).

Ganz Cooney, seeing Jim Henson's Muppets on the *Ed Sullivan Show*, knew they would provide just the right level of absurdity to appeal to children. She saw in the Muppets and Jim Henson a creative playful spark that was missing in children's television (Lapinski, 1998). Henson initially hesitated to join the Children Television Workshop because he did not perceive himself as a children's entertainer. Despite those hesitations, he signed on in 1968. According to Peggy Charren, director of *Action for Children's Television*, "He owed part of his success to Joan for creating *Sesame Street*. And Joan owed part of her success to him" (Lapinski, 1998). After agreeing to work with the Children's Television Workshop, Henson developed a new set of characters that today are known around the world, *Big Bird, Bert, Ernie, Oscar the Grouch,* and more.

Sesame Street debuted on November 10, 1969. The original programs reflected Ganz Cooney's belief that no one figure should play a starring role; rather the whole cast should reflect the diversity of America (Williams-Rautiolla, n. d.). Ganz Cooney argued for a multi-racial cast and representation of both men and women. "Strong black characters were there from the beginning; Hispanics Luis and Maria joined in 1972" (Moreau, 1989, p. 88). Gordon, played by show producer Matt Robinson, provided a strong father figure for child viewers. Kanfer (1970) noted that many of the targeted children in the viewing audience had no father in the home; Gordon provided a strong, authoritative role model. Countering his authoritative tone was Loretta Long, the actress playing his wife. Her character, as described by Kanfer, was syrupy sweet. Rounding out the human cast were Bob McGrath, a high-spirited music teacher, and Will Lee, a gruff grocer with a very warm heart (Kanfer, 1970). The diversity of cast members has continued to develop, reflecting Ganz Cooney's commitment to representing all viewers.

The human cast was complemented by a variety of characters found in no other program, the Muppets. These zany creatures became some of the most beloved characters in American television. According to Kanfer (1970), Big Bird received more fan mail than any of the human hosts.

The commercial networks were delighted that Sesame Street was so successful; it relieved them of the responsibility to provide strong educational programming (Kanfer, 1970; Polsky, 1974). They did offer support through the early days of *Sesame Street*. Two days before *Sesame Street's* debut, NBC preempted programming to air a special preview of the program (Polsky, 1974). In part this support can be attributed to the relationship Ganz Cooney developed with broadcasters. John White, President of NET, said Ganz Cooney's personality was primarily responsible for the success of the project (Polsky, 1974). The program received support from the three major networks in the form of spot announcements and discussion on television news programs.

Even with the success of their initial programs, Ganz Cooney and her team received a lot of criticism. Traditionalists worried that television would replace teachers, but Ganz Cooney responded, "TV has a very important role to play in education. Still, it's just a big cold box, and just can't replace a loving teacher who cares about a child" (Kanfer, 1970, p. 66). Criticisms ranged from McLuhan, who considered the program naïve, to Bronfenbrenner, a psychology professor who argued the interactions among the characters were too unrealistic. Ganz Cooney's responses to the criticism ranged from dismissal to serious consideration. To McLuhan she responded that his argument was irrelevant; to Bronfenbrenner, the children we target have more than enough conflict, mayhem and upset in their lives; they don't need it in their television programs too (Kanfer, 1970). In response to suggestions from the National Organization for Women, Ganz Cooney created an additional role for Loretta Long; no longer is she only a housewife; she is also a nurse (Kanfer, 1970). Ganz Cooney is careful to note that not all ideas were accepted.

> I say no a lot . . . I'm looking for a kind of project that fits with what I feel our mission is: educational television and high quality children's programming. Everything we do, we do because we want to do it. First we ask, "Is it consistent with our mission?" Then we ask, "Can we raise the money to meet the budget?" The two things have to go together (Gilbert & Moore, 1981, p. 298).

Thanks to Ganz Cooney's strong guidance, the show has remained consistent with that vision and goal.

Throughout the development of the Children's Television Workshop and *Sesame Street*, Ganz Cooney has remained dedicated to the model first developed in the 1960s. In the original proposal for funding, Ganz Cooney emphasized the importance of using research to develop a well-defined curriculum for the program. "*Sesame Street* was the first series to employ empirical research as an integral part of its production; formative research was—and continues to be—used on an ongoing basis to inform production decisions" (Truglio & Fisch, 2001, p. xvi). Although the curriculum of early *Sesame Street* programs was narrow in scope, usually covering only five or six subjects, today's programs encompass more than 200 different topics. "'We started out thinking that it might teach simple things', [Ganz] Cooney explains. 'We learned you could do so much more'" (Moreau, 1989, p. 88).

To Ganz Cooney's credit, summative research has supported her vision as well. Research on *Sesame Street's* effect on preschool viewers has consistently revealed significant cognitive gains (Mielke, 2001; Moreau, 1989). Each segment is designed to achieve measurable instructional goals such as "recognition of numbers one through ten and simple counting ability" (Polsky, 1974, p. 42). In her proposal Ganz Cooney wrote, "we would expect, also, that a child who had regularly watched the show would have grown culturally; in his appreciation of arts and crafts, his familiarity with basic music concepts, his general knowledge about the world" (Polsky, p. 42). Ganz

Cooney's commitment to creating a show that could stand alone was a driving force in the decision not to include at-home projects. According to Polsky, Ganz Cooney believed the program must be a success on its own merit, not requiring additional materials for children to use at home.

After the first few successful years, the Children's Television Workshop branched out to include other age groups. In 1971, the team created *The Electric Company,* a program for children 8 to 12 years of age that emphasized reading. Following the CTW model, Ganz Cooney and her team integrated the unique aspects of television production with sound empirical research to produce the show. Other programs developed under the CTW model include *Feelin' Good, The Best of Families, 3-2-1-Contact,* and *Square One TV.* All of these shows have since ceased production, primarily for economic reasons (Alexander, n. d.).

Ganz Cooney remained in the role of president of the Children's Television Workshop until 1990. At that time she took over the roles of chair of the organization. Throughout her career at the helm of the Children's Television Workshop, Ganz Cooney has remained a strong advocate for children and educational television. Citing a quote attributed to her, Ganz Cooney affirmed her belief that "If you travel the road to the top, you don't travel many other roads" (Gilbert & Moore, 1981, p. 298). She recognized that she made sacrifices but believes the secret to a happy life is a balance between work and personal life. Ganz Cooney's personal life changed as she traveled her road to the top. She and husband Tim Coone separated and divorced. Ganz Cooney later married Pete Peterson, an executive on Wall Street.

PROFESSIONAL LIFE

An important part of who Joan Ganz Cooney is can be found in her professional role as an executive of the Children's Television Workshop. As the president and then chief executive officer and chair of the organization, Ganz Cooney has shown doubters her ability to be a "gutsy and effective administrator" (*Forbes*, 1975, p. 43). In an interview with *Forbes* magazine, Ganz Cooney said, "I'm tired of only being called the lady from Sesame Street" (p. 44). She is proud of her executive skills and prefers to be the boss, rather than be bossed. People working for her agree. Mike Dann, a Children's Television Workshop consultant, said, "I've worked for 15 network presidents. Joan Cooney is the most flexible" ("Boss is better," 1975, p. 44).

As the only female member of Board of Directors of First Pennsylvania Corporation, Ganz Cooney was regarded by female employees of the organization as a hero ("Boss is better"). In addition to serving on the Board of

Directors for First Pennsylvania Corporation, Ganz Cooney was the first female to serve on the boards of Xerox Corporation and May Department Stores (Collins & Esposito, 1978). She has since served as a director for Johnson & Johnson, and Metropolitan Life Insurance Company (Williams-Rautiolla, n. d.). In discussing her role as a director, Ganz Cooney noted that so few women served as directors in the 1970s because the pool from which corporations selected directors was typically CEOs. Women rarely served as CEOs at that time. Referring to her own position, she stated that as a female CEO of a non-profit organization that created programming for children, she was seen as non-threatening and a "twofer, or even better, a threefer" (Collins & Esposito, 1978, p. 78). That is, not only was she not threatening as a woman, she represented media, education and kids in the expertise she brought to the board.

Ganz Cooney, considered a leader among women and in her field, stated that a key to her success was perseverance (Lloyd, 1986). She developed a single-mindedness that allowed her to identify her course and stay with it to the completion of the task. Honored by *Working Woman* magazine with induction into the Working Woman Hall of Fame in 1986, Ganz Cooney discussed the struggles and triumphs of being a leader in her field. One of the frustrations that she has faced has been the role of government regulation of children's television. She stated,

> It's been terrible in my business that they will not regulate the network[']s quality of the shows. Every country recognizes children as a unique population. But we are the only country that doesn't demand that you do something for children. And it's a tragedy because I know television could be quality television (Lloyd, 1986, p. 160).

Ganz Cooney continued her crusade for children's television. In 1988 she spoke about the need for change in our educational system. She argued that an extended school day and a longer school year are the only viable remedies for improving education (Kramer, 1988). Ganz Cooney also suggested that school systems must examine the way time is used in classes. She argued that television should be thought of as a positive force, rather than the current conception held by most parents and teachers. She said,

> the bias against TV is staggering. Parents and teachers are so convinced TV is a *destructive* force they won't even think about how to use it constructively — despite the success of something like *Sesame Street*. . . we want kids to read, and we know that TV is a thief of time. But we can't keep moaning about the fact that not only kids but all of us are getting more and more of our information from TV. And if we are honest about it, we know that TV is often the catalyst

that drives us to read more about something we only learn in sketch from the tube (Kramer, 1988, p. 19).

TODAY'S SESAME WORKSHOP

Ganz Cooney, long an advocate of meeting children's educational needs through television, continues as chair of the Executive Committee of the Sesame Workshop. The Children's Television Workshop changed its name in 2000 to better represent the media world of today's children ("We've changed," 2000).

Ganz Cooney strongly emphasized the need to adapt to changes in the audience. She noted that when the show began, four year olds were the primary audience. Today, children begin school earlier, and three year olds are the focus of programming (McClellan, 1998).

AWARDS AND HONORS

Joan Ganz Cooney has received well-deserved recognition for her visionary efforts from many organizations. The Christophers honored Ganz Cooney in 1989 by awarding the James Keller Award for "outstanding service to children around the world" (Christopher Awards, 1989, p. 281). The James Keller Award is given to individuals who have contributed to the well-being of young people in a meaningful way. The Christophers believe that Ganz Cooney's work with the Children's Television Workshop exemplifies an individual who used her power and responsibility to change the world for the better (K. Hutcheson, personal communication, November 29, 2001). About the same time, Ganz Cooney was the first recipient of the Lowell Award from the Corporation for Public Broadcasting. The Ralph Lowell Award "recognizes outstanding individual contributions to public television" ("Ralph Lowell Awards," 2000). Lowell, a philanthropist and banker, founded the WGBH Educational Foundation and was influential in the development of the Carnegie Commission on Educational Television. Through his efforts the Public Broadcasting Act of 1967 was passed, establishing the Corporation for Public Broadcasting.

The National Education Association recognized Ganz Cooney's contribution to the education of children by bestowing upon her the Friend of Education Award in 1978 (Newell, 1997). "The award recognizes individuals whose leadership, acts, and support have raised the level of excellence in American public education" ("Friend of Education," 2001). Ganz Cooney received the

Silver Satellite Award from American Women in Radio & Television. This award recognizes individuals who make outstanding contributions to the broadcast industry ("Silver Satellite," 2001).

In 1995, Ganz Cooney was recognized for her tremendous contributions to the development of educational television by then-President Clinton. In his address awarding the Presidential Medal of Freedom, Clinton noted that the shows of the Children's Television Workshop,

> have helped teach a generation of children to count and to read and to think. They also teach us more about how we should live together. We all know that Grover and Kermit reinforce rather than undermine the values we work so hard to teach our children, showing kids every day what it means to share, to respect differences, and to recognize that it's not easy being green (Clinton, 1995, p. 2).

In 1998, JC Penney Company awarded the Juanita Kreps Award to Ganz Cooney for her pioneering efforts in the field of educational television and for "chang[ing] the landscape of children's television programming" (PR Newswire, 1999, p. 1). The $20,000 educational grant that is part of the award was donated to a special project of the Children's Television Workshop at Ganz Cooney's request. Juanita Kreps was a noted educator and economist who served as the first woman U. S. Secretary of Commerce and the first woman board member for the JC Penney Company.

Also in 1998, Ganz Cooney was inducted into the National Women's Hall of Fame for her achievement in education. Ganz Cooney was inducted into the *Broadcasting & Cable's* Honor Roll of the Fifth Estate. People who have made a significant contribution to the broadcast industry are honored for unparalleled excellence and service (Broadcasting & Cable, November 9, 1998). Also recognized by the Television Academy for her contributions, Ganz Cooney was inducted into their Hall of Fame in 1990 (*People Weekly*, 1990). In celebration of Women's History Month 1999, Barnes and Noble Bookstore, selected Ganz Cooney as an outstanding woman in journalism and entertainment (Business Wire, 1999).

Joan Ganz Cooney and the Children's Television Workshop have earned 76 Emmy awards including a Daytime Emmy for Lifetime Achievement (Golden & Findlen, 1998). In addition, the Children's Television Workshop has received two Peabody Awards (Rohan, 1998), the first in 1970 after less than six months on the air ("TV's switched-on," 1970).

KIDSNET is an organization that assists parents in using broadcast media positively for their children. In 1999 they created an award honoring Shari Lewis, creator of Lambchop. The award is presented to people or organizations that "demonstrat[e] a continued commitment to providing superior educational and entertainment content for children" (KIDSNET, 2001). Joan

Ganz Cooney shared the honor with Lloyd Morrisett and Jim Henson in 2001. Director Karen Jaffe said, "We are proud to give this years' honor to the creators of *Sesame Street,* a show which has become the single largest teacher of children, reaching over 120 million kids in more than 140 countries" (KIDSNET, 2001).

Joan Ganz Cooney's impact on children, television, and the media industry cannot be underestimated. The tremendous number of honors and awards that have been accorded Ganz Cooney, the Children's Television Workshop, and her collaborators reflect the esteem America holds for her and her contributions. Perhaps her impact is best summed up in her biographical sketch on the National Women's Hall of Fame, "Perhaps no other woman in the latter quarter of the 20th century has influenced the education of so many children as has Joan Ganz Cooney" ("Women of the Hall," 1998).

REFERENCES

Alexander, A. (n.d.). *Children's Television Workshop.* Retrieved July 12, 2001, from: http://www.mbcnet.org/ETV/C/htmlC/childrenste/childrenste.htm

American Women in Radio and Television Web page. (2001). *Silver Satellite Award.* Retrieved June 15, 2001 from: http://ww.awrt.org/awards/silver_satellite.html

Christopher Awards. (1989, March 15). *Christian Century, 106,* 281.

Clinton, W. J. (1995, October 2). *Remarks on presenting the Presidential Medal of Freedom.* Weekly compilation of Presidential documents. Retrieved July 12, 2001, from: http://www.ibiblio.org/pub/archives/white...-Remarks-in-Medal-of-Freedom-Presentation.html

Collins, E. G. C., & Esposito, A. I. (1978, January-February). A woman in the boardroom. *Harvard Business Review, 56,* 77–86.

Corporation for Public Broadcasting Web page. (1996). *Recipients of the Lowell Award.* Retrieved July 12, 2001, from: http://www.cpb.org.about/media/annualreports/1996/awardlowellpast.html.

Corporation for Public Broadcasting Webpage. (2000). *The Ralph Lowell Award: Outstanding Contributions to Public Television.* Retrieved July 16, 2001, from: http://www.cpb.org.about/media/awards.lowell/

Ganz Cooney, J. (2001). Forward. In S. M. Fisch & R. T. Truglio (Eds.). *G is for growing: Thirty years of research on children and Sesame Street* (pp. xi–xiii). Mahwah, NJ: Erlbaum.

Gilbert, L., & Moore, G. (1981). *Particular passions Talks with women who have shaped our times.* New York: Clarkson N. Potter, Inc.

Golden & Findlen (1998). *Remarkable women of the Twentieth Century: 100 portraits of achievement.* New York: Friedman/Fairfax Publishers.

Grannan, C. (n. d.). *Top 100 women of the millennium #13 Joan Ganz Cooney.* Retrieved July 12, 2001, from: http://www.women.com/news/top100/013.html.

Kanfer, S. (1970, November 23). Who's afraid of big, bad TV? *Time*, 60–73.

KIDSNET. (2001). *Second annual Lambchop Award* . Retrieved September 18, 2001, from: http://www.kidsnet.org/lambchop/postrelease2.html.

Kramer, M. (1988, June 13). A presidential message from Big Bird. *U.S. News & World Report*, 19.

Lapinski, S. (1998). *The gift of Jim Henson: Friends, family, and colleagues remember the man who conjured up the Muppets*. Retrieved July 12, 2001, from: http://www.sesameworkshop.org/sesame/beat/article/0,2044,75182,00.html.

Lloyd, K. R. (1986, November). America's secret weapon. *Working Woman*, *11*, 158–162.

McClellan, S. (1998, October 12). Web feat for Big Bird. *Broadcasting & Cable*. Retrieved June 15, 2001, from: http://www.findarticles.com/cf_0/m0BCA/1998_Oct_12/53096610/print.jhtml

Mielke, K. W. (2001). A review of research on educational and social impact of Sesame Street. In S. M. Fisch & R. T. Truglio (Eds.), *G is for growing: Thirty years of research on children and Sesame Street* (pp. 83–96). Mahwah, NJ: Erlbaum.

Moreau, D. (1989, July). Change agents: Joan Ganz Cooney created *Sesame Street* 20 years ago. Now it's an institution. *Changing Times, 43*, 88.

National Education Association Webpage. (2001). *Friend of Education Award*. Retrieved November 25, 2001, from: http://www.nea.org/nr/nr000705.html

National Women's Hall of Fame. (1998). *Women of the Hall: Joan Ganz Cooney*. Retrieved July 12, 2001, from: http://www.greatwomen.org/profs/cooney_j.php

Newell, L. A. (1997). *The rich and famous: UA style*. Retrieved July 12, 2001, from: http://wildcat.arizona.edu/papers/91/5491_1_m.html

Palmer, E. L., & Fisch, S. M. (2001). The beginnings of *Sesame Street* research. In S. M. Fisch & R. T. Truglio (Eds.), *G is for growing: Thirty years of research on children and Sesame Street* (pp. 3–24). Mahwah, NJ: Erlbaum.

Polsky, R. M. (1974). *Getting to Sesame Street: Origins of the Children's Television Workshop*. New York: Praeger.

PR Newswire (1998, October 19). *JC Penney Company announces winner of Juanita Kreps Award*. Retrieved June 16, 2001, from: http://www.findarticles.com/cf_0/m4PRN/1998_Oct_19/53093403/print.jhtml

Public TV: The forgotten 12 million. (1969, November 14). *Time*, 96–98.

Rohan, V. (1998, November 15). Bert, Ernie, and friends turning 30. *The Record Online*. Retrieved July 12, 2001, from: http://www.bergen.com/yourtime/sesame15199811153.htm

This year's TV Hall of Famers get great reception. (1990, January 22). *People Weekly, 33*, 42–43.

Truglio, R. T., & Fisch, S. M. (2001). Introduction. In S. M. Fisch & R. T. Truglio (Eds.), *G is for growing: Thirty years of research on children and Sesame Street* (pp. xv–xxi). Mahwah, NJ: Erlbaum.

TV's switched-on school. (1970, June 1). *Newsweek*, 68–71.

We've changed our name! (2000). *Sesame Workshop*. Retrieved November 29, 2001, from: http://www.sesameworkshop.org/corporate/namechange/0,5236,,00.html

Williams-Rautiolla, S. (n.d.). *Joan Ganz Cooney*. Retrieved July 17, 2001, from: http://www.mbcnet.org/ETV/C/htmlC/cooneyjoan/cooneyjoan.htm

Wright, J. C., Huston, A. C., Scantlin, R., & Kotler, J. (2001). The early window project: *Sesame Street* prepares children for school. In S. M. Fisch & R. T. Truglio (Eds.), *G is for growing: Thirty years of research on children and Sesame Street* (pp. 97–114). Mahwah, NJ: Erlbaum.

Chapter Eighteen

Frances Benjamin Johnston: Mother of Photojournalism

Cynthia M. Lont

Her spectrum of photographic work was enormous—rich and poor, black and white, men and women, famous and obscure, young and old—whether recording proud workers, famous Americans, or scenic splendor, she composed a portrait that evoked a true and lasting visual suggestion of the age. (Daniel and Smock, 1974, p. 3)

In 1974, I wrote a paper for a History of Photography class. The assignment was to research a famous photographer, assumed by the professor and the class to be male. In my library research (there was no web access in 1975), I came across the name Frances Benjamin Johnston. Odd, that name wasn't in my textbook although Johnston had taken many historical photographs between 1864 and 1952. My professor had never heard of her. Maybe she wasn't important, I thought. Yet she'd photographed Mark Twain and Susan B. Anthony. I set out on the most frustrating yet rewarding experience of my graduate career. I discovered articles and photographs by Frances Benjamin Johnston ranging from a 1907 piece in *Harpers'* to photographs in the *Saturday Review*. Her success as a photographer of her time was apparent as I uncovered magazines filled with her work—photographs she took of President McKinley the eve of his assassination, portraits of the Roosevelts, Joel Chandler Harris, Booker T. Washington, and Alexander Graham Bell. Intertwined with these photographs was the story of a woman who was both Victorian and rebel, of a great photographer who was independent, artistic, and entrepreneurial yet swept under the rug by historians.

This absence of women from media history was not uncommon until the 1970s. Women, whether they were part of the printing process during the American Revolution or worked as contemporary newscasters, were ignored, dismissed, or relegated to the fashion pages of women's magazines. Scholars, mostly female, rediscovered women who created media but whose contributions were forgotten or eliminated from media history. Well-documented in books such as Ross's *Ladies of the Press* (1974), Marzolf's *Up from the Footnote: A History of Women Journalists* (1977), and Beasley and Gibbons's *Women in Media: A Documentary Sourcebook* (1977), this "reclamation" movement focused on women past and present who created news. These "reclamation" scholars and I were rediscovering women's contributions to media and society. Why is the reclamation movement important to note here? Because although the first books reclaiming women's role in the history of the media were written in the 1970s, there are still few references to women who create media. Try to find historical information about Connie Chung or someone lesser known like Mary Garber, one of the first women sports writers. If you find anything, it will be about their personal lives (what they wear, to whom they are married) in magazines such as *People* or *Glamour*. Do you think their male counterparts, Dan Rather or Howard Cosell, are discussed only in such magazines?

Is Frances Benjamin Johnston in the history of photography textbooks? Could she easily slip from those pages into oblivion again? Those of us who believe women have been completely integrated into media history need only look at the lack of information about women of color who have contributed to the media. Those who don't know their history are doomed to repeat it.

THE VICTORIAN AND THE REBEL

Background

Frances Benjamin Johnston was born in Grafton, West Virginia, on January 15, 1864. She was the only child of four who survived past the first year. She spent her childhood in Rochester, New York. Sometime between the ages of 10 and 12, she and her family moved to Washington, DC, where her father, Anderson Doniphon Johnston, became head bookkeeper for the United States Treasury Department. Her mother, Frances Antoinette Benjamin, was "one of the leading journalists of her day." The "Lady Correspondent" for the *Baltimore Sun,* she was featured in the *Rochester Democrat and Chronicle*, specializing in coverage of Congress (Berch, p. 11). There is little doubt that Johnston's mother's position as a journalist (an unusual position for a woman in the 1800s) guided Johnston. Johnston's mother influenced Frances' educational route, her view on the role of women, her access to famous people and places, her feelings about women's accomplishments, and her expectations of herself.

Johnston's early education was at home. At age fifteen, she took classes in Washington, D.C., with a group of eight girls. By eighteen, she attended Notre Dame Convent in Govanston, Maryland, and by 1883 (at the age of 19) she studied art at Academie Julian (the leading art school for those who were not French) in Paris. Unlike her female classmates, Johnston attended art school to learn art, not to meet a husband. Unlike most art schools of the time, Academie Julian allowed women to learn alongside men.

After art school, Johnston returned to Washington, D.C., and replaced a friend as a correspondent for a New York paper. Many editors liked illustrations to accompany news stories, so Johnston's drawings helped sell her articles. She soon discovered photographs were a selling point for her stories and wrote George Eastman, inventor of roll film and friend of the family, to send her a camera that would take good pictures for newspapers. This was the start of Johnston's career as a photographer. Johnston's background as an artist influenced her use of the camera as more than just a tool for documenting news but as a way to say something about her subjects. Johnston used the camera to reflect her subjects' personalities, their roles, and their positions of authority.

EARLY WORK (1885–1917)

Photographs of Places

Johnston's first magazine article appeared in 1889 in *Demorest's,* a general circulation magazine. The article, entitled, "Uncle Sam's Money," included photographs and drawings depicting the way U.S. money was minted in Washington, D.C. In many of the photographs, women and men, African-Americans and Euro-Americans, young and old stood side by side as they made money by hand. There was no retirement age, so many people worked into old age. The workers recognized no barriers between Blacks and Whites, or between men and women. In the rest of American society in 1889, men and women, Blacks and Whites rarely worked together. Johnston's picture not only showed how money was made but showed the breaking down of social barriers among those working in the U.S. mint.

In early 1890, Johnston built a studio in her parent's rose garden in Washington, DC, a workshop where she later took portraits of the Roosevelts, Mark Twain, Susan B. Anthony, and Booker T. Washington. Her studio also served as a meeting place for her friends, many of whom were part of the art movement popular on the East Coast. Johnston and her friends, artists, poets, playwrights, and actors, called themselves "The Push." In many ways, their views mocked much of the Victorian tradition Johnston publicly upheld. The light side of the "The Push" can be seen in a photograph of the members dressed up in costumes and in a poem her Push friends gave to her:

Frances is our hostess, Frances is our joy.
She gives us many a party, likewise many a toy.
So here's to Frances' great success, with coal and bread and butter.
Long may she wave and entertain, and often snap the shutter
(Daniel and Smock, p. 21).

Johnston lived two lives—the traveled photographer, often photographing those in the White House, playing the part of the Victorian lady—and the hostess for this Bohemian art group. Her dual nature is represented through the photographs she took, the friends she kept, and even where she lived. Her very existence as an unmarried career woman with a profitable business was unusual at the time.

A good example of Johnston's adventurous nature occurred in 1891, when Johnston traveled to Shenandoah City, Pennsylvania, to photograph the conditions in the Kohinoor Mines. The mines were dark, and the use of the magnesium powder flash necessary to photograph the interiors was dangerous. Having used a flash technique before, Johnston decided to try it. Although it took her four hours to complete three negatives, she left the mines unharmed. The photos were somewhat flat but deemed successful. In addition to photographing the mines, Johnston photographed the workers and their families. She stated, "I confess to the strange charm of the people, their labor, and their country. I would like to go back some day. I shall be very sorry if I don't" (Daniel & Smock, 1974, p. 43).

In 1899, Johnston shot a series of photographs of Hampton Institute, established in 1868 in Hampton, Virginia, for African and Native Americans by Samuel Chapman Armstrong, former commander of an African American regiment and head of the Freedman's Bureau for Northeastern Virginia. The photos from this series, once again, demonstrate how Johnston often used subjects which contrasted with one another. In one photograph, we see a Native American student showing his peers (African Americans) his Indian Tribal dress, while in the background is a stuffed eagle and Remington's painting of the U.S. Cavalry. This juxtaposition of two quite opposing forces within the same photograph demonstrates how Johnston documented the happenings of the day but integrated, sometimes subtly and sometimes not so subtly, political statements.

Not all her peers in the photography field, especially male photographers, accepted Johnston. Alfred Steiglitz, one of the better-known photographers of the time, was opposed to her selection as one of the judges for the Philadelphia Photographic Society, a big honor. Steiglitz's concern was the way she posed her subjects (Berch, pp. 29–30). Some of her peers argued that Johnston's work was not as "womanly" as that of other women photographers. There is no evidence that this lack of support or criticism bothered Johnston or changed how she approached her work. Johnston's primary desires were to travel, take photographs, and support herself. Most of her projects allowed her to do just that. She was not above a little commercialism to make sure the money came in to support other new and exciting projects.

In the summer of 1899, Johnston left on a European vacation. Before she sailed, her agent suggested she take photos of Admiral Dewey because few had been taken since his return from Manila. She tracked down Theodore Roosevelt, then Assistant Secretary of the Navy, who gave her a note of recommendation. Johnston caught up with Dewey in Naples, and he allowed her to take pictures on board his ship and travel with the crew. She worked well with Dewey and his men and even filled out an enlistment card while on board. She was rated "excellent" in everything from seamanship to marksmanship but received low marks for sobriety. The pictures were taken on August 5th, but by the 11th her agent still had not received them. Meanwhile, another photographer, J.C. Hemment, published photos of Dewey. Johnston had, in fact, given her photos to Hemment to deliver while she went off on another adventure. Hemment held onto her photos until his were published and then gave them to her agent. In some ways, this misplaced trust in others is one of Johnston's weaknesses. She was not frivolous with her trust, but she appeared to believe in the good nature of people until proven wrong. Once she was wronged, she went after those who wronged her with a vengeance.

In 1902, Booker T. Washington asked Johnston to photograph Tuskegee Institute, an educational institution established in 1881 for African Americans. Part of Tuskegee's mission was to train African Americans to return to their communities to build other schools for the Black community. Washington believed photographs of the work at Tuskegee would help attract donors (Berch, p. 59). George Washington Carver and Johnston took the train together to Tuskegee. Since the train was late in arriving, they headed out to a friend's home for dinner. Several hours later, Johnston returned with one of the three African American men with whom she had dined. The local white people, believing Johnston to be "dallying" with Black men, started to shoot and chase both Johnston and her companion. Both were lucky to escape with their lives. Johnston was livid and wanted to call her friends in Washington. Booker T. Washington felt it was better for him to handle the situation, because if word were to leak out, donors might be less likely to contribute. After this experience, George Washington Carver called Johnston, "the pluckiest woman I ever saw" (Harlan, p.3).

Photographs of People

Frances Benjamin Johnston was the White House photographer for several Presidents. In 1898, Johnston took pictures of then President William McKinley and, separately, pictures of his wife, Ida Saxton McKinley, a former cashier in Johnston's father's bank in Ohio who married McKinley in 1871.

On September 6, 1901, President McKinley was assassinated while attending the Pan American Exposition in Buffalo, New York. Many photographers claimed to have taken his last photograph. George Eastman discovered Johnston had used one of his cameras for the last shot and fought for her photo's rightful place. While the argument continues over who took the last picture of McKinley, I have little doubt it was Johnston.

With few exceptions, all her subjects look unsmilingly at the camera. Many of the men are surrounded by their work while women are more fancily dressed than the men and often are posed in front of neutral backgrounds. Often, Johnston took portraits of famous people and their families. John Phillip Sousa, the March King, is in his uniform standing outside while a portrait of his wife and daughters shows them beautifully dressed and positioned inside. Booker T. Washington appears in both a solo portrait and another with his two sons.

In 1902, Johnston took photographs of then President Theodore Roosevelt's children. Up to that point, the President had been reluctant to place his children in the limelight. But Johnston had known the Roosevelts through her mother and had a long association with their family. Johnston's photographs include the teenaged Alice Roosevelt in her riding clothes holding a puppy, a young Quentin Roosevelt with a playmate, and Quentin and Kermit Roosevelt standing alongside the White House police. Johnston photographed Theodore Roosevelt Junior in the garden holding his parrot, Eli. These portraits of life as a President's children were less formal than Johnston's normal portraits and more like snapshots of everyday life.

Johnston took many portraits of well-known people of her time, including Alexander Graham Bell, scientist and teacher of the deaf, but best known as the inventor of the telephone. A portrait of suffragist Susan B. Anthony shows her in front of her desk, surrounded by her work. This was an unusual background for one of Johnston's female subjects and may reflect her view of the importance and seriousness of the Women's Rights Movement. The writer Mark Twain was photographed in his famous all-white suit. Books surrounded steel magnate and philanthropist Andrew Carnegie. Although Johnston was well known for her portraits, beginning about 1918 she shifted to another type of subject.

LATER WORK (1918–1944)

Photographs of Things

In the early 1920s, Johnston began photographing buildings and gardens, especially those in the South. By 1926, she earned a commission to photograph Chatham near Fredericksburg, Virginia. This project continued for eight years and resulted in five books on the architecture of colonial churches in Virginia, the plantations of the Carolinas, and the early architecture of Georgia. In 1930 (at the age of 66) she received a $26,000 Carnegie grant to photograph southern architecture in nine states. The American Institute of Architects elected her an honorary member in 1945.

Frances Benjamin Johnston went into semi-retirement in 1940 in New Orleans, where she had purchased a townhouse on Bourbon Street. In 1947, she donated her prints, negatives, and correspondence to the Library of Congress. In 1952, she died in New Orleans at the age of 88.

HER BUSINESS SIDE

Johnston didn't come from money nor did she marry into money; yet she brought in enough income to travel and to photograph the sights of the day. She was not above taking photographs she knew would sell well or packaging her photographs for their best resale (in brochures, books, etc). It appears through her letters that she was often disappointed with those she hired as assistants. Most often, it seems she had good reason to be unhappy with their work. In some cases, her employees did not do the job they were hired to do, stole her equipment, sold it, or left her with debts. Johnston, however, was not afraid to go after those who cheated her, and she was persistent until they made amends, returned the equipment, or paid her back in some fashion.

JOHNSTON'S RELATIONSHIPS

Johnston's strongest ties were with other women. A very strong bond existed between Johnston and her mother, who was a positive role model, allowing Johnston to grow and be more adventurous than many of her female contemporaries. Her mother's sister, Cornelia Hagan, also known as Aunt Nin, influenced Johnston in this same way.

Johnston's bohemian artist friends appear in her collection of photographs, but there is no reference to "romantic relationships" with men. There is some question as to the eight-year relationship Johnston had with Mattie Edwards Hewitt. Hewitt, originally married to photographer Arthur Hewitt, divorced in 1909 and moved to New York City to live with Johnston, who had moved to New York that same year. Hewitt and Johnston opened up a business, specializing in architectural photography including stately homes and gardens. Their business and personal relationship ended in 1917. In letters from Hewitt to Johnston, there are references to Hewitt's love for Johnston, but whether that love was meant in a platonic or more romantic sense is hard to discern. If read with an eye of the times when single women frequently lived together, even bought homes together, these references alone are not proof that a romantic lesbian relationship existed between the two women. Of course, it does not disprove that relationship. It is interesting that although Johnston left her photographs and correspondence to the Library of Congress, some 2500 square feet, little material reflects on her long-term relationship with Hewitt. This may be a part of Johnston's life which will go unsolved . . . rumored but unproven.

CONCLUSION

It is hard to talk about a photographer's work without seeing the photographs, but Frances Benjamin Johnston is reflected through who and what she chose to photograph. Johnston led two lives. To gain access to those she photographed (and get paid for it), she was the amenable Victorian with a well–connected mother. In her personal life, Frances Benjamin Johnston was a rebel who relished her friends, her club, and her art. She broke the roles prescribed for women, which often put her in precarious and dangerous situations. While other women married men for financial stability, Johnston came up with new projects to finance her life and her work. Many of her writings include letters to those who owed her money or those who tried to take advantage of her (Berch, p. 132), but when she died at 1952 she was living in her own home, financially independent.

The two books highlighting Johnston's life reflect in many ways the difference between the way we reclaimed women in the media in the 1970s and reclamation in the twenty-first century. It was enough for Peter Daniel and Raymond Smock to discover that there was a woman photographer whose contribution to history was significant and to emphasize that few people knew of her life although many knew her photographs. Even the title of their book, *A Talent for Detail: The Photographs of Frances Benjamin Johnston* (1974), is quite neutral. Bettina Berch's major work, *The Woman behind the Lens* (2000), is quite different. It is not only Johnston's work which is important in this book; Berch also showcases the person, her lifestyle, her influence at the time, and the role model she provided. One could argue that the "new" reclamation movement is not just about reclaiming what women in the media created but how they as role models affected generations to come and how the content of that media might be different from what men at the time were creating. Do we believe that a woman's eye would differ from that of a man's during the late 1800s and early 1900s?

Johnston rarely allowed social or physical boundaries to interfere with her work. Her instinctive eye for narrative, her desire for adventure, her patience and persistence on assignments, and her ability to elbow her way into situations has led some scholars to call her the mother of photojournalism.

Figure 18.1.   Library of Congress, Prints & Photographs Division, [re-production number, LC-USZ62-64301]

REFERENCES

Beasley M.H., & Gibbons, S.J. (1997) *Women in Media: A Documentary Sourcebook.* Washington, DC: Women's Institute for the Freedom of the Press.

Berch, B. (2000). *The Woman Behind the Lens: The Life and Work of Frances Benjamin Johnston, 1864–1952.* Charlottesville and London: The University of Press of Virginia.

Beverlin, H. (2001, April 27). Grafton woman was a pioneer in photography. The Mountain Statesman, pp x-xx.

Daniel, P., & Smock, R. (1974). *A Talent for Detail*, New York: Harmony Books.

Harlan, L.R. et al (1972–1979). *The Booker T. Washington Papers.* Urbana: Illinois: University of Illinois Press.

Johnston, F. B. (1907). "The Eagle's Perch Abroad: The Shabby and Discreditable Housing of the Foreign Representatives of the United States in Many Lands When Uncle Sam is Landlord." *Harper's*, May 18, 725–727.

Marzolf, M. (1977) *Up from the Footnote: A History of Women Journalists.* New York: Hastings.

Photographer's Gallery: Frances Benjamin Johnston (2002, Janaury 2). *The White House Historical Association.* Retrieved from: http://whitehousehistory.org.

Ross, I. (1974). *Ladies of the Press: The Story of Women in Journalism by an Insider.* New York: Harper and Arno Press.

Weiss, M. R. (1975). "The Formidable Frances Benjamin Johnston" *Saturday Review*, August 23, 73–75.

Women Photographers: UCR/California Museum of Photography (2002). Retrieved from: http://cmp.ucr.edu/site/exhibitiojns/wome/johnston.html.

Chapter Nineteen

Recontextualizing "The Change": Rhetorical and Performative Constructions of Menopause in *Cybill*

Dacia Charlesworth

In the introduction to *Feminist Television Criticism*, the authors note that "Since the 1970s, feminists have become increasingly interested in television as 'something more than a bad object, something that offers a series of lures and pleasures, however limited its repertoire of female roles'" (1997, p. 1). Thirty years later, while still finding value in television, critics continue to argue that women's roles are limited. In addition, actors themselves now acknowledge how restrictive women's television roles can be. For example, Cybill Shepherd developed and produced the series *Cybill* in 1995 because of her frustration over the lack of worthwhile roles for women her age (Shepherd, 1998, p. 69). Working against the cultural perception, best articulated by Gail Sheehy (1991), that encourages our society to view aging women as invisible, women like Shepherd are extraordinary because they demand that attention be paid to aging women as well as to the experiences aging women encounter.

Menopause is one experience that most aging women encounter, and it serves to mark women as invisible. The invisibility of menopause, however, may be slowly fading. Currently, 1.3 million American women experience menopause every year; in 2010 that number will double, and in 2010 a total of 60 million women will experience or already will have experienced menopause (Baum, 1993). Now that "baby-boomers" are at or nearing menopause, the communicative taboos surrounding menopause may become less severe.

The topic of menopause has received much scholarly attention and is generally studied from biomedical, socio-cultural, or feminist perspectives. Researchers working within the biomedical perspective are most interested in quantifying women's experiences with menopause and hormone replacement therapy. In the sociocultural perspective, scholars question or contest the cultural and medical constructions of menopause. Members working within feminist perspectives tend to offer readers a more positive view of menopause that differs from the predominantly negative cultural view of menopause. Feminist perspectives are unique because women's voices, experiences, and views are privileged above all else. Despite this research, especially the research conducted from feminist perspectives, few have investigated the ways in which women are attempting to transform the primarily negative stereotypes associated with being a menopausal woman via mediated forms of communication.

Thus, in this essay, I examine the ways in which American television depicts menopause by analyzing the situation comedy *Cybill*. *Cybill* is unique because the experiences of the main character, Cybill Sheridan, parallel the experiences of the star, Cybill Shepherd. Not only has Shepherd discussed her experiences with menopause publicly, but her series was unlike the few television programs that even addressed menopause, e.g., *All in the Family* and *Designing Women*, in that it dealt with menopause directly and frequently. As an executive producer, Shepherd also had the luxury of having greater control over the material that was written about menopausal women and the way her character performed the role of menopausal woman. Taking into account these factors as well as Shepherd's own commitment to feminism, I posit that Shepherd's performance and conceptualization of a menopausal woman offers viewers an emancipatory character that may serve to empower women.

To examine Shepherd's depiction of a menopausal woman, I conduct a textual analysis of two episodes of Cybill that focus specifically on Shepherd's attempt to recontextualize and re-present menopause. The two episodes I analyze are entitled, "When You're Hot, You're Hot" and "Some Like It Hot." In these episodes, Shepherd's character, an affluent, heterosexual Caucasian woman, communicates about her experiences with menopause openly, challenges the negative stereotypes surrounding menopausal women, and questions the medical community by using "alternative therapies" instead of hormone replacement therapy (HRT). According to Dow (1992) a major objective of feminist rhetorical criticism of television is to examine which particular views of women audiences are encouraged to accept as well as what function these views might serve; thus, I consider the ways in which Shepherd selects, reflects, and deflects particular types of realities in her portrayal of a menopausal woman.

This essay, then, is divided into three parts. The first part presents a contemporary account of the ways in which menopause is perceived in our culture. Here, I focus specifically on the medicalization of menopause and the communicative taboos surrounding menopause. Next, I examine the rhetorical and performative strategies utilized in *Cybill* to reconstruct and challenge the cultural prototype of a menopausal woman. Finally, I offer conclusions and implications of this analysis for feminist rhetorical criticism, media criticism, and everyday life performance.

CYBILL, EMANCIPATORY CHARACTERS, AND RHETORICAL STRATEGIES

Cybill aired on CBS for four seasons from 2 January 1995 to 13 July 1998. The Carsey-Werner Company, the producers of *Cybill*, described the situation comedy in the following manner:

> *Cybill* is a sexy, sophisticated series, comically dealing with single parenthood, divorce, sex and dating over forty, from a realistic and fresh perspective. Cybill Shepherd stars as Cybill Sheridan, a woman who has it all: two spiteful daughters, two clingy ex-husbands, an outrageous best friend, an unstable future, and a house on an eroding LA hillside. But with humor and determination, Cybill braves each new challenge that comes her way, while having the time of her life discovering that life after forty is anything but downhill (Carsey-Werner Company, 2001).

As evidenced by the description above, the character Cybill is clearly no June Cleaver. At the time *Cybill* aired, it was unusual for a situation comedy to focus specifically on the life of a woman over the age of forty. *Cybill* was a relatively popular show; the first year the show premiered, it averaged a 10 Nielsen rating (percentage of televisions with households) and a 16 Nielsen share (percentage of individuals actually watching television at that time and who are watching the show). In 1996, the ratings for the series jumped 26 percent to a 12.6 rating and a 19 share. In terms of adult viewers, *Cybill* fared well. For adults in general, *Cybill* had a 7.4 rating; for women between the ages of 25-54, *Cybill* had an 11.1 share in 1996 (Rice, 1996, p. 15). *Cybill* was also popular with members of the Hollywood Foreign Press Corps, as Cybill Shepherd received the 1995 Golden Globe for Best TV Actress in a Musical or Comedy. In general, *Cybill* is an ensemble show and frequently features Cybill's best friend, Maryann Thorpe, a wealthy, shallow, but loveable divorcee; Cybill's second ex-husband, Ira Woodbine, a whiny, neurotic author; and Cybill's youngest daughter, Zoey, a sarcastic, intelligent young woman.

Cybill as an Emancipatory Character

The two episodes that focus specifically on Cybill's experience with menopause and thus form the foundation of this analysis include "When

You're Hot, You're Hot" (original air date: April 29, 1996) and "Some Like it Hot" (original air date: October 6, 1997). In the first episode, Cybill, starring in a production entitled *Sex and Sensibility,* supposedly produced by Aaron Spelling, receives a visit from her second ex-husband's mother-in-law, discovers that she is pre-menopausal, has a horse wander into her backyard, and decides to try some herbal remedies to help calm the signs of perimenopause. In the second episode, Cybill prepares for a visit from her mother, continues to deal with the signs of perimenopause, and tries to explain to her mother and Maryann why she does not want to take HRT.

These episodes are significant in that Cybill Shepherd, the writers, and other executive producers of *Cybill* decided to make menopause the explicit focus of these episodes and chose to deal with it openly and directly. Through these episodes, this television program continued to break new ground and placed women's health issues in the spotlight, if only for thirty minutes. After performing a rhetorical analysis of these two episodes, it is clear that Cybill has the potential to serve as an emancipatory character for viewers.

Cybill serves as an emancipatory character in these episodes because she offers readers an alternative way to break free from the controlling cultural influence faced by women experiencing menopause. Cybill offers viewers autonomy, especially as it relates to issues surrounding menopause, on several different levels. First, by utilizing non-euphemistic language when discussing menopause, Cybill presents viewers with a way to challenge the communicative taboos pertaining to menopause. Second, by providing viewers with details of how menopause is affecting her and then by dealing with menopause according to her own plan, Cybill offers viewers a detailed example of how they may also deal with menopause on their own terms or may encourage others who are experiencing menopause to do so. Finally, by confronting and critiquing the cultural ideals and expectations placed upon aging and menopausal women, Cybill invites viewers to question these standards or, if they have already questioned these ideals, supplies viewers with a repertoire of arguments they may use to confront others who hold women to these unattainable standards.

From the very beginning of the first episode, Cybill does not use euphemisms when talking about bodily processes. After filming a brief scene for *Sex and Sensibility*, Cybill begins complaining to her on-screen daughter about how hot the set is. The actor playing her daughter, bundled up in a parka, says "Are you like, totally mental? It's totally arctic." As Cybill picks up her layers of garments and begins to fan herself under her dress, her daughter says, "You're like, acting all weird. You're way hot and cranky. Like when my mom went through the change." Cybill, shocked at this remark, says "Menopause. Are you like, mental?" Although "the change" is a widely-known euphemism for "menopause" in our culture, Cybill chooses to use the word "menopause," thereby demonstrating to the young woman (and viewers alike) that it is perfectly acceptable to use the medical term.

In the next scene, Maryann and Cybill are in the restaurant they frequent and are being served by the waiter who always takes care of them. Cybill begins by telling Maryann about her experiences with perimenopause and Maryann asks if Cybill still has her "friend" even though she is perimenopausal. Cybill asks Maryann if she is 12 because of her use of the euphemism "friend." Instead of answering Cybill's question, Maryann responds, "You know, Aunt Flo." One reason for Maryann's use of the euphemisms for the menstrual flow may be because the waiter had just brought them their salads. However, even though the waiter is there, Cybill tells Maryann, "Just say it! Period Period Period!" The waiter is carrying a pepper mill and responds to Cybill saying "Period" by asking, "Fresh ground valium? Say when." Cybill does not answer the waiter but does go on to answer Maryann's question: "Sometimes my period is regular, sometimes I skip a month, and lately I've been spotting a lot." The waiter, looking aghast, stops grinding, says "When," and exits. Later in the same scene, Cybill starts taking her clothes off in the restaurant during a hot flash and then stands up and pours ice water down her shirt and moans, "Oh, yeah" while most of the patrons in the restaurant are looking at her, but she does not seem to care.

The scene described above is noteworthy for several reasons. First, Cybill chides Maryann for using euphemisms that reinforce the shame attributed to menstruation. Second, she discusses her experiences with menopause in a public, rather than a private, setting. In that same vein, she also does not attempt to hide her hot flash from public view. In fact, she calls even more attention to herself when she begins removing layers of clothes, stands up, and pours ice water down her shirt. Finally, the waiter serves as a cultural reflector when, upon hearing Cybill say the word "period" repeatedly, he thinks she is crazy or, at the very least, abnormal, and offers her valium. In addition, when Cybill begins describing her menstrual flow in detail, he becomes visibly uncomfortable and decides leave even though he is not finished with his task. This scene humorously depicts what may happen if women decide to communicate about and experience menopause openly and shamelessly. In the end, it is Maryann and the waiter who are embarrassed, not Cybill.

In the second episode, Cybill uses the word "menopause" to get a rise out of Virginia, her mother, a very prim and proper woman from Memphis. Upon hearing Cybill say "menopause," Virginia becomes flustered and excuses herself from the room. Later on in this episode, Virginia becomes upset and tells Cybill that she has ruined her Christmas because all she is doing is talking about her menopause and nobody wants to hear about it. When Cybill points out that her mother used the actual word, Virginia responds, "See, now you've got me cussing like a sailor." The audience is invited to identify with Cybill by recognizing how silly Virginia is being when she equates saying the word "menopause" with cussing like a sailor. Just as was the case with Maryann and her use of euphemisms for the menstrual flow, Cybill points out how ridiculous it is for grown women not to communicate openly about their bodily processes.

In addition to speaking openly about menopause, Cybill also assists viewers who have not yet experienced menopause by providing them with clear descriptions of her experience. Understandably, Cybill's signs of menopause become more intense in episode two, as over a year has passed since the broadcast of the first episode. In the first episode, Cybill remarks to Maryann, "pre-menopause is really something. One minute I'm freezing, the next I'm burning up. No one told me these hot flashes were gonna be so hot," and she tells Ruth, her ex-mother-in-law with whom she shares a close relationship, "I knew it would happen someday. I'm hot, can't sleep at night, and I'm sick of drinking dirt." During episode two, Cybill becomes more frustrated and tells Maryann that she is still hot, sick of feeling hot inside, of feeling everything intensely, of feeling everything with her whole body, and of feeling as if she is bubbling and bursting. In this episode, Cybill also comments on her memory loss and even forgets what time she is supposed to pick her mother up from the airport. As Cybill notes, however, memory loss can have its advantages because she will soon forget that her mother is visiting. During this episode Cybill also decides to keep a journal, and in it she writes of her night sweats, foot cramps and weird black hairs sprouting from her chin. In these passages, Cybill offers a fair representation of menopause. She discusses the negative and inconvenient effects of menopause while offering viewers some clear advantages of the effects.

Not only does Cybill describe her experiences with menopause in detail, she also encourages viewers to describe menopause in a positive manner. In essence, Cybill reconceptualizes and reclaims menopause through her use of language. In episode one, Cybill discusses her menopause "symptoms," but in episode two, Maryann mentions a symptom of menopause, and Cybill corrects her by saying "Not symptom. Sign. Menopause is not a disease. It's a natural transition." By encouraging Maryann to think about the significance and impact of her language choice, Cybill also demonstrates to viewers that when one mentions "symptoms" of menopause, she implies that almost all women will someday become disease-stricken. In episode two, Cybill also substitutes "power surge" for "hot flash" when talking to Maryann; however, she uses the term "hot flash" when talking to her daughter Zoey. By using the term "power surge," Cybill makes use of an expression many feminists have utilized in an attempt to put a more positive spin on the derogatory "hot flash." "Power surge" invites viewers to think of the changes going on in the menopausal body as not only powerful but positive. Throughout both episodes, Cybill's careful language choices, and her corrections of others' choices, show viewers how to subvert the cultural notion that menopause is somehow too debilitating a taboo to discuss.

Moreover, Cybill serves as an emancipatory character by the way she deals with menopause. In both episodes, Cybill makes it apparent that *she* is experiencing menopause and that *she alone* will decide what to do with her body. As may be expected, however, other characters have ideas of their own. When first learning that Cybill is perimenopausal, almost all the characters to whom she discloses this piece of information have negative reactions. When Cybill's on-screen daughter suggests Cybill is menopausal, Cybill replies, "Are you like mental?" But after being exposed to this idea, Cybill seems to accept that she is perimenopausal and does not react negatively to the label again, only to the signs of perimenopause. Cybill tells Maryann, who retorts, "Thank goodness this will never happen to me." Ira whines, "Aw, geez, no. I'm too young for you to go into menopause." Zoey also responds selfishly: "I realize that this is a tough time for you . . . but it would help me to be supportive if I could make insensitive jokes at your expense." Although Zoey's response is perfectly aligned with her character, it is significant that the two people Cybill relies on most, her ex-husband and her best friend, do not even ask Cybill how she is feeling or even if she wants to talk about her experiences; they only seem to care about themselves.

The only positive reaction is from Ira's mother, Ruth, who is now postmenopausal. Ruth tells Cybill that life does not end because of menopause. She then tells her about post-menopausal bliss: "it's liberating. You have all this energy, and you don't have to care what people think. You can do things you wouldn't ordinarily do, like buy your granddaughter a car and get a tattoo of Elmer Fudd on your ass." It is in this scene that Ruth establishes herself as a guide for Cybill. She provides her with her own experiences and strives to let Cybill know that she will get through this and be fine. This scene is a good example for viewers because it could encourage those who have not yet experienced menopause to talk with someone who has and could also encourage those who have experienced menopause to share their wisdom with others.

Upon learning that she is perimenopausal, Cybill begins to engage in nontraditional treatments. After her on-screen daughter suggests that she may be menopausal, the next scene shows that Cybill has since become educated in the ways of homeopathic medicine as it relates to menopause. She tells Maryann that she has been reading about menopause and natural supplements. She empties out her purse that contains several bottles and jars: "I've got teas, tinctures, infusions, Yellow dock—I think that's for hot flashes, scull-cap for sleeplessness, oat straw, tea, dandelion root, black cohosh for breast tenderness." She admits that she is confused about what herbs to take and seeks assistance from a Chinese herbalist later in the episode.

In the second episode, Cybill visits an acupuncturist and keeps a journal so that her daughters can "understand that menopause is just another life change. Like puberty. You grow, and become a more complete person . . . and in both cases, a little hairier." She is also supplementing her diet; for example, she eats tofu dogs for estrogen and asparagus for breast tenderness. Cybill eventually becomes confused with all the information: "One book says exercise, another says stay in bed. One says herbs are good for you, another says herbs grow facial hair. One even says retreat from the world." It is interesting to note that Cybill never seeks the council of a physician, although this is the usual protocol followed by most women with a health care provider. The fact that she does not even mention a health care provider seems to be an implicit critique of the medical community and sends the message to women that they should read about menopause first and try to deal with it themselves before seeking help from members of the medical community. This perspective has advantages and disadvantages. One advantage is that women can become informed about menopause on their own and decide for themselves the types of action they would like to take. A disadvantage is that women may not receive all the information they need or may not be alerted to vitamin and mineral deficiencies they may have.

Although Cybill may be content with the non-traditional approach, almost all of the other characters question her choices. These occurrences demonstrate what other women who follow Cybill's path may expect. Maryann, Cybill's best friend constantly criticizes Cybill's approach to dealing with the signs of perimenopause. In the first episode dealing with menopause, she asks Cybill why she's being "medieval" when Cybill reports that she does not want to take HRT. Maryann then refers to HRT as a perk of living in the twentieth century. This statement implies that Cybill's methods are outdated, primitive, and invalid.

Cybill's herbal supplements prove to be a constant source of amusement for Maryann, who makes fun of Cybill when she is taking her supplements from a dropper by saying she looks like a hamster. When looking at all the bottles and jars Cybill has removed from her purse, Maryann picks up a bottle, commenting, "St. John's wort—you know you can have those burned off." Maryann makes this comment after she has recommended that Cybill try HRT and Cybill argues, "I don't want to medicate this away. I want to experience it." Even though Maryann is only joking, the joke is at Cybill's expense and conveys the message that Cybill does not have Maryann's complete support. This lack of support is later made clear in this episode when Maryann tells Cybill, once again, "just take the drugs."

In episode two, Cybill's mother, frustrated that Cybill has the audacity to even talk about menopause, becomes fed up: "If you ask me, Cybill, you should just take the hormone pills! Now, millions of women take them everyday. . . . Just try the pills. You'd be doing everybody a favor." To make matters worse, Maryann sides with Cybill's mother: "Cybill, if the hormones would make things easier . . ." Before Maryann can even finish, Cybill interrupts her and leaves. At the end of this episode, however, viewers learn that Maryann is trying to get Cybill to take HRT because she knows if Cybill "makes it through" the "hormonal hurricane" without them, she will expect Maryann to do the same. Maryann's admission, then, provides viewers with a sympathetic portrayal of Maryann: She is not as strong as Cybill and does not want to try to experience menopause without the assistance of HRT.

Besides Ira's mother, Cybill eventually receives the most support from Ira. In episode two, after Maryann has sided with Cybill's mother in an attempt to get Cybill to try HRT, Cybill goes to Ira's house for some comfort and reassurance that she is not crazy for dealing with perimenopause her own way. Ira tells Cybill that what she is doing is fine: "You've always done things your own way, Cyb. What would be crazy is if you stopped now." Essentially, Cybill's non-traditional methods of dealing with menopause are only endorsed by her ex-husband. She cannot count on her best friend, mother, or daughter to support her choices. This alerts viewers to the fact that if they wish to go against culturally sanctioned behaviors, they must be prepared to deal with the fact that those they care about may be unable to support their decisions.

In addition to encouraging viewers to communicate openly about menopause and try alternate therapies for experiencing menopause, Cybill is also an emancipatory character because she explicitly confronts and critiques cultural expectations for aging and menopausal women. When she first learns that she is perimenopausal, Cybill tells Maryann, "No way am I becoming invisible when the wolf whistles stop. I'm going to be one loud, brassy, and in-your-face menopause mama." She knows from the beginning that she is not going to equate her sexuality with youth and will not rely on other's (read: men's) approval to feel attractive. In these two episodes, the writers also effectively use secondary stories that parallel Cybill's experiences with being perimenopausal.

In the first episode, an old mare wanders into Cybill's backyard. Cybill contacts the owners of the mare and is shocked to learn that the horse's days are numbered because she is going to be turned into dog food. When Cybill learns of this, she tells the man who has come to pick up the horse, as well as the others in the room, "Just because she's old doesn't mean she has no value.

She's strong, she's vibrant, she has great legs, and I'm sick and tired of everyone telling her to take hormones." In this excerpt, Cybill directly addresses our youth obsessed culture and attempts to show that just because individuals, be they equine or human, are old, they are still a vital part of our culture with something to contribute. I found it particularly interesting that the writers choose to use a mare in this story. It makes sense to use a horse, since older horses are often referred to as "old nags" and are "put out to pasture," something Cybill sees happening to older women in our culture, but what I found remarkable about the use of the horse (and I am almost sure this is coincidental) is that Premarin, the most popular brand of HRT, is derived from the urine of pregnant mares.

In the second episode, Cybill finds out that the producers of her "one good movie" are making a sequel, and everyone from the original cast will be reprising their roles except for Cybill. Cybill simply and succinctly critiques Hollywood standards by stating, "I'm too old to play myself ten years later!" Given this piece of information and the pressure she is feeling from her mother and Maryann to begin taking HRT, Cybill goes to Ira's house to watch her performance in this movie. After she interrupts Ira's date, he is kind enough to see that Cybill is upset and needs to talk, so he asks her what the matter is. She responds, "See, they're making this sequel without me. I had to see what I had then that they think I don't have now. But the truth is, I have more to offer. I can't make them see that. It's like menopause. . . . I can't make them see that I'm not crazy just because I don't want to take drugs to make it go away." Confused, Ira asks if the movie people want her to take HRT. Cybill answers that it is not the movie people but her mother and Maryann: "They just want me to shut up, just go gently into that good night." Again, Cybill addresses the notion that once women begin aging, they are expected to know their place and essentially become invisible.

Cybill also comments on the impossible physical ideals of women in our culture and the steps they have to go through to obtain and retain these ideals. In the first episode, Cybill and Maryann visit an herbalist, a very young looking Chinese woman. When the herbalist leaves the room, Cybill remarks that she looks great and bets that she is at least 50. Maryann says that if the herbalist is a day over 40, she will drink as much of the bark juice as Cybill does. When the herbalist returns, Cybill asks her how old she is. The woman replies that she is 67. Maryann and Cybill are dumbfounded. Cybill asks her how long she has been taking herbs and the woman tells her, "Since June. My plastic surgeon told me they'd help me heal faster." While this is an amusing segment, it suggests that the only reason Maryann would take herbs or "drink bark juice" would be to improve upon or sustain her external appearance. The play on the stereotypical images of Eastern cultures is also amusing. After all, who would expect a Chinese herbalist to have plastic surgery? This scene demonstrates the pressure placed on all women to conform to American culture's impossibly high beauty standards.

Later in the episode during Cybill's shoot, viewers also learn that Cybill's older on-screen daughter has had plastic surgery. The actor tells Cybill that she has had "enough excess skin removed to build a couple of little fat kids" and Cybill begins to compare herself to the other woman and wonders if she should have plastic surgery. Cybill does not blame the actor for having surgery; instead, she claims "It's society's fault. It makes women feel ashamed about getting older." Later Cybill announces, "No way am I going to mutilate this body just because the culture we live in tries to force women to aspire to some impossible ideal." Cybill then looks at her image in a spoon and adds, "Then again, never say never."

The next scene begins with Cybill lying on what appears to be an examining table with Maryann and Ruth, her ex-mother-in-law, at her side. Cybill says she cannot believe she is doing this. She wonders how long she will have to keep the bandages on and asks what if it does not look the way she wanted. Maryann offers Cybill a shot of courage from a fifth of tequila while Ruth tells Cybill that she needs to remember "this is symbolic of the passage into the next chapter of your life." Then viewers see a tattoo artist approach Cybill, saying, "One Pepe Le Pew coming up." Cybill asks the man to make it small and then Ruth asks him if he also does body piercing. This segment is noteworthy because it illustrates how menopause, even perimenopause, marks a transition in Cybill's life. Fortunately, she is accompanied by two women, one who has served as a guide, always offering a positive perspective and the other who has served as a foil, always questioning Cybill's decisions but in the end supporting her as well. Ruth is portrayed as a hip older woman who is finally able to do what she has always wanted because she now wears the badge of "post-menopause." In turn, Cybill pays homage to Ruth, emulating her by getting a cartoon character tattooed on her body.

Cybill offers a valuable critique of the cultural expectations placed upon women in terms of beauty and aging and also critiques the medical community. When she walks into the herbalist's shop, she tells Maryann, "See, isn't this more interesting than a sterile pharmacy?" She also notes, "Western medicine doesn't have all the answers. Some of these herbs have been around for thousands of years." By showing herbs as an alternative to HRT, valuing what has been in existence for a long time, and noting the sterile, dry nature of Western medicine, Cybill presents viewers with a different option for experiencing menopause.

So as to not seem one-sided, I must note that the writers of these episodes also highlight some negative aspects of Eastern medicine. After drinking some herbs,

Cybill asks Maryann if she wants to go lick the driveway due to the disgusting taste in her mouth. Cybill also tells Ruth that she is sick of drinking dirt. Although these herbs do offer Cybill some comfort in episode two, the writers inform viewers that taking natural supplements is not going to be enjoyable. In the end, though, Western medicine does come out looking like the (invisible) villain trying to force Cybill to take HRT. The writers missed a good opportunity to demonstrate that by partnering with the right physician, patients may assume a major role in their health care. Given the history of the medical community and HRT, however, perhaps the writers assumed that most women would be talking with their physicians anyway, and they wanted to encourage women to locate and read information about menopause from various sources on their own. Moreover, by not having Cybill visit a physician, the script allows us to view Cybill as independent, free-thinking, and in control.

Perhaps the principle critique of Western medicine appears in episode two. While Cybill and Maryann are at the acupuncturist, Maryanne once again asks Cybill about the hormones: "I saw an ad for them in a magazine. The woman was dancing with her husband. She looked ecstatic. Of course, maybe it was the five carat ring on her finger. Or maybe it wasn't her husband. The point is, she was radiant." Cybill answers: "Next time, look at the back of the ad. It's filled with disclaimers and warnings. I don't want to take synthetic hormones just because an ad tells me to. Or because a doctor tells me to. That's what happened to our mothers." Yet again, Maryann focuses only on the importance of her external appearance and buys into the commodification of menopause. That is, she will willingly purchase her youth and vitality at any cost. Cybill, on the other hand, is more concerned with the possible negative physical effects of HRT; the hormones may improve the condition of her skin, but they may also increase her risk of certain cancers. Even if viewers do not pick up on the dichotomy between Maryann and Cybill, they may look closely at the next advertisement for HRT they see in a magazine.

As an emancipatory character, Cybill encourages viewers to talk openly and directly about menopause in a way that does not categorize menopause as a disease. She invites viewers to experience menopause in their own ways by doing whatever they feel comfortable with and allowing others that same luxury. She also demonstrates how one may confront, critique, and subvert cultural standards of beauty for aging and menopausal women.

CONCLUSION

As demonstrated in this analysis, the character Cybill offers viewers a realistic portrayal of what menopause may be like. Shepherd and the other writers and producers took a great risk when they decided to talk explicitly about menopause. They also managed to strike a perfect balance between seriousness and comedy. It is easy to imagine how the writers could have gone for some easy laughs at Cybill's expense; however, Cybill continually reaffirms that menopause is not life-threatening or even life-ending—it just is.

One of the most important contributions of these two episodes is Ruth's character. She offers women an option they are not used to seeing: a Gap-wearing, traveling, pot-smoking, hip mother/grandmother who, because of menopause, is now able to enter the "Me Me Me phase" of her life, as she describes it to her son. For Ruth, menopause becomes an excuse for her to do what she may have wanted to be doing all along but was unable to because of household and child rearing responsibilities.

Ruth exemplifies how post-menopausal women may be able to subvert cultural constructions of menopause and use them to their advantage. Since our culture seems to mark menopausal women as unstable, crazy, dangerous, and/or invisible, Ruth acts upon her desires and can always fall back upon the excuse, "Menopause made me do it." With this subversion, however, comes the danger of further reifying the cultural beliefs that menopausal women are to be feared. An important question to be asked, then, is why are menopausal women to be feared? One obvious answer is that these women are behaving as men have been socialized to behave; that is, they are putting their own desires and goals first and not considering the consequences. By marking these women as dangerous or frightening, members of our culture learn that a woman behaving as a man is not acceptable. Hence, through this labeling, the status-quo or, more specifically, gendered roles are maintained. This non-acceptance or fear of menopausal women is demonstrated in episode one when Cybill's on-screen daughter discusses how weird her mother was during menopause and when Maryann tells Cybill that when her mother went through menopause, she lived under the sink for a few years. With the baby-boomers entering (and some now exiting) menopause, I hope this perception may begin to change or, at the very least, begin to be questioned more. Cybill Shepherd, however, managed to accomplish her goal; she not only improved the lives of women on television, she also improved the lives of those women who are experiencing or will experience menopause and now feel they may not only talk about it but may even decide for themselves how to experience it.

REFERENCES

Baum, G. (1993, December 5). The menopause generation: Once upon a time, there was the Pepsi generation. Then came the Me generation. Now get ready for the next baby-boomer obsession. *Los Angeles Times*.

Boston Women's Health Book Collective. (1992). *The new our bodies, ourselves: A book for and by women.* New York: Simon and Schuster.

Brunsdon, C., D'Acci, J., & Spigel, L. (1997). *Feminist television criticism: A reader.* Oxford, Clarendon Press.

Carsey-Werner Company. *Cybill.* Retrieved November 15, 2001 from http://www .carseywerner.net/cybill_eng.htm.

Dow, B. (1992). Femininity and feminism in *Murphy Brown. The Southern Communication Journal, 57.2,* 143-155.

Rice, L. (October 28, 1996). *Cybill* sees more defections. *Broadcasting & Cable, 126.45,* 15.

Sheehy, G. (1991). *The silent passage: Menopause.* New York: Random House.

Shepherd, C. (June 29, 1998). Meno-peace. *People,* 69-74.

Trainer, D. (director), & Wallem, L. (writer). (October 6, 1997). *Cybill* [Television Program]. Some like it hot [Episode #406].

Weyman, A. (director), Bishop, E. A., & Jaffee, S. N. (writers). (April 29, 1996). *Cybill* [Television Program]. When you're hot, you're hot [Episode #221].

Wilson, R. (1962). Roles of estrogen and progesterone in breast and genital cancer. *Journal of the American Medical Association, 182,* 327-331.

———. (1966). *Feminine forever.* New York: M. Evans.

———, & Wilson, T. (1963). The fate of the nontreated post-menopausal woman: A plea for the maintenance of adequate estrogen from puberty to the grave. *Journal of the American Geriatrics Society, 11,* 347-361.

Selected Bibliography

Allen, D. and Rush, R.P. (Eds.). (1996). *Women Transforming Communications: Global Intersections.* Thousand Oaks, CA: Sage Publications.

Ammu, J. (2000). *Women in Journalism: Making News.* Delhi, India: Konark Publishers.

Armatage, K. (Ed.). (1999). *Gendering the Nation: Canadian Women's Cinema.* Toronto: University of Toronto Press.

Baehr, H. and Gray, A. (Eds.). (1996). *Turning It On: A Reader in Women and Media.* New York: St. Martin's Press.

Bathla, S. (1998). *Women, Democracy, and the Media: Cultural and Political Representations in the Indian Press.* Thousand Oaks, CA: Sage Publications.

Braden, M. (1996). *Women Politicians and the Media.* Lexington: University Press Of Kentucky.

Brunsdon, C. and D'Acci, J. (Eds.). (1997). *Feminist Television Criticism: A Reader.* New York: Clarendon Press.

Carter, C. and Branston, G. (Eds.). (1998). *News, Gender, and Power.* New York: Routledge.

Cortese, A.J. P. (1999) *Provocateur: Images of Women and Minorities in Advertising.* Lanham, MD: Rowman & Littlefield.

Creedon, P.J. (1993). *Women in Mass Communication, Revised Edition.* (1993). Newbury Park, CA: Sage Publications.

Cuklanz, L.M. (2000). *Rape on Primetime: Television, Masculinity, and Sexual Violence.* Philadelphia: University of Pennsylvania Press.

Dow, B.J.(1996). *Prime-time Feminism: Television, Media Culture, and the Women's Movement since 1970.* Philadelphia: University of Pennsylvania Press.

Fineman, M. and McCluskey, M.T. (Eds.). (1997). *Feminism, Media, and the Law.* New York: Oxford University Press.

Flanders, L. (1997). *Real Majority, Media Minority: The Costs of Sidelining Women in Reporting.* Monroe, ME: Common Courage Press.

Gallagher, M. (2001). *Monitoring Gender in the Media.* London, UK: Zed.

Gammel, I. (Ed.). (1999). *Confessional Politics: Women's Sexual Self-Representation In Life Writing and Popular Media.* Carbondale, IL: Southern Illinois University Press.

Hall, A.C. (Ed.). (1998). *Delights, Desires, and Dilemmas: Essays on Women and the Media.* Westport, CT: Praeger.

Halper, D.L. (2001). *Invisible Stars: A Social History of Women in American Broadcasting.* Armonk, NY: M.E. Sharpe.

Inness, S.A. (1999). *Tough Girls: Women Warriors and Wonder Women in Popular Culture.* Philadelphia: University of Pennsylvania Press.

Jackson, S. and Jones, J. (Eds.). (1998). *Contemporary Feminist Theories.* New York:New York University Press.

Kamalipour, Y. R. (Ed.). (1997). *The U.S. Media and the Middle East:Image and Perception.* Westport, CT: Praeger.

Kitch, C.L. (2001). *The Girl on the Magazine Cover: the Origins of Visual Stereotypes In American Mass Media.* Chapel Hill: University of North Carolina Press.

Lent, J.A. (1999). *Women and Mass Communication in the 1990's: an International Annotated Bibliography.* Westport, CT: Greenwood Press.

Lont, C. (Ed.). (1996). *Women and Media: Content/Careers/Criticism.* Belmont, CA:Wadsworth Publishing Company.

Lorfing, I. (1997). *Women, Media, and Sustainable Development.* Beirut: Institute for Women Studies in the Arab World.

Martinez, D.P. (Ed.). (1998). *The Worlds of Japanese Popular Culture: Gender, Shifting Boundaries and Global Cultures.* Cambridge, UK: Cambridge University Press.

Mayne, J. (2000). *Framed: Lesbians, Feminists, and Media Culture.* Minneapolis: University of Minnesota Press.

Mbilinyi, D.A.S. and Omari, C.K. (Eds.). (1996). *Gender Relations and Women's Image in the Media.* Dar es Salaam: Dar es Salaam University Press.

Meyers, M. (1999). *Mediated Women: Representations in Popular Culture.* Cresskill, NJ: Hampton Press.

Munshi, S. (Ed.). (2001). *Images of the 'Modern Woman' in Asia: Global Media, Local Meanings.* Richmond: Curzon.

Norris, P. (Ed.). (1997). *Women, Media, and Politics.* New York: Oxford University Press.

Onslow, B. (2000). *Women of the Press in Nineteenth Century Britain.* New York: St. Martin's Press.

Rapping, E. (1994). *Media-Tions: Forays into the Culture and Gender Wars.* Boston: South End Press.

Redding, J.M. and Brownworth, V.A. (1997). *Film Fatales.* Seattle, WA: Seal Press.

Rodriguez, C.E. (Ed.). (1997). *Latin Looks: Images of Latinas and Latinos in the U.S. Media.* Boulder, CO: Westview Press.

Ross, K. (2002). *Women, Politics, Media: Uneasy Relations at the New Millennium.* Cresskill, NJ.: Hampton Press.

Sochen, J. (1999). *from Mae to Madonna: Women Entertainers in Twentieth-Century America.* Lexington: University Press of Kentucky.

Singh, U. (2001). *New Woman and Mass Media*. Jaipur, India: Surabhi Publications.

———, (Ed.). (1995). *Feminism, Multiculturalism, and the Media: Global Diversities*. Thousand Oaks, CA: Sage Publications.

Valdivia, A.N. (2000) *A Latina in the Land of Hollywood and other Essays on Media Culture*. Tucson: University of Arizona Press.

Van Zoonen, L. (1994). *Feminist Media Studies*. Thousand Oaks, CA: Sage Publications.

Vavrus, M.D. (2002). *Postfeminist News: Political Women in Media Culture*. Albany: State University of New York Press.

Index

269

About the Contributors

Kimiko Akita taught at colleges in Japan while free-lancing for an English magazine. She is a doctoral candidate in the School of Interpersonal Communication at Ohio University.

Michele Tracy Berger is currently an Assistant Professor of Political Science and Women's Studies at the University of North Carolina, Chapel Hill. Her research interests include AIDS activism, sex work, and health policy. She is working on an ethnographic study about the lives of stigmatized women (formerly drug users and sex workers) with HIV/AIDS who became politically active in Detroit.

Linda Brigance is an Associate Professor in the Communication Department at the State University of New York at Fredonia where she teaches courses in rhetorical theory and criticism, persuasion, and gender.

Dacia Charlesworth is a Visiting Assistant Professor at Robert Morris University. Her primary research interests center on taboo topics, women's health, and media studies. Specifically she focuses on the intersections of rhetoric and ideology and how these two elements shape everyday life performances.

Giovanna Del Negro is an Assistant Professor of English at Texas A&M University. She has co-authored a book entitled *Identity and Everyday Life: Essays in the Study of Folklore, Music, and Popular Culture*, which explores core issues in social and cultural theory. Her work on performance, popular culture, and piazza strolling has appeared in the *Journal of American Folklore* and *Midwestern Folklore*.

Linda Y. Devenish has taught at several colleges and universities in the United States. She primarily conducts research on adult daughter-father conflict. She received training in conflict mediation at Hamline University Dispute Resolution Institute and has served as a mediator.

Margaret O. Finucane is an Assistant Professor of Communication at John Carroll University in University Heights, Ohio. She has recently published research on spousal coviewing and biographies of women who were instrumental in the development of local news in their communities.

Gloria Gadsden is an Assistant Professor of Sociology at Fairleigh Dickinson University. Her areas of expertise include gender, race, sexuality, popular culture, and deviance.

Catherine M. Gillotti is an Associate Professor of Communication in the Department of Communication and Creative Arts at Purdue University Calumet. She specializes in interpersonal communication, focusing on interpersonal communication in the health care context. She has authored book chapters and articles on physician-patient communication and bad news delivery.

Angela High-Pippert is an Assistant Professor of Political Science and Women's Studies at the University of St. Thomas. Her research and teaching interests include women and politics, political participation, public opinion, and public policy. Her most recent publication appears in *Women and Politics.*

Reiko Ishiyama received her Master's Degree in Communication at Tokyo Women's Christian University. Currently, she is a doctoral student in Communication at Seijo University, Japan. Her research interests include gender and mass communication.

Barbara L. King is an Associate Professor of Communication at Carroll College, Waukesha, Wisconsin, where she teaches courses in advertising, research methodology, and feature writing. Her research interests include gendered communication and organizational culture.

Cynthia M. Lont is Professor and Chair of the Communication Department at George Mason University in Fairfax, Virginia. She has authored several books and articles on women and the media, subcultural media (women's music), and visual communication theory.

Xin-An Lu is an Assistant Professor in the Speech and Theatre Arts Department at Shippensburg University of Pennsylvania. His research interests include organizational communication, communication technology, visual rhetoric, and intercultural communication.

Lori Montalbano-Phelps is an Assistant Professor of Communication at Indiana University Northwest. Her research areas include performance studies, narrative studies, gender, and rhetorical communication.

Tom Reichert is an Assistant Professor in the Department of Advertising and Public Relations at the University of Alabama. His primary research interests include message and advertising effects, images of women and men in the media, and the influence of sexual appeals on message processing and persuasion.

Tina Richardson is currently teaching at the American University of Sharjah in the United Arab Emirates, where she has successfully structured composition courses around environmental issues. Tina's research focuses on the intersection of literature and the environment, particularly environmental justice issues illuminated by feminist theory and perspectives.

Abhik Roy is an Assistant Professor in the Department of Communication and Culture at Howard University. His work has appeared in the *Howard Journal of Communication, Journal of Applied Communication, Journal for Language and Intercultural Communication, Journal of Popular Culture,* and *International and Intercultural Communication Annual.* He is the author of *Selling Stereotypes: Images of Women in Indian Television Commercials.*

Shinichi Saito is an Associate Professor in the Department of Communication at Tokyo Women's Christian University. His research interests include the effects of mass media, social psychology of communication, and quantitative research methods. His most recent publications include chapters in *Images of the U.S. around the World, Handbook of the Media in Asia,* and the *Asian Communication Handbook* as well as several journal articles.

Orly Shachar is an Associate Professor in the Department of Mass Communication at Iona College, New Rochelle, New York. Her research focuses on gender imagery and genderized communication in science journalism and medical discourse.

Audrey Vanderford is a doctoral candidate in Comparative Literature at the University of Oregon. Her research interests include the political performances of anarchist and radical environmental groups. She has published essays on street theater, pie throwing, and treesitting.

About the Editors

Theresa Carilli, Professor of Communication and Creative Arts, teaches at Purdue University Calumet. She has published two books of plays, *Familial Circles (*Guernica, 2001) and *Women As Lovers* (Guernica, 1996), co-edited an anthology, *Cultural Diversity and the U.S. Media* (SUNY, 1998), and guest edited a theater issue of *Voices in Italian Americana*. She has published several performance texts and articles which explore the connection between culture and the creative process.

Jane Campbell, Professor of English at Purdue University Calumet, is the author of *Mythic Black Fiction: the Transformation of History* (University of Tennessee Press, 1986/2002). Her work has appeared in *Callaloo: A Journal of African and African American Arts and Letters, Obsidian, Black Women in America, The Oxford Companion to Women's Writing in the U. S., the Dictionary of Literary Biography, the Heath Anthology of American Literature, Belles Lettres*, and *U. S. Media and the Middle East: Image and Perception.*